Ultimate Azure Data Engineering

Build Robust Data Engineering Systems on Azure with SQL, ETL, Data Modeling, and Power BI for Business Insights and Crack Azure Certifications

Ashish Agarwal

www.orangeava.com

First Published: July 2024

Published By: Orange Education Pvt Ltd, AVA™

Address: 9, Daryaganj, Delhi, 110002, India

275 New North Road Islington Suite 1314 London,
N1 7AA, United Kingdom

ISBN: 978-81-97651-14-4

Scan the QR code to explore our entire catalogue

www.orangeava.com

Dedicated To

In the Loving Memory of My Late Grandfather

Sh. Kanhaiya Lal Ji Goyal

My Inspiration

About the Author

Ashish Agarwal currently works as an Engineering Architect in the Azure SQL Engineering team at Microsoft, where he works with large and complex SQL modernization projects spanning from SQL On-Premises to Azure IaaS and PaaS platforms.

He holds an Honors Bachelor's degree in Computer Science Engineering from BMIT, Jaipur, Rajasthan, India, affiliated with Rajasthan Technical University, Kota, Rajasthan, India. He earned the title of Best Outgoing Student in Computer Science Engineering for his graduating batch. He has worked at top product-based companies, FinTech organizations, as well as large MNCs across various domains.

An Azure Data Engineer, Business Intelligence SME, and Data Warehousing professional with over 13 years of extensive experience across multiple industries. He has hands-on experience and expertise in handling multiple projects across geographies and delivering solutions with minimal supervision.

He also has vast experience as a business expert for various domains, collaborating with various business partners to understand their needs and derive critical business metrics to help in business growth and resolve problems.

Ashish is currently working on the Azure data engineering stack, Azure data migration from heterogeneous source systems, SQL Server 2019, Azure Analysis Services, and Power BI for implementing business solutions. He has also written and contributed to Microsoft Tech community blogs.

He has a history of working closely with business users to understand and translate business requirements into effective business intelligence solutions. His domain knowledge includes Risk Management (Credit Card Industry), Human Resources, Nano Semiconductor, In-Store Solutions, Retail, and Pharmaceuticals.

When not working on technical projects, Ashish enjoys reading books, listening to music, and writing poetry.

About the Technical Reviewer

Narendra Ragho Angane is a Principal Engineering Architect Manager for the SQL CSE/Ninja Team at Microsoft Engineering, specializing in SQL Server and Azure Data Services. With over 25 years of experience in data and software technologies, he leads a team of engineering architects, providing top-tier service for complex SQL, Oracle, PostgreSQL, Mainframe, and Sybase workload modernizations.

Narendra holds a bachelor's degree in commerce from Mumbai University, a postgraduate diploma in computer applications, and several certifications in data science, computer programming, and RDBMS. He has completed the Data Science Degree Program and Azure Data University program from Microsoft, as well as a Business Model Innovation course from Microsoft-INSEAD. He has also passed numerous Microsoft-certified exams, including Developing Microsoft Azure Solutions and Architecting Microsoft Azure Solutions.

Before joining Microsoft in 2010, Narendra worked with Wipro Technologies, Hostway Solutions, Scalability Experts, and Lilavati Hospital, focusing on database administration, performance tuning, upgrades, migration, data warehousing, and business intelligence.

Acknowledgements

Embarking on the journey of writing *Ultimate Azure Data Engineering* has been a wonderful experience, and I am deeply grateful to the individuals who have played a crucial role in bringing this book to fruition. This endeavor wouldn't have been possible without the unwavering support, guidance, and expertise generously shared by many.

Firstly, my heartfelt thanks go to the Microsoft Azure community and all my mentors who helped immensely in shaping this book. The Microsoft Documentation and Learning Guide is an invaluable resource available at https://learn.microsoft.com/, which served as a guiding light, enriching the content and ensuring accuracy. Special gratitude is extended to the technical reviewer, Mr. Narendra Angane, whose meticulous reviews and insightful feedback enhanced the book. His dedication and expertise have been invaluable in refining the content and ensuring its accuracy.

To my family, thank you for your unwavering support. Your encouragement and understanding have been a constant source of strength throughout this writing journey.

To all those at the publication house who have contributed in various capacities, your collective efforts have enriched this endeavor. I appreciate the collaborative spirit that has fueled the creation of *Ultimate Azure Data Engineering*.

Finally, to the readers, thank you for choosing this book as your source of knowledge. May it be a valuable companion on your journey to master the concepts of Azure and navigate the dynamic world of Azure Data Engineering.

Preface

In the fast-evolving and expanding landscape of Data Engineering, embracing a public cloud that seamlessly blends power with elegance is paramount. Welcome to *Ultimate Azure Data Engineering* - a journey that transcends the ordinary and propels you into the extraordinary realm of Data Engineering in Azure Cloud, a public cloud ecosystem that has etched its name as a cornerstone in the modern cloud era.

This book comprises 10 chapters, each one is a complete module, serving as your comprehensive guide to mastering Data Engineering and Azure Cloud Concepts. It covers a wide array of topics, ranging from the fundamentals to advanced techniques. Whether you are a seasoned developer looking to expand your skills or a newcomer eager to dive into Azure development, this book has something for everyone.

This book is specially targeted at those who are embarking on a journey to level up their skills in data engineering, database concepts, and Azure cloud, even with no prior experience on the subject. Readers will be able to achieve great results after finishing this book.

Chapter 1. Introduction to Data Engineering: This chapter exposes you to the fundamental concepts, techniques, and tools required for a solid understanding of data engineering. You will learn about the modern data ecosystem and the roles that Data Engineers, Data Scientists, and Data Analysts play in it. It covers the various components that comprise the Data Engineering Ecosystem.

Chapter 2. Understanding SQL and RDBMS Concepts: The chapter explores the concepts of SQL Server and Relational Database Management Systems, which are essential for learning Data Engineering Concepts on Azure. The RDBMS is the most widely used database system in businesses all over the world. It offers a dependable technique for storing and retrieving massive amounts of data while balancing system performance and ease of deployment.

Chapter 3. Data Engineering: Azure Versus On-Premises: This chapter compares the data engineering approaches in on-premises and Azure environments using SQL Server, which is a popular relational database system that can manage both transactional and analytical tasks. Our focus will be on four key aspects: data ingestion, data transformation, data storage, and data security.

Chapter 4. Azure Cloud Concepts: This chapter discusses the principles of the Azure cloud, how data systems are evolving, and the implications they have for data professionals. You will also explore the differences between cloud and on-premises data solutions, as well as some examples of business scenarios that use cloud technologies. In addition, you will learn about the roles and responsibilities of a data engineer and how they connect with other data and AI roles.

Chapter 5. Working with Heterogenous Data Sources: This chapter covers one of the main aspects of data engineering: handling different kinds of data sources where the company's data may be stored. Our goal is to create a unified and consistent data source that serves as a "Single Source of Truth" when working with a Data Warehouse solution.

Chapter 6. ETL Concepts: This chapter covers the main aspects of data engineering, which involves performing ETL (Extract, Transform, and Load) operations on data from different sources. ETL is a process of getting data from one or more source systems, changing it based on some business rules and needs, and putting it into a destination system, such as a data warehouse or a data lake. ETL helps businesses to combine, merge, and examine data from various sources and get insights or make decisions.

Chapter 7. Database Design and Modeling: This chapter discusses database design, which is an essential component in building, developing, implementing, and maintaining enterprise data management systems. A good database design makes management easier, improves data quality, and reduces costs. The main objectives of database design in DBMS are to create logical and physical models of the planned database system.

Chapter 8. Performance Best Practices and Data Security: This chapter discusses how to improve performance and secure data in data engineering projects. Performance is a crucial factor in database engineering, as every data engineering project must deliver timely and efficient solutions for data ingestion and transformation (ETL) that meet the data quality and availability expectations of the downstream systems. These systems use the data for extraction, analysis, and reporting purposes at different levels, supporting the decision-making process of the end users.

Chapter 9. Data Visualization and Application in Real World: This chapter introduces the ideas of data visualization and how it can be used in real-world situations. Data visualization helps data professionals to communicate a message with data. Here is an extensive guide on data visualization. Data visualization is the representation of information and data using visual tools such as charts, graphs, maps, and others.

Chapter 10. Data Engineering Certification Guide: This chapter discusses the data engineering certifications and how one can pursue them for personal skill assessments and improvements or to meet the organizational requirements for a specific role.

This book is a hands-on guide filled with practical examples, real-world scenarios, and best practices. We hope this journey through Data Engineering empowers you to build robust data engineering architecture solutions and enhances your skills in the field of Data Engineering in Azure.

Happy Learning!

Get a Free eBook

We hope you are enjoying your recently purchased book! Your feedback is incredibly valuable to us, and to all other readers looking for great books.

If you found this book helpful or enjoyable, we would truly appreciate it, if you could take a moment to leave a short review with a 5 star rating on Amazon. It helps us grow, and lets other readers discover our books.

As a thank you, we would love to send you a free digital copy of this book, and a **30%** discount code on your next cart value on our official websites:

www.orangeava.com

www.orangeava.in (For Indian Subcontinent)

☑ **Here's how:**

Leave a review for the book on Amazon.

Take a screenshot of your review, and send an email to **info@orangeava.com** (it can be just the confirmation screen).

Once, we receive your screenshot, we will send you the digital file, within 24 hours.

Thank you so much for your support – it means a lot to us!

Colored Images

Please follow the links or scan the QR codes to download the ***Images*** of the book:

You can find code bundles of our books on our official Github Repository. Go to the following link to and QR code to explore the further:

https://github.com/orgs/ava-orange-education/repositories

Please follow the link to download the Colored Images of the book:
https://rebrand.ly/7962a5

In case there's an update to the code, it will be updated on the existing GitHub repository.

Errata

We take immense pride in our work at **Orange Education Pvt Ltd,** and follow best practices to ensure the accuracy of our content to provide an indulging reading experience to our subscribers. Our readers are our mirrors, and we use their inputs to reflect and improve upon human errors, if any, that may have occurred during the publishing processes involved. To let us maintain the quality and help us reach out to any readers who might be having difficulties due to any unforeseen errors, please write to us at :

errata@orangeava.com

Your support, suggestions, and feedback are highly appreciated.

DID YOU KNOW

Did you know that Orange Education Pvt Ltd offers eBook versions of every book published, with PDF and ePub files available? You can upgrade to the eBook version at **www.orangeava.com** and as a print book customer, you are entitled to a discount on the eBook copy. Get in touch with us at: **info@orangeava.com** for more details.

At **www.orangeava.com**, you can also read a collection of free technical articles, sign up for a range of free newsletters, and receive exclusive discounts and offers on AVA™ Books and eBooks.

PIRACY

If you come across any illegal copies of our works in any form on the internet, we would be grateful if you would provide us with the location address or website name. Please contact us at **info@orangeava.com** with a link to the material.

ARE YOU INTERESTED IN AUTHORING WITH US?

If there is a topic that you have expertise in, and you are interested in either writing or contributing to a book, please write to us at **business@orangeava.com**. We are on a journey to help developers and tech professionals to gain insights on the present technological advancements and innovations happening across the globe and build a community that believes Knowledge is best acquired by sharing and learning with others. Please reach out to us to learn what our audience demands and how you can be part of this educational reform. We also welcome ideas from tech experts and help them build learning and development content for their domains.

REVIEWS

Please leave a review. Once you have read and used this book, why not leave a review on the site that you purchased it from? Potential readers can then see and use your unbiased opinion to make purchase decisions. We at Orange Education would love to know what you think about our products, and our authors can learn from your feedback. Thank you!

For more information about Orange Education, please visit **www.orangeava.com**.

Table of Contents

CHAPTER 1

Introduction to Data Engineering

Introduction

This chapter exposes you to the fundamental concepts, techniques, and tools required for a solid understanding of **data engineering**. You will learn about the modern data ecosystem and the roles that data engineers, data analysts, and data scientists play. The data engineering ecosystem is made up of various components. It comprises many data types, formats, and data sources. Then, we have sequences of data processing steps that transform raw data into analytics-ready data commonly called data pipelines. Data pipelines can be batch or streaming, depending on the frequency and latency of data ingestion and processing. Data pipelines enable data engineers to automate data workflows, ensure data quality and reliability, and deliver timely and accurate data to data consumers. Data pipelines collect data from a variety of sources, turn it into analytics-ready data, and make it available to data consumers for analysis and decision-making. This data is processed and stored in data repositories such as relational databases, non-relational databases, data warehouses, data marts, data lakes, and big data stores. Data integration platforms bring together diverse data sources to create a single perspective for the user.

Structure

In this chapter, we will discuss the following topics:

- Basic Concepts of Data Engineering
- Difference Between Data Engineering, Data Analysis, and Data Science
    - Data Engineering
    - Data Analysis
    - Data Scientist
- Modern Data Ecosystem
- Source Systems, Formats, and Data Types

- Basics of ETL Concepts
    - Extract
    - Transform
    - Load
- Relational and Non-relational Databases
- Data Warehouse and Data Marts
- Data Lake, Big Data Store, Lakehouse, and Delta Lake

Basic Concepts of Data Engineering

Building systems that facilitate data collecting from a variety of source systems and then make it useful for analysis and decision-making after appropriate data cleaning, validating, and transforming is referred to as **data engineering**. Most of the time, this data is utilized to facilitate further analysis and data science, which frequently includes data processing, cleansing, validating, transforming, and machine learning, typically requiring significant computing and storage to make the data usable.

Data engineering helps to collaborate with teams of business intelligence engineers, data scientists, and data analysts.

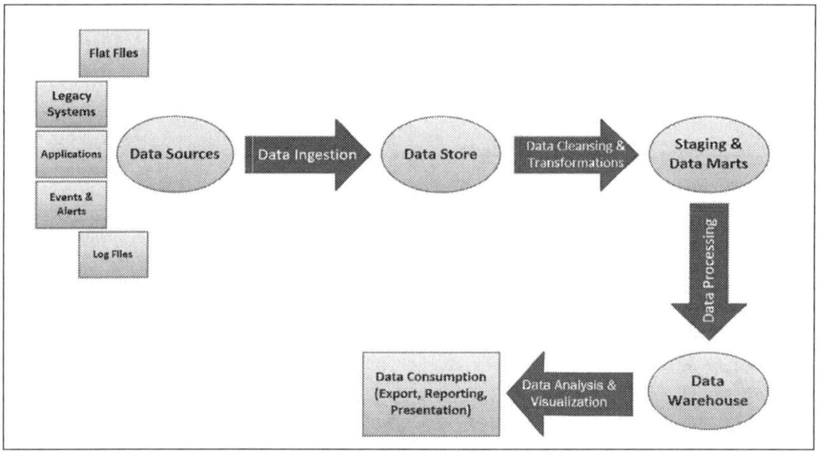

***Figure 1.1**: Data Engineering Architecture Overview*

The preceding figure illustrates how a typical data engineering project's overall architecture look like. The very first step is understanding the **source systems** from which we are expecting the data to flow into the system.

The complexity, accessibility, and availability of the source systems play a crucial role while designing the data pull or extraction process of the raw data, which will eventually be used for **Data Ingestion** and further processing.

We will be discussing the various types of data sources and systems in depth in the later chapters of this book.

Difference Between Data Engineering, Data Analysis, and Data Science

When it comes to defining various job roles related to the data world in any small, medium, or large enterprise, there are basically three major categories to consider: data engineers, data analysts, and data scientists.

On a high level, these roles will sound very similar to each other and are often considered to be the same in the data community, especially for aspiring engineers who are looking to pursue their careers in the database space.

In this section, we will learn about the key aspects of each of the roles and what makes them different from each other.

Data Engineering

Systems that help data scientists and analysts do their jobs are developed and optimized by **data engineers**.

Every business relies on the reliability of its data and the ease with which users may access it. The data engineer makes certain that all data is appropriately received, converted, stored, and made available to other users.

Roles and responsibilities

Data engineers lay the groundwork for data analysts and scientists to build upon. To manage data at a very large scale, data engineers frequently employ sophisticated tools and approaches while building data pipelines. Data engineering has a far stronger emphasis on software development skills than the other two job pathways.

In larger organizations, data engineers may concentrate on using data tools, maintaining databases, or building and managing data pipelines. Regardless of the specific role, a skilled data engineer allows data scientists or analysts to concentrate on finding analytical solutions rather than transferring data from one source to another.

The attitude of a data engineer frequently places greater emphasis on constructing and optimizing. Examples of the kinds of projects a data engineer could be working on include:

- Construction of APIs for data consumption
- Integrating fresh or external datasets into pipelines of data already in use
- Using fresh data to do feature modifications for machine learning models

- Continually testing and monitoring the system to guarantee optimum functioning

Data Analyst

Data analysts add value to their organizations by gathering data, analyzing it to find answers to problems, and conveying the findings to assist management in making choices. Data cleansing, analysis, and data visualization are frequent tasks carried out by data analysts.

The term **data analyst** may be used differently, depending on the industry (for example, "*business analyst*," "*business intelligence analyst*," "*operations analyst*," or "*database analyst*"). Regardless of title, the data analyst is a generalist who can integrate into a variety of roles and teams to support others in making better data-driven decisions.

A traditional company might become data-driven with the help of a data analyst. Their main duty is to aid others in keeping track of their progress and concentrating as best as they can.

Roles and responsibilities

How can a marketer utilize analytics data to aid in the rollout of their next campaign? How can a salesperson choose the right demographics to target? How can a CEO comprehend the fundamental causes of current business growth? The data analyst responds to each of these queries by doing analysis and presenting the findings.

In the larger area of data, data analyst roles are frequently "*entry-level*" occupations, but not all analysts are at this level. Data analysts are essential for businesses that separate technical and business functions because they are skilled communicators who are also knowledgeable about technological tools.

A skilled data analyst will remove uncertainty from business choices and contribute to the success of the entire organization. By merging several reports, analyzing fresh data, and translating the results, the data analyst acts as a useful link between various teams. This, in turn, enables the organization to keep an accurate pulse on its expansion.

The precise abilities needed will vary based on the needs of the firm; however, the following are some typical tasks:

- Data preparation and organization
- Use descriptive statistics to gain a broader perspective on their data
- Examine intriguing trends in the data

- Make dashboards and visualizations to aid in the interpretation and decision-making of data for business
- Deliver the findings of technical analysis to external or internal teams or commercial clients
- Both the technical and non-technical aspects of an organization benefit greatly from the work of the data analyst. The analyst promotes stronger team connections by conducting exploratory analysis or describing executive dashboards.

Data Scientist

A **data scientist** is an expert who uses their knowledge of statistics and available machine learning algorithms to develop machine learning models, make predictions, and provide crucial business insights.

Similar to a data analyst, a data scientist still needs to be able to clean, analyze, and visualize data. A data scientist can also train and improve machine learning models and will have greater depth and competence in these areas.

Roles and responsibilities

A data scientist is someone who can add a great deal of value by addressing more complicated and open-ended problems, making use of their expertise in cutting-edge statistics and algorithms. The scientist concentrates on making accurate forecasts for the future, while the analyst concentrates on comprehending facts from both past and present viewpoints.

By applying both supervised (such as classification and regression) and unsupervised learning (such as clustering, neural networks, and anomaly detection) techniques to their machine learning models, the data scientist will be able to unearth hidden insights. They essentially develop mathematical models that will enable them to recognize trends and make precise forecasts more effectively.

Examples of work done by data scientists include the following:

- Assessing statistical models to assess the reliability of the analyses
- Creating more accurate forecasting algorithms with machine learning
- Testing and ongoing improvement of machine learning model accuracy
- Creating data visualizations to highlight the findings of sophisticated analysis

Data scientists approach and view the world from a completely new viewpoint. The data scientist will pose new queries and develop models to make predictions based on fresh data, whereas an analyst may describe trends and interpret those findings in business terms.

Modern Data Ecosystem

A data ecosystem is a collection of business applications and infrastructure that is used to gather and analyze data. It allows businesses to develop improved marketing, pricing, and operational strategies by helping them better understand their consumers.

Data engineers, data analysts, and data scientists all play a part in the current data ecology. The ecosystem for data engineering consists of a variety of parts. It contains many data sources, formats, and data kinds. Data pipelines collect information from many sources, turn it into data that is suitable for analysis, and then make it accessible to data consumers for analysis and decision-making.

These data are processed and stored in data repositories such as relational databases, non-relational databases, data warehouses, data marts, data lakes, and big data stores. For the benefit of the data consumers, data integration platforms aggregate several types of data into a single perspective. Building data platforms, creating data stores, and collecting, importing, wrangling, querying, and analyzing data are all parts of a typical data engineering lifecycle.

It also includes data governance, compliance, security, monitoring, and changing system performance to ensure the system is operating at its best in a highly optimal way.

The evolution of technology at a rapid pace is leading to the development of several heterogeneous data formats categorized into two major types, that is, structured and unstructured data. This can further be seen in multiple data formats, for example, textual data, images, video streams, chats, data output or conversations, real-time events, various social media platforms, legacy systems, and many more.

Now considering so many diverse and continuously evolving data sources, we need to have a robust data engineering system to make this data insightful for enterprises to be able to use it for an effective decision-making process.

Source Systems, Formats, and Data Types

When it comes to source systems, in modern times, we not only have a variety of source systems but also disparate systems in terms of the formats, the way they store the data, manage the data, transfer data between systems, and extract or export of the data to the downstream systems.

The flexibility of the source systems in the modern data ecosystem to produce or generate a variety of data formats requires a solid data engineering architecture to be in place for a seamless and easy-to-manage process.

In this section, you will learn about the best practices and standards followed to manage this complexity.

Source Systems

The phrase **source systems** should not be used arbitrarily to refer to some systems and not others. When we refer to source systems, we are referring to the data sources that make up a certain data warehouse, which is our starting point when using the phrase. Many businesses follow the Common Data Model, also referred to as CDM, which are mostly connected so that they may also serve as source systems for one another.

However, when we discuss data-generating systems, we may differentiate between those that produce new data and those that do not. A cash register is an example of a system that generates data because, as it scans things, it also creates new data. These files then provide the shop with information about which products, when they are leaving the store, and at what price. The business has the option of deleting the data from the register when the day is done, the client has left, and the register is balanced, but we don't always want to do so because this data may be utilized for many other purposes.

The data-generating system becomes a source system for one or more data warehouses, such as Data Lake, Data Mart, or Delta Lakes, when we decide to preserve the data. We may do a wide range of studies and business initiatives based on the information in the data warehouse (for example, inventory management, supply chain management, earnings analyses, multi-purchase analyses, and more).

Several instances of sources that provide data include:

- **Geospatial Data:** This information, when combined with an app user's location, can lay the groundwork for several new services: we can notify the user that one of our cafés is now within driving distance, and by displaying this message, they can receive a special discount.
- **HR Systems:** This is the information that comes from several employee management programs, which hold the data for the overall organization right from hiring, onboarding, attendance management, payroll, transfers, and termination. Examples of such systems are Workday, Taleo, Tally, and more.
- **Hospital Management Systems (HMS):** These are software applications that handle the administrative, clinical, and financial functions of hospitals and other healthcare facilities. They can store and process data such as patient records, medical histories, prescriptions, lab reports, billing, insurance, inventory, and more. Examples of such systems are Epic, Cerner, Meditech, and others. By analyzing this data, hospitals can enhance the quality of care, lower costs, increase efficiency, and comply with regulations.
- **Reminder Programs:** When clients don't pay their bills on time, these programs remind them. By analyzing the data, we may perform credit scoring and deal situations according to the payment histories of the customers.

- **Banking and Financial Systems:** These are software applications that deal with the main functions of banks and other financial institutions, such as deposit accounts, loans, investments, payments, transfers, and more. They can store and process data, such as customer information, transaction records, balances, interest rates, fees, and others. Systems, such as Oracle FLEXCUBE, Temenos T24, Finacle, and others, are a few examples. Banks and financial institutions can use this data to better their products and services, manage risks, follow regulations, and increase customer satisfaction and loyalty.
- **Telemetry, Monitoring, and Security Systems:** These are software applications that track and examine data from devices or systems that are hard or impossible to reach, such as satellites, aircraft, vehicles, power plants, and more. They can report data like location, speed, temperature, pressure, fuel level, performance, faults, and so on. Systems, such as LabVIEW, PRTG Network Monitor, SolarWinds, and more, are a few examples. This data can help telemetry, monitoring, and security systems improve operations, avoid and fix failures, ensure safety, and give feedback and control.
- **Wearable Devices or Machines:** These are small gadgets that track our physical activity, heart rate, SpO2, walking, running, or sleep activity, and accordingly notify us by analyzing this data over a certain period.
- **Internet of Things (IoT)**: Now, a growing number of gadgets can send sensor data. This information focuses on how the devices – which might be anything from hearing aids to televisions – are used. The information can then be applied to new product development or service enhancements.
- **CRM Programs:** These systems store call and conversation histories from clients. This is essential consumer data that may be used to examine complaint behavior and determine what the company needs to improve. Additionally, it might reveal which clients use a lot of service resources and are consequently less valuable. It serves as an input for improving customer management procedures.
- **ERP Systems:** This data comprises accounting management systems, which record financial transactions for the organization using accounting forms. If we wish to reveal correlations between initiatives and whether outcomes were as anticipated, it can be tied to KPI data.
- **Billing Software Systems**: These systems print invoices to specific clients. We may do segmentations based on behavior, values, and other criteria by looking at this data.
- **Data on Social Media**: This information may be used to gauge the mood of both individuals and groups. It may be quite helpful for employees who manage corporate social relationships since it will provide information on how the public and important influencers see the organization. This type of market

surveillance may be initiated by analyzing the positive and negative terms that are linked with a company using text mining.

- **Wikipedia**: These databases might aid intelligent robots conducting consumer interactions in comprehending complex linkages. For instance, references for a person's name that may be connected to a particular product, place, company, or historical instances or events.

Source Data Formats

The various source systems that we talked about in the preceding section have their own way of sending data to the downstream systems, and this is called data push from the source systems.

Another way of taking data from the preceding source systems is the data pull using any ETL/ELT tools.

Most of the source systems are designed in a way that the data present would be structured data, and hence even the extracted data would be in a **structured format**, but still, we can have some of the source systems outputting data in the form of **unstructured data**.

Unstructured data is typically an unorganized form of data that has no predefined formats or structure attached to it, which makes it a bit difficult to be able to read, process, or analyze. Examples of unstructured data are images, audio files, voice notes, video files, and binary large objects data, which are mostly related to the qualitative aspects of the data.

Unlike unstructured data, **structured data** is much more organized, consistent, easy to store and search, and quantitative in manner.

In the modern data ecosystem, we also have a concept of semi-structured data, which is a mix of both structured and unstructured data. The best example of semi-structured data can be an image captured using any digital media that can store details about the image like date and time, location, and people tagging.

So, in the preceding example, the photo itself becomes unstructured data, while the details related to the photo or what we can call metadata of the photo can be stored as structured data in the form of a table.

Another example could be the online survey forms wherein we fill out the details, such as name, city, age, address, and more. And along with that, we are requested to upload some documents as proof like PAN cards, Identity Proofs, and so on.

The following are some examples of various source data formats:

- There could be source database systems, such as Mainframes, Oracle, Sybase, Teradata, or SQL servers, which will have data stored in a structured format.

- There could be some applications that might be sending data in the form of files, for example, CSV files, text files, excel files, XML files, JSON files, and more.
- There could be systems that might have the data present in the forms of images, videos, PDF files, and more.

It is very crucial to understand the source systems before we proceed with designing any data engineering solutions in terms of the schema of this data output, the frequency at which the data is being changed or updated, the frequency at which new data comes into the system or gets archived away from the system to be able to design a robust architecture for any data engineering solution.

Data Types

The sorts of data that can be stored in database objects like tables are determined by their data types. Each column in a table has a name and a data type, and every table has columns.

Both options are available when building the table. The data type establishes the potential types of interactions and informs the database of what to anticipate from each column. Use the **`"int"`** data type, for instance, if you want a column to only contain integers.

SQL contains several data types, each having its own importance and usability as per the need of the data to be stored. It is equally important to have the right data types defined for the data to be stored for effective memory management, data storage, considering space usability and requirements, and most importantly, the usability of the data while implementing the business rules and statistical functions where we implemented these business rules for analyzing the data, processing the data, and building business metrics for decision making.

We will be discussing in detail each data type in SQL Server and other major database systems used across the industries, along with the implementation scenarios in the later chapters of the book.

Basics of ETL/ELT Concepts

Data is extracted, converted (cleaned, sanitized, and scrubbed), and then loaded into an output data container during the three-step *extract, transform, and load* (ETL) *process*. It is possible to combine data from one or more sources and output it to one or more locations. ETL processing is normally carried out by software programs, although system administrators can also perform it manually. ETL software often automates the entire procedure and can be executed manually, automatically, as a batch of tasks, or on a recurring basis.

An ETL system that has been appropriately built takes data from source systems, enforces data type and data validity criteria, and ensures the data is structurally compliant with the output requirements. For application developers to create applications and end users to make decisions, certain ETL systems may also supply data in a presentation-ready format.

An ETL process is one of the most crucial and an integral part of any data engineering system architecture.

Alternatively, another way to integrate data is *extraction, loading, and transformation (ELT)*, where the data is first moved to the destination and then transformed there. This approach leverages the computing power and storage space of the target system to speed up the data transfer and store multiple versions of the raw data. The main difference between ETL and ELT is the order of steps and the location of the data transformation. ETL changes the data before moving it to the ETL tool or on a separate server, while ELT changes the data after moving it to the destination.

Moreover, ETL often needs a more precise definition of the data models and schemas beforehand, while ELT allows for more agility and adaptability. The decision between ETL and ELT depends on several factors, such as the type and volume of data sources, business needs, available resources, and analytics objectives.

In the modern data ecosystem, ELT is especially suitable for cloud-based data warehouses or data lakes that offer high scalability and flexibility.

As abbreviated, it has three major components. First, it extracts the data from source systems. Second, the transformation of data as per the business requirements, which includes cleaning of data, the transformation of data types as per the need, the merging of data, and many more, and finally loading the data into a destination, which typically can be any data warehouse system or into a data lake in the form of files.

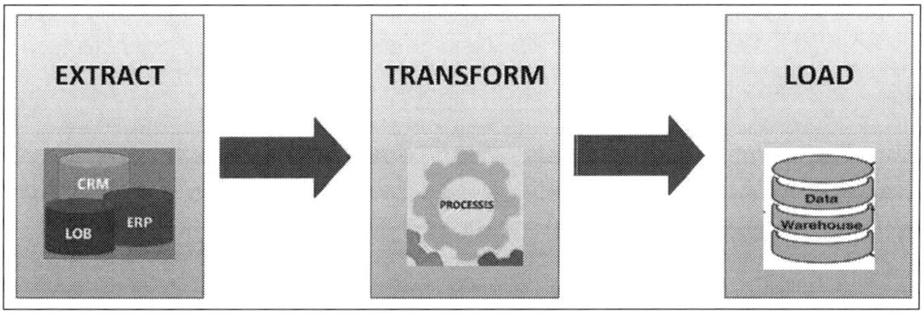

***Figure 1.2**: ETL Overview*

Extract

The very first stage of an ETL process is data extraction where you can manually extract the data from any of the source systems. It could be either push or pull, where either we go and pull the data from source systems or the source system pushes the data via a certain mechanism.

We do have a very robust set of tools specially designed for ETL processes that provide us with inbuilt tasks to connect to various kinds of source systems to be able to pull the data. Microsoft Business Intelligence Suite, popularly known as MSBI, contains one of the most powerful ETL tools, which is known as SQL Server Integration Services (SSIS).

The solution designed using SSIS is called a package, and it enables us to have an end-to-end control flow to build a data engineering solution and a data flow to be able to extract the data from various source systems.

In the Azure cloud world, we are one of the most powerful data transformation capabilities, which is the Azure Data Factory, commonly known as ADF. This has the concept of pipelines that make this data flow seamlessly from various source systems to target systems.

Transform

Once the data is extracted from the source systems, it may or may not be usable in a straightforward manner, and hence it would require some transformations to be able to make the data usable in the downstream systems.

These transformations could be as simple as pulling from two different datasets and merging them into one, or transforming the data types coming from heterogeneous systems with incompatible data types to enable them to be merged together.

The transformation section provides a powerful pack of features that also enables us to design the package or the solution based on specific business requirements in a GUI-based approach with minimal coding needs.

Load

The last and final part of this process is loading the data into destination systems after the transformations have been applied to the data, and now the data is ready as per the target architecture of the data warehouse systems.

The business might need us to load the data either into data marts, data warehouses, data lakes in the form of files or multiple other destinations.

It could be requirements wherein we need to load the data into flat files or excel files based on the needs of the business, and subsequently, these files will be delivered in a push mechanism to the end user either in the form of an e-mail on some preset frequency, for example, daily, weekly, or monthly emails or can be loaded into some file share or cloud storage like Azure BLOB storage from where it can be again passed on to further downstream systems.

Some business requirements may also involve loading the data into universal data formats, such as JSON, XML, or Parquet files. These formats are widely used for data interchange and processing across different platforms and applications.

They have some advantages over relational databases, such as:

- **JavaScript Object Notation (JSON)**: It is a lightweight and human-readable format that can store and represent complex data structures, such as arrays and nested objects. It is easy to parse and generate by various programming languages and web services. JSON is often used for RESTful APIs and NoSQL databases.
- **Extensible Markup Language (XML)**: It is a markup language that can define and structure data using tags and attributes. It can also support schemas, namespaces, and validation rules to ensure data consistency and quality. XML is often used for data exchange and integration among heterogeneous systems and applications.
- **Parquet**: It is a columnar storage format that can efficiently compress and encode large-scale datasets. It can preserve the schema and metadata of the data and support complex data types, such as maps and arrays. Parquet is often used for big data analytics and machine learning on platforms like Apache Spark and Hadoop.

Additionally, we can create Azure Landing Zone, which is a set of best practices and guidelines for creating a scalable and secure cloud environment on Microsoft Azure. It helps organizations to accelerate their cloud adoption journey and optimize their cloud governance, security, and operations. Azure Landing Zone consists of four key components: core platform, identity and access management, security and compliance, and monitoring and operations.

Relational and Non-relational Databases

Data is stored in **relational databases** as tables with rows and columns.

A table in a relational database contains data, which is subsequently connected to data in other tables by the use of special identification keys. A primary key, which uniquely identifies a row in one table, links with a foreign key, which uniquely identifies a row of data in a different table, to build associations between the tables.

In essence, relational databases are made to hold structured data or data that is well-defined and can be readily standardized inside a table, such as names, dates, and amounts. The most popular programming language for interacting with relational databases in relational database management systems (RDBMS) is Structured Query Language (SQL).

Well-defined structured data may be stored, retrieved from, and modified using relational databases. They are simple to utilize.

The following are some of the most popular relational databases:

- Microsoft SQL Server (on-premises)
- Azure SQL database
- Azure SQL managed instance
- PostgreSQL or Azure Database for PostgreSQL
- MySQL or Azure Database for MySQL
- Oracle
- Sybase
- Teradata
- Mainframe DB2

A **non-relational database** is a sort of database that stores data in whichever format is most appropriate for the type of data being saved rather than in tables. In essence, non-relational databases are made to store unstructured data or data that is not easily standardized and has a vague definition, such as email messages, videos, photos, and business documents. A combination of organized and unstructured data can be stored in them as well.

Non-relational databases may be created in a variety of methods. Key-value stores, column-family data stores, graph databases, and document databases are a few of the most popular strategies. Though many NoSQL databases accept SQL queries, they are still considered non-relational and termed NoSQL because they do not utilize Structured Query Language.

The following are some of the most popular non-relational databases:

- MongoDB
- Amazon DynamoDB
- Apache Cassandra

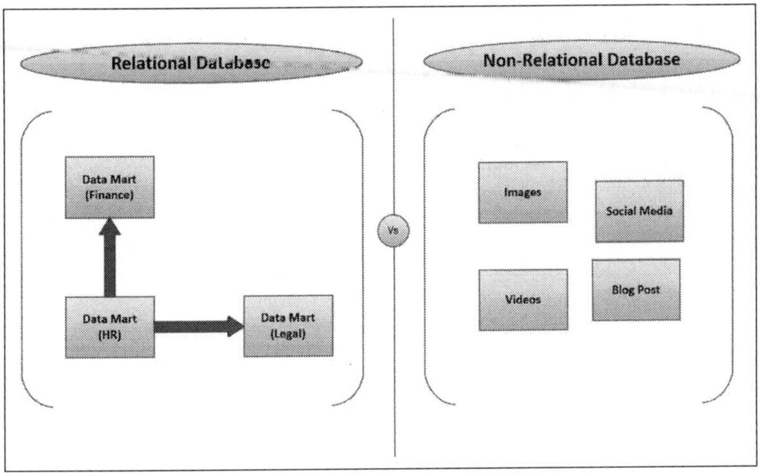

***Figure 1.3**: Relational vs. Non-relational Databases*

Data Warehouse and Data Marts

A **data warehouse** is a centralized location where all data of an organization is stored and organized for analysis. Data from client records to information from external cloud-based apps may be included in a data warehouse. It serves as the company's one-stop location for looking up any kind of data asset.

Additionally, a data warehouse facilitates data analysis and serves as the basis for all business analysis and data mining activities carried out by businesses.

Because it is read-focused and intended for analytical activities, a data warehouse differs from a database in this regard. Information from several databases may be included in a conventional data warehouse. A data warehouse is created by repeated procedures that extract information from real data sources, such as databases and cloud-based apps. A data lake may occasionally provide data to a data warehouse.

In an organization, a **data mart** is a centralized repository for information pertinent to a certain topic or problem. For its sales department and finance department, for instance, a company may build a data mart. It does not contain all the organization's data and is customized for a specific audience. Data marts frequently process data pertaining to a certain subject and cover that subject.

A data mart is additionally specialized and created with analytical needs in mind. If any database or source's data is pertinent to the target domain, it can contain information from many different sources. Data marts exist to prevent analysts from becoming overwhelmed with the organization's data and to make it simple for them to obtain data from several sources.

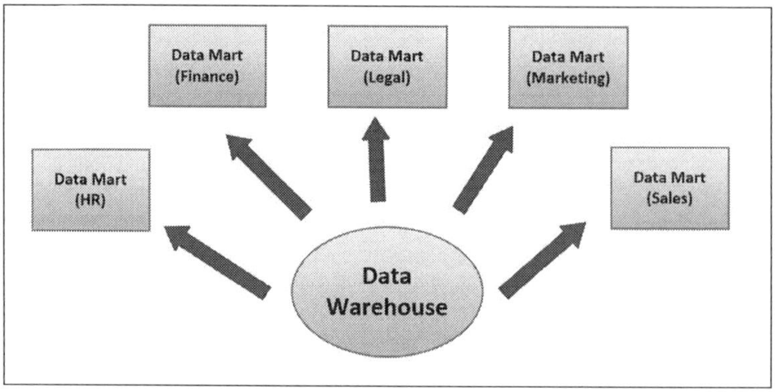

***Figure 1.4**: Data Warehouse vs. Data Marts*

Overall, a company's goals and available resources will determine whether to employ a data warehouse or a data mart. Data warehouses are a great answer in almost any circumstance due to their adaptability and flexibility. They can provide storage for a variety of data types and assist you in drawing valuable conclusions from them.

When you need to analyze a specific subset of data, data marts are an excellent solution. They provide similar capabilities to data warehouses, but they specifically customize your data to the issue you're trying to solve.

Data Lake, Big Data Store, Lakehouse, and Delta Lake

As we wrap up this chapter, let us give a quick overview of some other terms that are relevant to data engineering that you may come across in your journey. Data Lake, Big Data Store, Lakehouse, and Delta Lake are some of the words that refer to different methods of storing and processing huge volumes of data.

A **Data Lake** is a storage system that can hold any type of data, no matter how it is structured, formatted, or originated. Data lakes are commonly used for big data analysis, as they enable users to access raw data without any pre-set schema or transformation. Data lakes can be constructed on cloud platforms or on-premises servers, using distributed file systems like Hadoop and object storage services like Amazon S3 or Azure Data Lake Gen2, also known as blob storage containers.

A **Big Data Store** is a database system that can manage huge amounts of structured or semi-structured data, such as social media posts, weblogs, sensor data, and more. Big data stores are built to scale horizontally, meaning that they can grow by adding more nodes to improve their capacity and performance. Big data stores often use a non-relational or NoSQL model, which lets them store data in flexible formats and support different kinds of queries. Examples of big data stores are MongoDB, Cassandra, Elasticsearch, and others.

A **Lakehouse** is a system that combines the best of both worlds: a data lake and a data warehouse. A Lakehouse can handle any type of data, like a data lake, but also provides schema validation, quality assurance, and query optimization, like a data warehouse. A Lakehouse aims to provide a single platform for both batch and stream processing, as well as for both analytical and operational workloads. A Lakehouse can use technologies such as Apache Spark, Apache Parquet, and Delta Lake to achieve high performance and reliability.

A **Delta Lake** is a type of Lakehouse, created by Databricks. It is a storage layer that works on a data lake and provides features such as ACID transactions, schema evolution, versioning, and time travel. Delta Lake can manage both batch and stream data and allow both SQL and programmatic access. A Delta Lake can enhance the reliability and productivity of data engineering and data science workflows.

Conclusion

On a high level, this chapter has provided a basic and intermediate understanding of what data engineering is all about and how it is related or different from the other highly recognized job responsibilities, such as data analyst and data scientist.

In the next chapter, we will be focusing on the concepts of Relational Database Management System, otherwise referred to as RDBMS. To comprehend SQL and all other examples of current databases, including MS Access, SQL, MS SQL Server, and others, one must have a fundamental understanding of RDBMS.

Key Terms

- Heterogeneous and disparate data sources
- Data analysis and data science
- Extract, transform, and load
- Relational and non-relational databases
- Data warehouse
- Data marts
- Data Lake, Delta Lake, and Lakehouse

Chapter 2
Understanding SQL and RDBMS Concepts

Introduction

This chapter introduces the fundamental concepts, techniques, and tools required for a solid understanding of **SQL and RDBMS concepts**. RDBMS stands for Relational Database Management System. RDBMS is the basis for SQL and for all modern database systems like MS SQL Server, IBM DB2, Oracle, MySQL, and Microsoft Access. A relational database management system (RDBMS) is a program that allows you to create, update, and administer a relational database. Most relational database management systems use the SQL language to access the database.

Structured Query Language (SQL) is a programming language used to communicate with data stored in a relational database management system. SQL syntax is like the English language, which makes it relatively easy to write, read, and interpret.

Many RDBMSs use SQL (and variations of SQL) to access the data in tables.

Structure

In this chapter, we will discuss the following topics:

- Basic Concepts of RDBMS
- Components of RDBMS
    - Table
    - Column (Field or Attribute)
    - Record (Tuple)
    - Domain
    - Schema
    - Constraints
- Database Normalization

- Advantages and Limitations of RDBMS
- Basic Concepts of SQL
  - SQL Capabilities
  - SQL Commands and Types
- SQL Server and Client Architecture

Basic Concepts of RDBMS

Computer programs known as database management systems (DBMS) let users interact with databases. Users can write data, conduct queries, manage database access, and carry out any other database administration-related operations with the help of a DBMS.

Nevertheless, **DBMS** needs some sort of underlying model that specifies how the data is arranged to carry out any of these functions. Since its inception in the late 1960s, database software has made extensive use of the **relational model**, one of the method of data organization. In fact, as of this writing, four of the top five most-used DBMSs are relational.

Databases consists of logically modeled groups of data or information. No matter how or where the data is stored, any collection of data is a database. A database can even be found in a filing cabinet holding payroll data, a pile of hospital patient forms, or a company's collection of client data dispersed among several sites. Physical databases like this were the only ones available to government and commercial organizations that required them to keep information before storing and managing data with computers became commonplace.

There were no hypotheses, meanwhile, regarding how computers could arrange data logically and meaningfully. Storing unorganized data on a computer is one thing, but designing systems that let you add, retrieve, sort, and handle the data in other useful ways consistently is far more difficult. Many ideas for using computers to handle data were inspired by the requirement for a logical framework for data storage and organization.

How Relational Databases Organize Data

Tables, or relations, are the most basic components of the relational model and are recognized by both users and contemporary RDBMSs. A relation in a table is a collection of tuples, or rows, where each tuple shares a set of columns or attributes.

Components of RDBMS

There are several components of RDBMS, which can be categorized into three high-level sections: data structures, data integrity, and data manipulation.

Data structures consist of how particular data can be defined, what values it can take, and how we can use them in the database operations. Examples of data structures are stacks, queues, trees, linked lists, graphs, and so on.

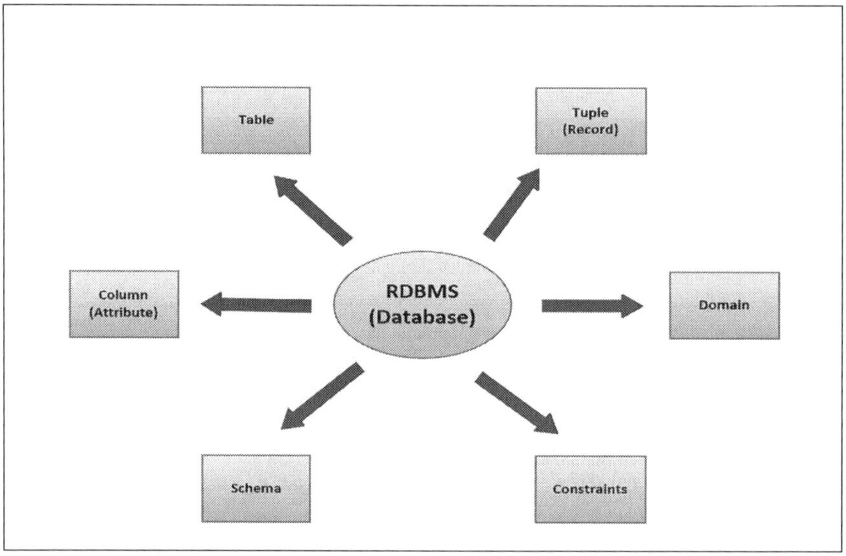

***Figure 2.1**: RDBMS components*

Table

Tables, which are database objects, are where data is kept in an RDBMS. This table, which has many columns and rows, is essentially an assortment of related data entries.

Recall that the most popular and basic type of data storage in a relational database is a table. An example of a Person table, which contains a person's ID, name, age, city, and country, is shown here:

ID	Name	Age	City	Country
1	Ashish	33	Hyderabad	India
2	Neha	34	Hyderabad	India
3	Ankita	30	Mumbai	India
4	Aayush	31	Mumbai	India
5	Rahul	33	Jaipur	India
6	Jhalak	32	Jaipur	India
7	Saransh	25	Ajmer	India

8	Anaisha	7	Hyderabad	India
9	Aaranya	3	Hyderabad	India

***Table 2.1**: Person table*

Column (Field or Attribute)

In a relational database, the fundamental building block is the column, which represents distinct characteristics defining each record within a table. These attributes, as they are formally termed, encapsulate the diverse facets of data. Each tuple, in turn, serves as a unique instance of the individuals, objects, events, or relationships stored in the database. Examples may range from lab test results and online sales to personnel information within an organization. Consider a table capturing teacher employment records at a school, where tuples encompass attributes such as date of admission, student name, subjects, and more. This relational structure provides a robust framework for organizing and managing diverse datasets, offering a comprehensive view of the interconnected information within a database.

You designate a data type when constructing columns, which determines the types of data that are permitted in that column. RDBMSs frequently create their own proprietary data types that might not be immediately convertible to comparable data types in other systems. Booleans, dates, numbers, and texts are a few examples of common data types.

Column names are also referred to as one of the attributes and are used to map data to the appropriate names.

In the preceding example of the Person table, ID, name, age, city, and country are all fields or columns.

ID	Name	Age	City	Country

Record (Tuple)

We have data in the database organized into different tuples. Under the properties, we refer to these tuples as rows. Here, the terms row, record, and tuple are used interchangeably.

ID	Name	Age	City	Country
1	Ashish	33	Hyderabad	India

In the preceding example, the row or record against the ID = 1 is a tuple, or most commonly called as a row, and it can be identified with a unique Identification based on various business scenarios.

Domain

The range of data that a database is allowed to hold is known as its domain.

- Example 1: Since age cannot be negative when referring to age, the domain is higher than 0. Let's see the same thing.
- Example 2: If there is a table for maintaining employees' payroll data and if it has a salary column, then it should only contain values higher than 0. So, this is called domain.

Most commonly, the date columns should be domain-bound and taken care of while dealing with the RDBMS operations and data insertion.

Schema

A schema is a table's composition. To put it simply, the database's schema consists of the columns and the kinds of data they hold.

The following table gives an overview of the schema of the Person table, that is, what is the type of a column, whether it is a computed column or not, what is the acceptable length, and so on.

Column Name	Type	Computed	Length
ID	`Int`	No	4
Name	`Varchar`	No	150
Age	`Int`	No	4
City	`Varchar`	No	100
Country	`Varchar`	No	100

Table 2.2: *Schema of the Person table*

Note: *Just for a note, let's not confuse the database schema with the schema of the table.*

A logical grouping of database objects, including tables, views, stored procedures, indexes, triggers, and functions, is referred to as a database schema in SQL Server. It is comparable to a container that a database user has constructed. The schema owner is the database user who generates the schema.

A database may contain one or more schemas, but a schema can only be part of one database.

A schema can include an unlimited number of objects.

We have access to several built-in schemas from SQL Server, such as "**`dbo`**", "**`guest`**", "**`sys`**", and so on.

Constraints

Constraints are rules or conditions applied to the data in a database table. When data is entered and kept up to date in our database, we wish to apply some guidelines for the correctness and maintaining the integrity of the data.

Constraints help us to preserve the correctness and integrity of our data. Our use case will determine whether we have constraints at the column or table level.

The following table lists the RDBMS constraints:

Sr. No	Constraint	Description
1	NOT NULL	Prevents the column from taking NULL values
2	DEFAULT	Sets a default value for the column
3	UNIQUE	Prevents duplicate values in the column
4	PRIMARY KEY	Helps to identify each record uniquely
5	FOREIGN KEY	Helps to identify each record in another database uniquely
6	CHECK	Applies certain conditions on the column data
7	INDEX	Helps in creating and the retrieval of records

***Table 2.3**: RDMS constraints*

Database Normalization

Data in a database is filtered and organized through the process of database normalization. The following justifies the requirement for database normalization:

- It aids in the removal of unnecessary information, enabling efficient use of the memory that is available.
- It aids in ensuring the logical accuracy of the data dependencies.

Following are the four major normal forms:

- **1NF or First Normal Form**: We make sure a database is free of multi-value records while it is in First Normal Form. For every attribute, there is a single value stored in each record.
- **2NF or Second Normal Form**: Builds on 1NF and ensures that all non-key attributes (columns) are fully functionally dependent on the entire primary key. Eliminates partial dependencies, where non-key attributes depend on only a part of the primary key.
- **3NF or Third Normal Form**: Builds on 2NF and ensures that there are no transitive dependencies. Eliminates dependencies where non-key attributes depend on other non-key attributes.

- **BCNF or Boyce Codd Normal Form**: A database must be in 3NF to be in BCNF form. In addition to this, we also need to verify the transitive dependency. If the database is in BCNF, there should not be any transitive dependencies.

Advantages and Limitations of RDBMS

Here are the advantages and limitations of RDBMS:

Advantages

- It aids in preserving the data's integrity.
- Relationships within the data are preserved and made easily accessible by RDBMS.
- We can use constraints to apply different types of tests on our data with the aid of RDBMS.
- We may access data via every component that is available, thanks to RDBMS.
- Relational databases offer significant advantage of widespread support for transactions within relational database management systems (RDBMS). A transaction is composed of a sequence of one or more SQL statements executed as a single unit. Adopting an all-or-nothing approach, all SQL statements within the transaction must be executed flawlessly for its success; any error will cause it to fail. This feature is instrumental in preserving data integrity during the modification of multiple rows or tables.
- Finally, relational databases offer a great deal of flexibility. They are effective even when dealing with massive volumes of data and have been utilized to create a wide range of applications. Additionally, SQL is incredibly powerful since it lets you add and modify data at any time, as well as change database schema and table structures without affecting already-existing data.
- One of the main benefits of transactions in relational databases is that they ensure the ACID properties, which are:
    - **Atomicity:** A transaction is either fully completed or not executed at all. If any part of the transaction fails, the entire transaction is rolled back and the database state is restored to what it was before the transaction started.
    - **Consistency**: A transaction preserves the validity of the database state by enforcing the integrity constraints, such as primary keys, foreign keys, and check constraints. After a transaction is committed, the database remains in a consistent state.
    - **Isolation**: A transaction is executed as if it is the only one running on the

database without interference from other concurrent transactions. The degree of isolation can be adjusted according to different levels, such as serializable, repeatable read, read committed, and read uncommitted.

  - **Durability**: A transaction's effects are permanent and persist even in the event of a system failure or power outage. Once a transaction is committed, the changes are recorded in a persistent storage device and cannot be lost or undone.

Limitations

- Horizontal scalability of a relational database can be challenging. The process of adding more machines to an existing stack to share the load that enables more traffic and speeds up processing is known as horizontal scaling or scaling out. This is frequently contrasted with vertical scaling, which entails improving an existing server's hardware – typically by increasing its RAM or CPU.
- Because the relational model is built to guarantee consistency – that is, clients querying the same database will always return the same data – it is challenging to extend a relational database horizontally. Consistency would be challenging to maintain when scaling a relational database horizontally across several machines since clients might write data to one node but not the others. Inconsistencies amongst the other nodes would arise from the probable delay between the initial write and the time when they are updated to reflect the changes.
- The relational model was created to handle structured data or data that fits into an established data type or is at the very least arranged in a preset way, making it simple to sort and search. This is another drawback of RDBMSs.

Basic Concepts of SQL

SQL, which stands for Structured Query Language, is a computer language used for relational database operations and inquiries. These queries may include updating, altering, or creating a new database. In the realm of technology, major database operations are referred to as CRUD operations or Create, Read, Update, and Delete.

The massive amounts of data that are produced nowadays must be stored in the database.

SQL is an indispensable tool for anyone working with data daily. Data can be added to a database using SQL.

Relational databases are used by SQL to process commands and queries. The phrase "*relational database*" denotes that information is kept and retrieved via relations or tables.

A table contains the necessary results that the command gives when we run it on SQL Workbench or a comparable program.

SQL Capabilities

- SQL can be used to query a database.
- CRUD (Create, Retrieve, Update, Delete) activities on a database are carried out via SQL.
- To update and modify the current data in the database, we utilize SQL.
- A database table that already exists can have views created over it using SQL.
- When we need to distribute permissions among many database users, SQL proves to be helpful.
- SQL is easy to use for database transactions since it can be used with nearly any computer language, including Python, Java, C++, and so on.

SQL Commands and Types

SQL executes user-provided commands to function.

Based on the features they offer, we can categorize the SQL commands into five groups:

- DDL (Data Definition Language)
- DML (Data Manipulation Language)
- DQL (Data Query Language)
- TCL (Transaction Control Language)
- DCL (Data Control Language)

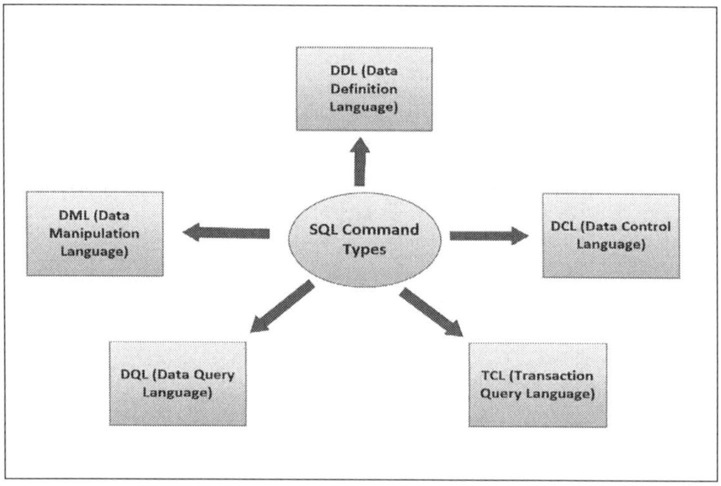

***Figure 2.2**: SQL commands and types*

The following table lists the various commands as part of all command types available in SQL:

Command Type	Command	Description
DDL	`CREATE`	Creates a new table, a view, or other object in the database
	`ALTER`	Modifies an existing database object
	`DROP`	Deletes an entire table, a view of a table, or other objects in the database
	`TRUNCATE`	Truncates the entire table in a go
DQL	`SELECT`	Retrieves the data stored in the database created by us and the data we store in the database
DML	`INSERT`	Populates and add data to the database already existing
	`UPDATE`	Changes the data that is already saved in the database
	`DELETE`	Deletes the existing records of a database
DCL	`GRANT`	Grants access to a designated group of people to carry out tasks
	`REVOKE`	Revokes all previously issued or rejected authorizations
TCL	`COMMIT`	Saves a transaction into the database permanently
	`ROLLBACK`	Rolls back a transaction to any stored state and restores the database to the last commit state. It can also be used in conjunction with the SAVE POINT command.
	`SAVEPOINT`	Allows us to quickly access a transaction's necessary point at any time by storing it in a temporary location

***Table 2.4**: SQL command and types*

SQL Server and Client Architecture

SQL Server has two main parts: server components and client components. The server components run on a machine that has SQL Server installed and offer the main features of the database system. The client components are programs or tools that link to the server components and let users work with the data.

- **Server Components**
  - **Database Engine:** The core component responsible for storing, processing, and securing data. It includes the query processor, storage engine, and other essential components.
  - **SQL Server Instance**: An installation of SQL Server on a machine. Each instance can host multiple databases.
  - **Databases**: Containers for data storage organized into tables, views, stored procedures, and other database objects.
- **Client-Server Interaction**
  - **Client:** Applications or tools that initiate requests and interact with the SQL Server. Examples include desktop applications, web applications, and other database management tools.
  - **Server:** The machine hosting the SQL Server instance.
- **Communication**
  - **Protocols:** SQL Server uses various protocols for communication. Commonly used protocols include TCP/IP and Named Pipes.
  - **Ports:** SQL Server communicates over specific ports, and the client needs to connect to the correct port to establish a connection.
- **Client Tools**
  - **SQL Server Management Studio (SSMS):** A graphical user interface tool used for managing SQL Server databases, executing queries, and performing administrative tasks.
  - **SQL Server Data Tools (SSDT):** An integrated development environment for designing, developing, testing, and deploying SQL Server databases.
- **Command-Line Tools**: SQL Server provides command-line tools like `sqlcmd` for executing SQL commands and scripts.
- **Connection Process:** The client initiates a connection to the SQL Server instance by providing the necessary connection information, such as server name, authentication details, and database name. The SQL Server processes the client's requests, which may include queries, updates, or other database operations. Results or responses are sent back to the client.
- **Security:** SQL Server implements security mechanisms, including authentication and authorization, to control access to the databases and ensure data integrity.

Microsoft SQL Server is a relational database management system (RDBMS). Tools and applications use Transact-SQL (T-SQL) to interface with an SQL Server instance or database.

SQL server can be installed on an on-premises machine, which could be a Windows or a Linux machine. We can also deploy this on a Linux container as well as any other IaaS platform, for example, an Azure virtual machine on Cloud.

The on-premises version of SQL Server is also known as the boxed product. The latest version of SQL Server available today is SQL Server 2022, which can be downloaded from the official site of Microsoft with appropriate licensing.

The core component of a SQL Server is a database engine that is used for storing, processing, and securing data. The database engine also provides controlled access and transaction processing to meet the requirements of the most demanding data-consuming applications within your enterprise. It also provides good support for business continuity.

The same database engine is used for many other products and services, which are listed as follows:

- Azure SQL database
- Azure SQL managed instance
- Azure synapse analytics
- Azure SQL edge
- Microsoft Analytics Platform System (PDW)

Client

Once you have the SQL Server installed and ready for the data storage processing and other important operations from a database engine perspective, we will need a client to be able to query the data you know on the server and do all other sorts of operations like data retrieval and so on.

There are many prominent client tools available in the market, but the most widely used is the SQL Server Management Studio (SSMS). We also have the latest tool available from Microsoft, which is Azure Data Studio, which can also be used to connect to the SQL servers posted on-premises as well as on Cloud and various SQL DB PaaS Services.

In this book, we will be widely using these client tools and their features while performing various SQL query exercises and other database operations.

Conclusion

In this chapter, we have learned about the concepts of Relational Database Management System, also referred to as RDBMS. This will help us to comprehend SQL and all other examples of current databases, including MS Access, SQL, MS SQL Server, and so on.

In the next chapter, we will be focusing on the major differential aspects of data engineering in an on-premises environment versus Azure Cloud. This will help you understand how the data engineering concepts are transforming as a part of Azure Cloud journey as compared to long-running on-premises setup and how we can leverage these for large-scale enterprise data estate modernizations.

Key Terms

- **RDBMS**: A relational database management system (RDBMS) is a program that allows you to create, update, and administer a relational database.
- **Normalization**: Data in a database is filtered and organized through the process of database normalization.
- **SQL Concepts**: Basic concepts are about the structured query language, semantics, syntax and operations related to SQL.
- **DDL, DML, DCL, TCL, and DQL**: These are the various types of SQL commands categorized as defining, manipulating, controlling, and querying.
- **SQL Client and Server Architecture**: A server hosts the database and is the underlying engine, and the client is used to connect to and perform operations on the server.

CHAPTER 3

Data Engineering: Azure Versus On-Premises

Introduction

Data engineering across on-premises and cloud is another intriguing subject that should be worked on and analyzed in terms of similarities and contrasts. Although the core concept remains the same, each public Cloud has its own set of advantages and disadvantages. The major changes that occur are in terms of data accessibility, ETL, storage, database engine, and security.

Data engineering entails creating, developing, testing, and up-keeping data pipelines that ensure the flow, alteration, and provision of data from diverse sources to different endpoints. It encompasses tasks, such as data collection, cleaning, merging, transfiguring, storing, warehousing, modeling, analyzing, and visualizing. Data engineering underpins various applications such as business intelligence, data science, machine learning, and analytics.

Off-site data engineering implies that data engineers deploy and govern their data framework on physical servers or virtual platforms within their firm's networks. This method grants total control and adaptability over the data setting but also obliges them to handle issues related to scalability, uptime, security, and upkeep.

Alternatively, Azure data engineering involves the use of Microsoft Azure's Cloud solutions and services to construct and operate data processes. This method provides benefits such as scalable operations, flexible resources, dependable security, and cost efficiency offered by the cloud, necessitating adjustments to the cloud-oriented architecture, tools, and recommended practices.

In this chapter, we will contrast the on-premises and Azure-based data engineering methods using SQL Server, which is a widely used relational database system capable of handling both transactional and analytical tasks. Our focus will revolve around four essential aspects: data intake, data alteration, data repository, and data safeguarding. Additionally, we will discuss multiple database engine options for SQL Server available on Azure, including IaaS (SQL Server on Windows\Linux), PaaS (SQL DB, SQL Managed Instance, SQL DB - Elastic Pools, SQL DB - Hyperscale).

Structure

In this chapter, we will discuss the following topics:

- Introducing Data Engineering Scenarios
  - Microsoft SQL Server and Business Intelligence Suite
  - Microsoft Azure
  - Overview of a Typical Data Engineering Solution
- Components or Stages Involved in Data Engineering
  - Homogenous and Heterogeneous Data Sources
  - Identifying the Source System(s) and Data
  - Deciding the Data Pull Checkpoint and Frequency
  - Building an ETL Solution Using an Appropriate Tool
  - Designing a Data Warehouse to Store Data
  - Deciding the Data Refresh Methodology (Full vs. Incremental)
  - Automating the Process and Scheduling Jobs
  - Building Reporting Systems for End-user Data Access

Introducing Data Engineering Scenarios

So when we talk about data engineering in the on-premises world, it is about how in the traditional world of data engineering can be used to design and develop an end-to-end solution architecture to deal with various types of source database systems or raw data store or scattered over multiple places and then taking that data, process it, transform it into meaningful data or structured data. The journey continues with an analytical lens, where the data undergoes thorough analysis, business rules are applied, and meaningful insights are unearthed. The goal is to channel this refined data into a designated destination, serving as a singular source of truth. This consolidated information powerhouse becomes instrumental for decision-making across various organizational facets, spanning operations, sales, marketing, finance, and beyond. It forms the backbone for informed decision-making at multiple levels within the organization, fostering efficiency and strategic prowess.

In an on-premises setup, all the above-mentioned steps are managed by the organization or an infra provider who will have a responsibility to provide the infrastructure required by the organization to fulfill all their data engineering needs that includes the physical machines, such as servers, the hardware needed for installing those servers, all the licenses for operating systems and subsequent software, the licenses for the other required software, for example, the antivirus and any other security related software, editors and integrated development environments, the database server software, for example, SQL Server, SQL client software to be able to connect to those server systems, for example, SSMS (SQL Server Management Studio), Azure Data Studio, and so on.

Additionally, the organization or the infrastructure provider will be responsible for any updates to this operating system or software, patching and maintenance activities, maintaining the backups and recovery of the database, and any other disaster recovery or high availability scenarios.

Another key challenging aspect of data engineering in an on-premises environment is keeping track of the hardware and software lifecycle which can become obsolete or reach its end-of-life. This might compromise the efficiency, safety, and dependability of both data warehouses and BI solutions. For instance, if the hardware is not updated to handle growing data volumes and processing needs, it may hinder or even disrupt loading and query operations, potentially leading to failures and data loss. Comparable issues arise with software; failing to update it can leave the data warehouse vulnerable to threats, glitches, or incompatibility problems with different tools and applications. Consequently, data engineers must keep an eye on hardware and software lifecycles and schedule appropriate updates, substitutions, or transitions. These activities can be costly, require significant effort, and carry inherent risks, especially in the case of extensive and intricate data warehouses. Additionally, it is crucial for data engineers to ensure that hardware and software adhere to company policies and standards, as well as comply with sector regulations and recommended practices, further complicating the data engineering tasks.

Microsoft SQL Server and Business Intelligence Suite

Business Intelligence (BI) is an interesting and useful field that can help businesses make better decisions based on data analysis. Microsoft Business Intelligence (MSBI) is a suite of tools that can help implement a data warehouse using SQL Server. Some of the tools included in MSBI are:

- SQL Server Integration Services (SSIS) is a tool that can extract, transform, and load data from various sources into a data warehouse.
- SQL Server Analysis Services (SSAS) is a tool that can create multidimensional cubes and models for data analysis and reporting.
- SQL Server Reporting Services (SSRS) is a tool that can design and generate reports from data sources.

These tools can work together to provide a complete solution for business intelligence.

Some of the additional modern day or Cloud world services are Synapse, Power BI, Azure Analysis Services, Azure Data Factory (ADF), Databricks, Microsoft Fabric, and so on.

Microsoft Azure

Microsoft Azure is a Cloud platform that offers various services and tools for data engineering, enabling data processing and analysis at scale.

Some of the main data engineering services that Azure provides are:

- Azure SQL Database and SQL Managed Instance are PaaS-managed database engine offerings provided by Azure.
- Azure HDInsight is a fully managed service that runs Hadoop and Spark frameworks for processing large datasets.
- Azure Databricks is a managed service that enhances data engineering and machine learning on an optimized platform. Built on Apache Spark, it provides a shared workspace, interactive notebooks, and smooth workflows. It integrates with multiple Azure data sources and services including Azure Blob Storage, Azure Data Lake Storage, Azure Cosmos DB, Azure SQL Database, and Azure Synapse Analytics.
- Azure Stream Analytics is a service that allows real-time data streaming and analytics.
- Azure Synapse Analytics is a fully managed data warehouse that can handle petabytes of data.
- Azure Data Factory is a fully managed ETL service that can transform and move data from different sources.
- Azure Blob Storage is Microsoft's object storage solution for the Cloud. It is optimized for storing massive amounts of unstructured data, such as text, binary, or files.

Overview of a Typical Data Engineering Solution

Let us consider a problem statement wherein we need to design a data engineering solution for a large enterprise dealing with multiple systems to cater to their business needs and data access solutions across multiple departments (*Figure* 3.1).

Sample Architecture - I

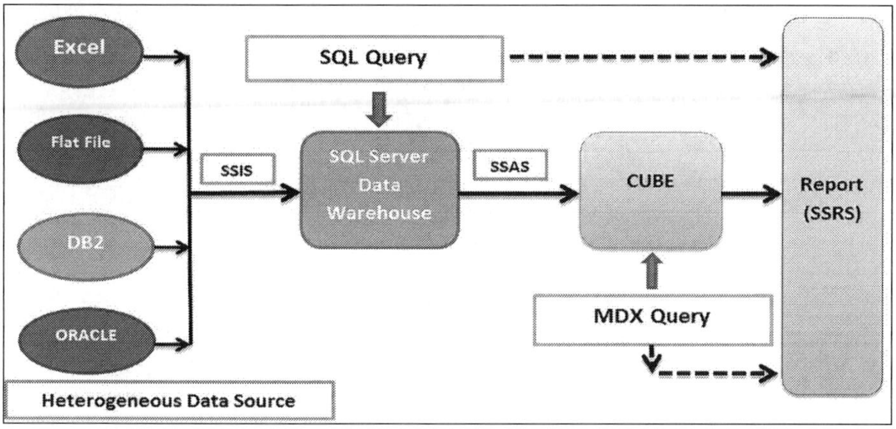

Figure 3.1: *Data Engineering Architecture Overview - On-Premises*

Figure 3.2 presents a compelling illustration of a data engineering solution architecture that embraces a diverse array of data source systems. These sources span from simple flat files to sophisticated in-house or custom application systems such as ERP and CRM. Serving as the lifeblood of our Data Warehouse, these sources undergo a meticulous *Extract, Transform, Load* (ETL) process, ensuring the seamless integration of data. Subsequently, the Data Warehouse yields a versatile output, serving various purposes such as Online Analytical Processing (OLAP) data analysis, data mining, and generation of Business Intelligence (BI) reports for data visualization, development of interactive dashboards, and even customized actions like alert generation. This exemplifies the multifaceted utility of a well-designed data engineering solution, demonstrating its efficacy in supporting diverse analytical needs, strategic decision-making, and tailored operational interventions.

Sample Architecture - II

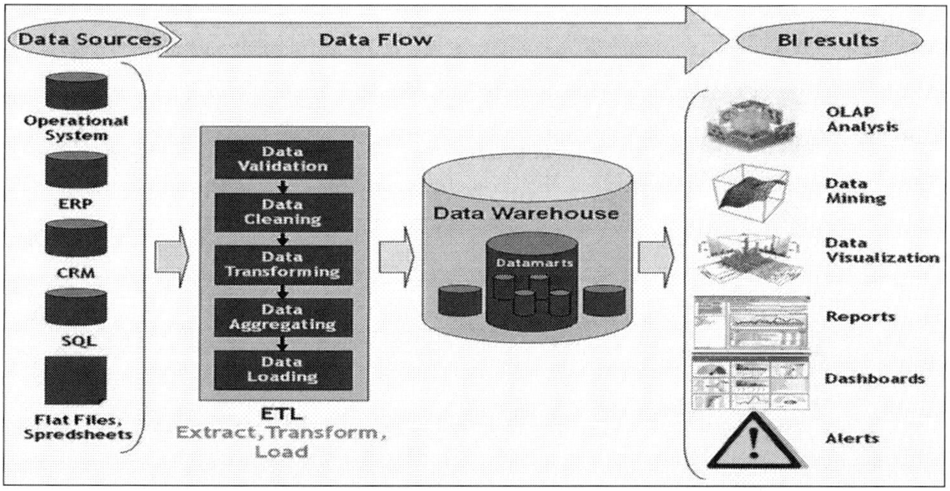

Figure 3.2: *Data Engineering Architecture (II) - On-Premises*

Figure 3.3 explains about data engineering on Azure Cloud where we have multiple source systems being used to either pull or migrate the data to Cloud into respective VM's on Azure as an Interim migration and then finally to respective PaaS databases services.

The data once migrated to Cloud is then being leveraged across various end tools like Power BI service on Cloud, Power Apps, Logic Apps, Azure functions, and so on.

Sample Architecture – III

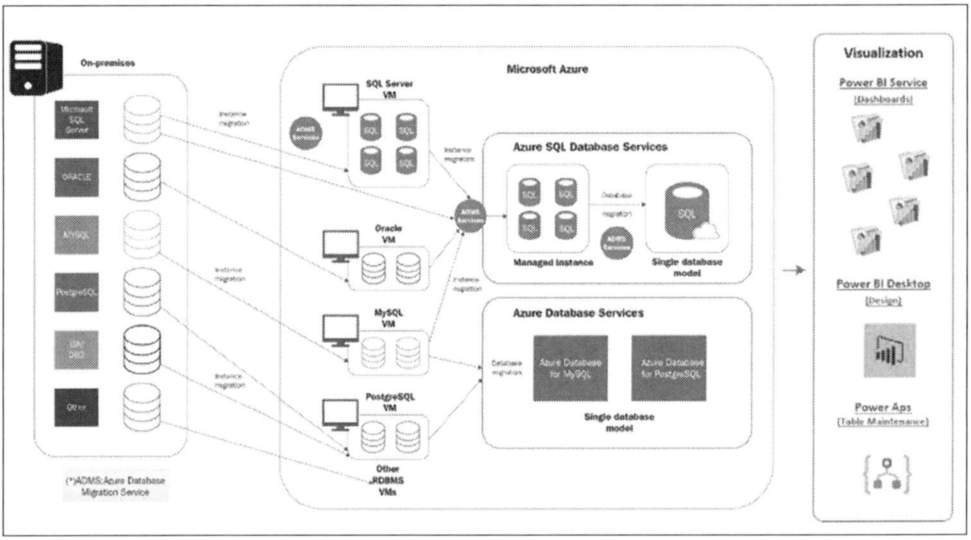

Figure 3.3: *Data Engineering Architecture Overview – Azure Cloud*

Components or Stages Involved in Data Engineering

There are several components or stages involved in a typical data engineering solution architecture as shown in the sample architecture(s): *Figures* 3.1 and 3.2, where we discuss data engineering in an on-premises world, and in *Figure* 3.3, where we discuss data engineering on Azure Cloud.

Let's talk about these components and stages in detail now:

Homogenous and Heterogeneous Data Sources

The very first component or the stage which is involved as part of any data engineering solution is a data source. When we build a solution considering SQL Server as a target database system, usually the source is termed as a heterogeneous data source or a mix of multiple data sources (as depicted in *Figure* 3.1). However, it is not necessary that the data source system in every data engineering solution would be heterogeneous source only.

There is a possibility that we might also have an SQL Server database on the source side as well (as depicted in *Figure* 3.2) which might be involved in a data engineering project and again land on another SQL Server database target based on business needs. A classic example of that could be migration from an older version of SQL Server to the latest version where a direct migration is not possible and we need to have a solution in place to transfer the data from the source to the target. Else, there might be a scenario where we cannot get rid of the source system completely due to further dependency of applications on the source SQL Server's version and requirement of the downstream systems configured or designed to read data only from the latest version of SQL Server database.

On a high-level heterogeneous data, sources can be categorized into the following categories, flat files or static data sources which require a manual update of the data or which are pushed from some external sources as part of the extract; secondly, it could be a live feed from some other ERP, CRM systems, or custom applications which will act as the OLTP systems. And finally, most of the solar system comprises of various database systems or data warehouses like Oracle, Mainframe systems, Sybase, Teradata, or SQL Server itself.

The data sources can be present in an on-premises environment, for example, the files placed on some file servers which are present in some Internet network or local servers or drives or it could be a standalone database instance, for example, on-premises SQL Server, Oracle database on the server, or it could be the output of a data desktop application which might be sending data locally to a remote storage or a local database.

Identifying the Source System(s) and Data

One of the most important parts of designing any data engineering solution is to have a deep understanding of the source system or systems in case there are multiple source systems, which are present within or outside the organization from where we need to collate the data and use the same to draw meaningful insights or perform certain sets of activities based on business needs.

The following points are to be taken care of when working with data sources:

- We need to be aware of all or a single data source involved in the process of the data engineering project we are working on so that we do not miss any data points later.
- We should have all the required access (primarily read-only) from the data source to extract the data.

- We should have a proper understating of how the data is managed or updated at source to decide how we can effectively use the source data.
- In the case of flat files, Excel files or Raw data file formats, we should procure proper naming conventions of files, extensions of files, Tab names in terms of Excel files, XML tag and XSD files in case of XML files, JSON files, and so on.
- In database systems, we should have detailed source schema documentation and understating of the database systems with proper business usage at a field and table level.
- We should be aware of any data processing happening at the source level as well to be able to leverage and use the correct finalized tables or interim tables based on our requirements.

Deciding the Data Pull Checkpoint and Frequency

Once we are done identifying the right data sources, the next important step in the process of designing any data engineering solution is to identify at what point of time, we should be extracting the data from the source and using it to load into our target data systems.

What makes this particular decision important is that if we keep on pulling the data without knowing the functioning or the data frequency or the business cases on which the source data is getting populated or updated then we will never be able to figure out what data is a new data or what data is an old data which we have already pulled and ultimately leading to data discrepancies into our target system and hence beating the purpose of the overall project or the solution which we are building on.

Let's see how we can decide and what factors we should consider when taking this call.

- Some systems are OLTP-based (Online Transaction Processing) and are driven by some sort of front-end applications like CRM or ERP systems. They have a continuous in-flow of data in both new record insertion as well as making updates to old records continuously.
- Some OLTP systems are only designed in a way to insert only new records, and no updates to the data can be done once entered, for example, sales portals (kiosks) in supermarkets.
- Some OLTP systems are designed in a way where they update the records but only for attributes and not the complete record. For example, e-commerce websites' orders where the order can be placed and if there are no issues then there is no change, if the order is cancelled then change in status, payments refund, or order date changed due to delivery issues but products ordered cannot be changed in most cases.

- In flat files data sources where the files are placed at regular intervals at some shared location and need to be ready to be pulled for further processing. These files can continuously receive new data, be updated with changes to existing data in new files, or experience deletions, rather than being limited to just insertions and updates.
- Some systems have logic to upload a full source dataset at some frequency, let's say, a full data input every month end and then a daily data updates file for the rest of the days of the month.
- Some systems just send a full cut-over dataset once when we take an input and then only incremental data on either hourly, daily, weekly, bi-weekly, or monthly basis to cater for changes to source data.

In a nutshell, there could be many more permutations and combinations of source data pull frequency and checkpoints apart from what has been covered above and every scenario is critical to be analyzed and then accordingly adjusted to make a decision to design the overall data engineering solution.

Also, any change in the way the source data system is generated, existing data engineering solutions need a change to be implemented to cater to the respective change at the source end and that's what makes the checkpoint and data extraction frequency analysis one of the key aspects of designing a data engineering solution.

Building an ETL Solution Using an Appropriate Tool

Once we are done with the finalization of the source systems and have gained an understanding of the data to be pulled along with the right frequency and business logic, we need to design an effective ETL (Extract, Transform, and Load) solution to fulfill those business requirements and convert them into a technical architecture design.

This is a three-step process, which includes extraction of the data from sources, transformation of the source data into meaningful and insightful data by cleaning of data, applying several transformational logics as per the business needs, for example, fuzzy grouping, merge logic, inserting of variables while loading, auditing logic, error logging and monitoring, and so on.

In this section, we will discuss the prominent tools, which can make our job seamless in designing this process in the following section in the on-premises as well as cloud world.

SSIS (SQL Server Integration Service)

SSIS is Microsoft's tool for ETL, which stands for *extraction, transformation, and loading*.

ETL is the process of moving and transforming data from different sources and formats into a unified data warehouse, data mart, or any other target system based on the requirements.

SSIS provides a platform for creating and testing solutions that perform ETL operations efficiently and effectively.

SSIS also offers graphical tools and wizards that make it easier to build and debug packages. Primarily, SSIS is an on-premises IDE (Integrated development environment) which was a part of BIDS (Business Intelligence Development Studio) and now a part of Visual Studio.

Below is how we can Download and Install SSIS developer tool on our system:

- Download and Install Visual Studio latest version (Visual Studio 2022 as of today)
- Download the SQL Server Integration Services Projects 2022
- Once we have both Visual Studio and SSIS installed, we need to create a new projectusing Visual Studio.

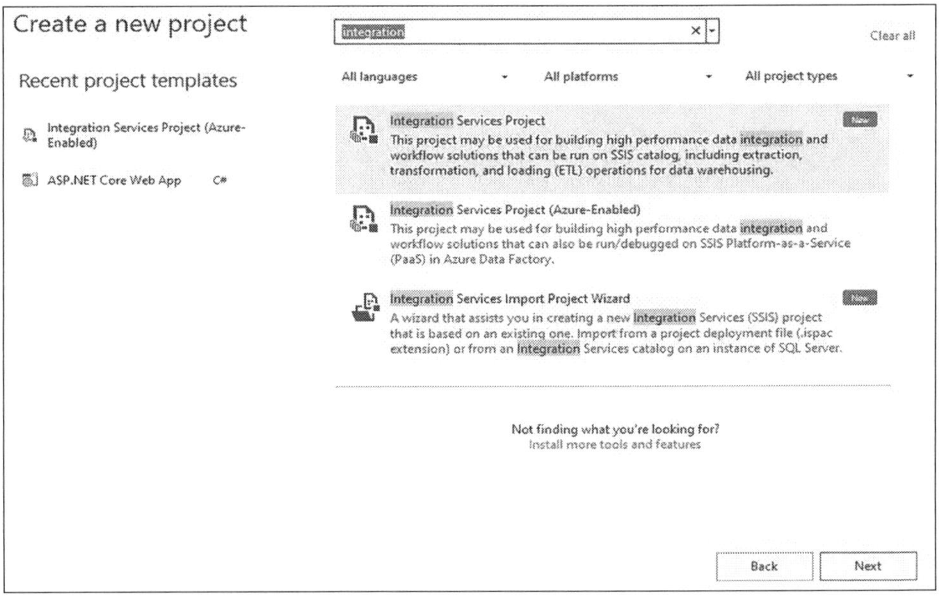

Figure 3.4: *Creating a SQL Server Integration Services Project*

As shown in *Figure* 3.4, there are three types of projects that we can create based on our requirements as explained here:

- **Integration Services Project:** This will be used for building workflow solutions for data warehousing on-premises and will be run through SSIS Catalogue (deployed on an on-premises SSIS Instance) or locally using IDE or via SQL Server Agent Jobs on SQL Server database engine.

- **Integration Services Project (Azure-Enabled):** This is a recently launched project type which gives an additional capability to debug/run the project on Azure Data Factory (*we will cover this soon in this chapter under the* Azure *section*) as an SSIS Platform-as-a-Service (PaaS).
- **Integration Services Import Project Wizard:** This project type enables us to create a solution by importing pre-built packages using either a deployment file, SSIS Catalogue, SQL Instance, or even from a file system.

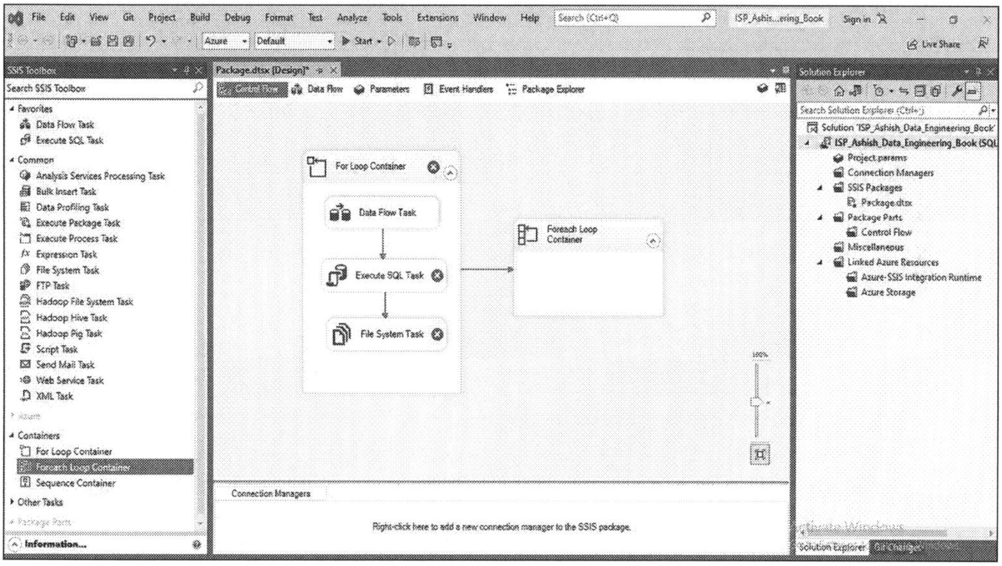

***Figure 3.5**: Sample SSIS Package Designer Overview*

Components of SSIS

SSIS **Control Flow** can perform workflow functions like sending email messages, FTP operations, data sources, and destinations. Control flow is the brain of the SSIS package. It helps you to arrange the order of execution for all its components. The components contain containers and tasks that are managed by precedence constraints.

SSIS **Precedence constraints** are components which direct tasks to execute in a predefined order. It also defines the workflow of the entire SSIS package. It controls the execution of the two linked tasks by executing the destination tasks based on the result of the earlier task – business rules which are defined using special expressions.

SSIS **containers** are units for grouping tasks together into units of work. Apart from offering visual consistency, it also allows you to declare variables and event handlers which should be in the scope of that specific container.

There are mainly three types of SSIS containers available:

- A Sequence Container
- A For Loop Container
- Foreach Loop Container

SSIS **Data Flow** component enables us to extract data from a wide variety of sources, such as SQL Server databases, Excel files, Oracle and DB2 databases, and so on. SSIS Data Flow Transformations are components that process, modify, or transform the data in the data flow. They can perform operations, such as sorting, filtering, merging, splitting, aggregating, pivoting, and converting data types.

Some of the common SSIS Data Flow Transformations are as follows:

- **Aggregate**: This transformation groups the input data by one or more columns and calculates summary statistics, such as count, sum, average, and so on for each group.
- **Derived Column:** In this transformation, new columns are introduced into the data flow, formulated using existing ones or variables.
- **Lookup:** This function conducts a lookup by combining incoming data with a reference set on specific match points, enhancing or checking the data through information retrieval from another source.
- **Merge:** By executing a merge join operation, this transformation unifies two ordered input sets into one, enabling the combination of different data origins or incremental loads.
- **Merge Join:** With this feature, an inner, left outer, or full outer join is applied to two ordered datasets, allowing for joining separate data sets based on shared keys or fields.
- **Pivot:** This transformation creates columns out of rows, by pivoting data around a chosen column and summing up distinct values, suited for reorganizing unstructured or transactional data into more analytical or organized shapes.
- **Sort:** This tool organizes input data in ascending or descending patterns based on one or multiple columns, setting the stage for other processes needing pre-arranged inputs, such as "*merge*" or "*merge join*".
- **Split:** Here, incoming data gets divided into various outputs according to row-specific conditions, thus segmenting the data into divergent flows according to operational logic or standards.
- **Union All:** It merges several inputs into a singular output, stacking all rows from each input, optimal for integrating varied data sources or union tasks.

SSIS **Connection Managers** are used to set up connections with source systems and target systems for data pull and data load respectively. There are additional connection managers, which are used to being able to connect to the files in the file system, FTP systems, SMTP connections to send e-mail, web services connections or to connect to a different SSIS package as well.

SSIS **Variables** are used to dynamically set or pass values to subsequent components or tasks in the package.

SSIS **Parameters** are much like variables, except that they can be set outside the package easily. They can be designated as values that must be passed in for the package to start.

SSIS **Event Handlers** are the simplest means of turning an SSIS script into a reliable system that is auditable, reacts appropriately to error conditions, reports progress and allows instrumentation and monitoring of your SSIS packages. They are easy to implement and provide a great deal of flexibility.

Azure Data Factory: Microsoft Azure

Azure Data Factory (ADF) is a tool that integrates data and has many advantages, such as being flexible, scalable, and affordable. Users can use Azure Data Factory to make and control data pipelines that can transfer and change data from different places and formats.

It is a tool that runs on Microsoft Azure cloud and integrates data. Users can use it to create, plan, and control data pipelines that connect and move data from many places and formats, both on the cloud and on-premises/other data centers.

Azure Data Factory helps users to transfer and change data fast and easily, so they can learn from the data and make smart choices. Azure Data Factory also has a user interface that does not need coding, which makes it simple to write and watch data pipelines.

Below is how we can provision an Azure Data Factory resource :

1. Please go to Azure Portal using the URL https://portal.Azure.com/
2. Click on **`Create a resource`** and select "**`Data Factory`**" as shown in *Figure 3.6*:

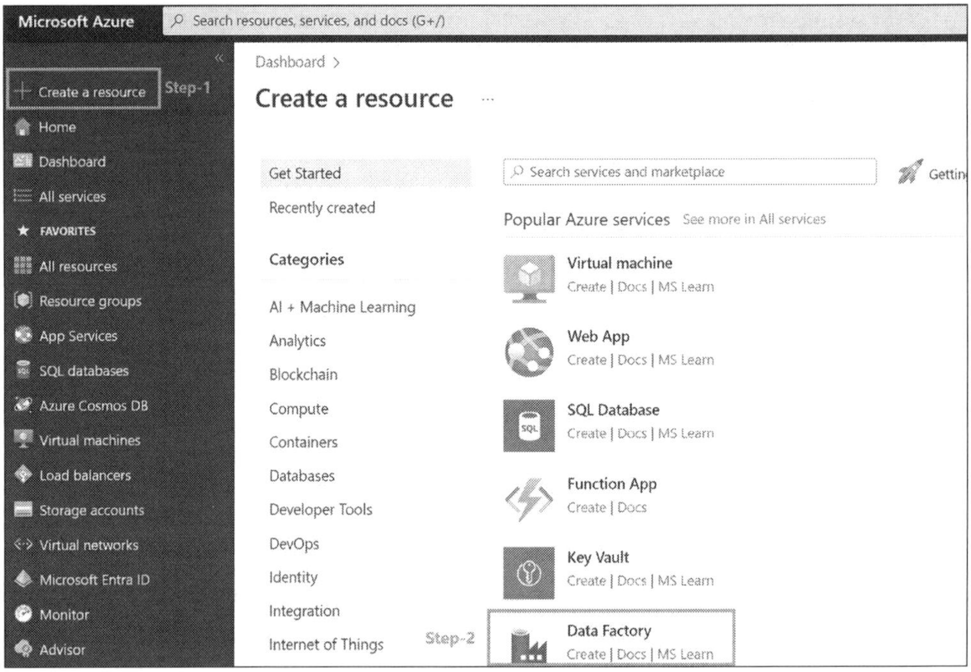

***Figure 3.6**: Provisioning an Azure Data Factory Resource via Portal*

3. The next screen will ask you to provide the necessary parameters to create the resource.

   a. **Subscription:** An Azure subscription is a logical container for your resources in Azure. It holds the details of all your resources as well as other details. You can have multiple subscriptions under one Azure account, and each subscription can have different billing and access policies. To create an Azure Data Factory resource, select an existing subscription or create a new one.

   b. **Resource Group:** An Azure Resource Group is used to manage multiple resources to effectively manage them within an organization based on departments, projects, modules, categories, and so on.

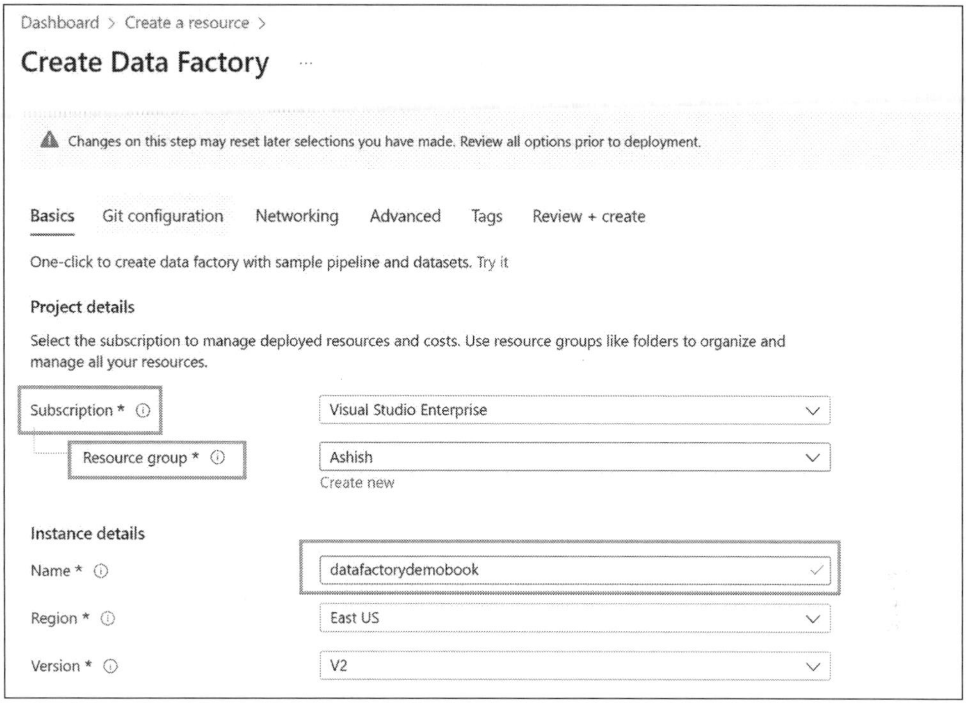

***Figure 3.7**: Parameters to Create Azure Data Factory*

The key components of Azure Data Factory are as follows:

- **Linked Service** : A linked service defines the connection and authentication information for a specific data source or destination. You can create multiple linked services for different data sources or destinations in your Azure Data Factory. For example, you can create a linked service for an Azure Blob Storage account, an Azure SQL Database, or an Amazon S3 bucket.

  Here are the steps:

  1. Go to the Azure Data Factory page and click the "**`Author & Monitor`**" button.
  2. Click the "**`New linked service`**" button and choose the data source or destination you want to connect to.
  3. Enter the information needed to connect, such as server name, database name, and credentials. Click the "**`Test connection`**" button to check if the connection works.
  4. Click the "**`Create`**" button to finish creating the linked service.

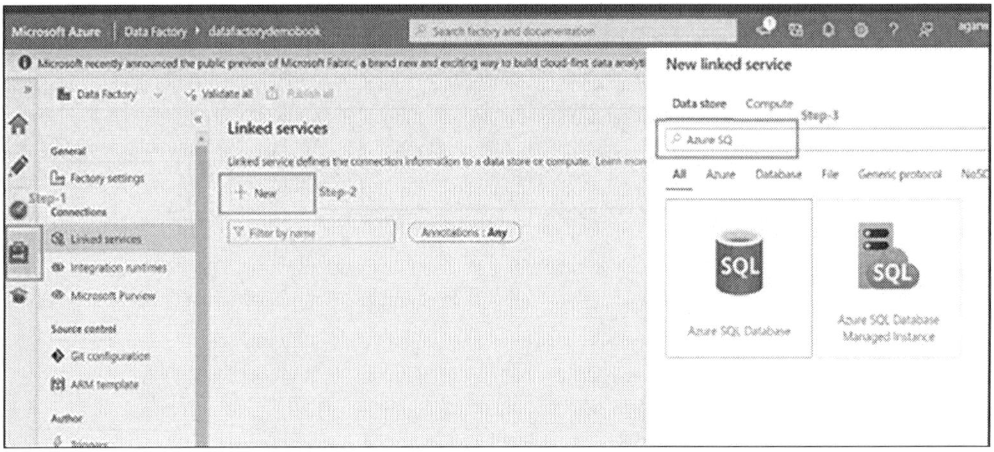

Figure 3.8: *ADF - Creating a Linked Service – Step 1*

5. Please fill the details for your linked service as shown in *Figure 3.9*:

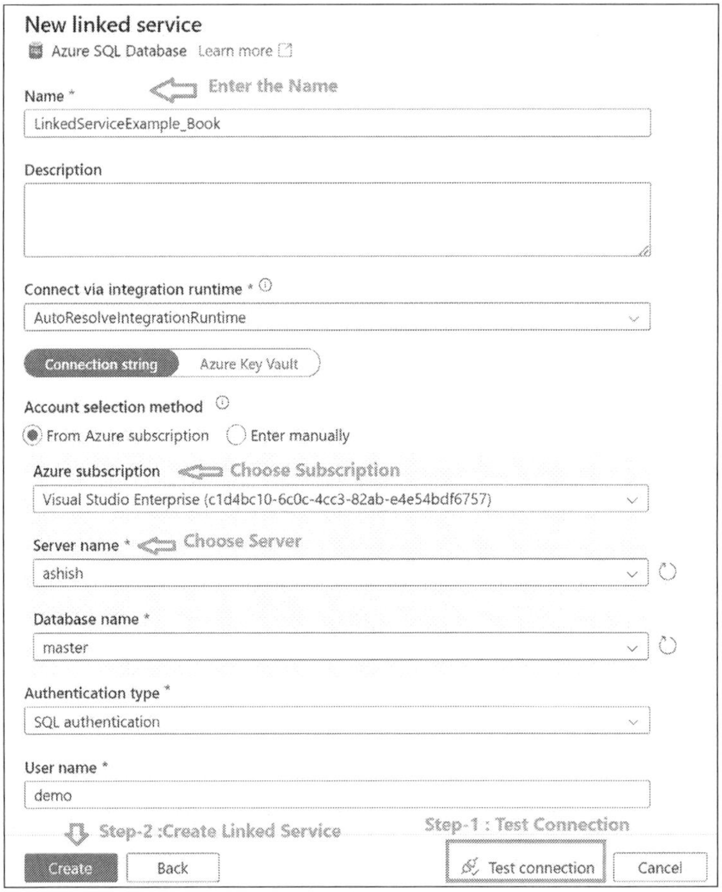

Figure 3.9: *ADF - Creating a Linked Service – Step 2*

- **Dataset:** To create a dataset, you need to represent a data source or destination. A dataset definition is a JSON file that specifies the properties of a dataset, such as its type, schema, structure, format, and linked service. You can create a dataset definition using the graphical interface or the code editor in Azure Data Factory. A dataset definition has the following components:
  - **`name`**: The name of the dataset.
  - **`properties`**: The properties of the dataset, such as:
  - **`type`**: The type of the data source or destination, such as AzureBlob, AzureSqlTable, or AzureCosmosDbCollection.
  - **`typeProperties`**: The type-specific properties of the data source or **`destination`**, such as **`tableName`**, **`fileName`**, or **`collectionName`**.
  - **`structure`**: The schema of data, such as columns, data types, and nullable values.
  - **`format`**: The format of the data, such as delimiter, encoding, or compression.
  - **`annotations`**: The custom properties or tags for the dataset.
  - **`folder`**: The folder where the dataset is stored in the data factory.
  - **`parameters`**: The parameters that can be used to dynamically configure the dataset.
  - **`linkedServiceName`**: The reference to the linked service that connects to the data source or destination.

  Here are the steps:

  1. Go to the Azure Data Factory page and click the "**`Author & Monitor`**" button.
  2. Click the "**`New dataset`**" button and choose the data source or destination for your dataset. Enter the information needed to identify the data, such as table name, file name, or folder path.
  3. Click the "**`Preview data`**" button to see if the data is correct.
  4. Click the "**`Create`**" button to finish creating the dataset.

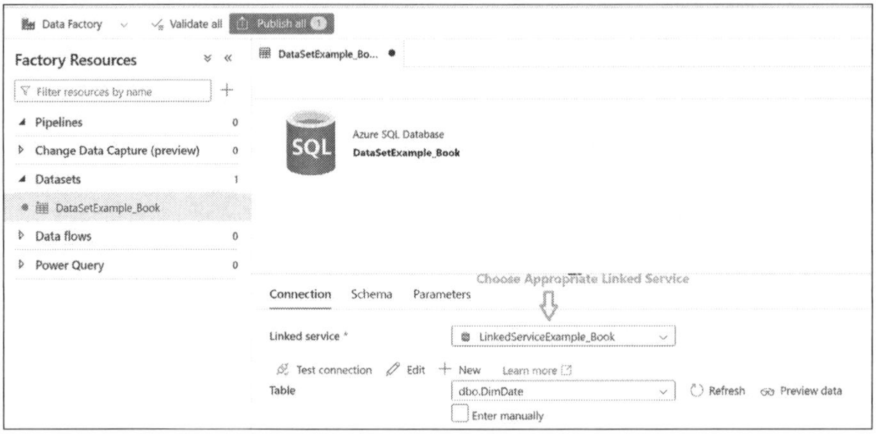

Figure 3.10: ADF - *Creating a Dataset using a Linked Service*

- **Pipeline:** To create a pipeline, you need to define a sequence of activities that move and transform data. A pipeline is a workflow that you can run and monitor.

  Here are the steps:

  1. Go to the Azure Data Factory page and click the "**`Author & Monitor`**" button.
  2. Click the "**`New pipeline`**" button and drag and drop the activities you want from the "**`Activities`**" pane to the "**`Pipeline canvas`**." Drag the green arrow from one activity to another to connect them.
  3. Enter the information needed to configure the activities, such as input and output datasets, linked services, and transformation logic.
  4. Click the "**`Validate`**" button to check if the pipeline is correct.
  5. Click the "**`Publish all`**" button to publish the pipeline.

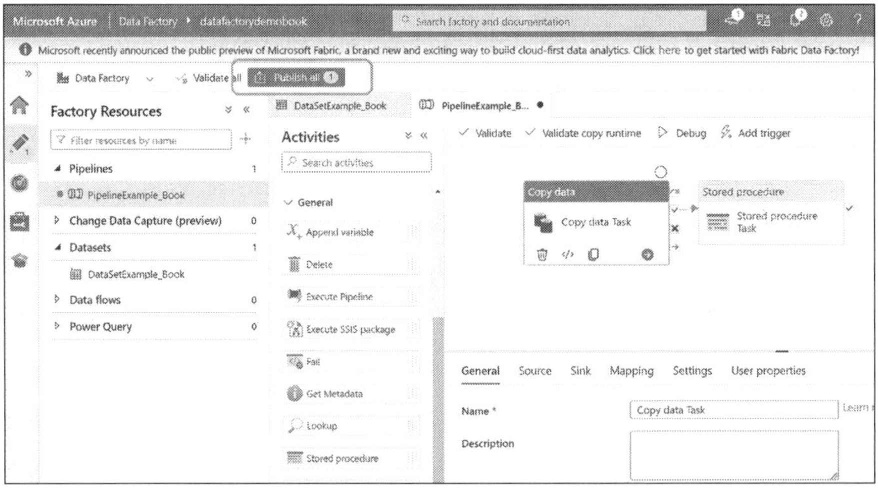

Figure 3.11: ADF - *Creating a Pipeline*

- **Leveraging a Template Gallery:** To build a pipeline from an established template, you can utilize the template gallery. This gallery includes a variety of templates catered to common tasks like data replication from one source to another, executing data transformations, or populating a data warehouse. Furthermore, it permits the creation and preservation of personalized templates for subsequent applications.

  Here are the steps:

  1. Navigate to Azure Data Factory and select the "**`Author & Monitor`**" option.
  2. Use the left panel to click the "**+**" and choose "**`Pipeline from template`**".
  3. Review the templates and pick one that fits your requirements.
  4. Enter the necessary parameters and connections for the chosen template.
  5. Deploy the pipeline by clicking on the "**`Deploy`**" button.
  6. If desired, modify the pipeline through the graphical interface or code view.

- **Monitoring and Managing Pipelines:** To monitor and manage pipelines, use the Azure Data Factory interface. You can see the status, activity runs, and triggers of your pipelines. You can also change the settings, connections, and triggers of your pipelines.

  Here are the steps:

  1. Go to the Azure Data Factory page and click the "**`Author & Monitor`**" button.
  2. Click the "**`Monitor & Manage`**" button and choose the pipeline you want to monitor or manage.
  3. Use the options on the page to see and change the details of your pipeline.

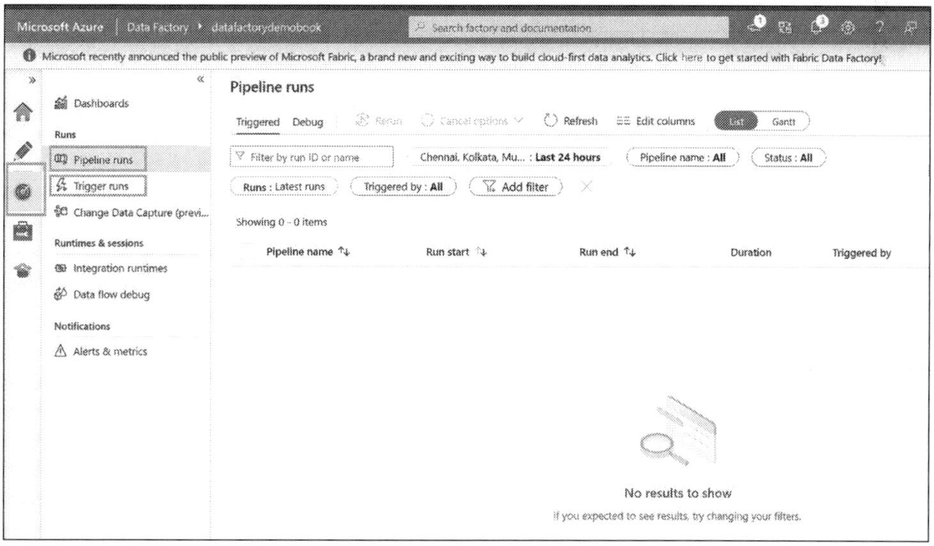

Figure 3.12: *ADF - Monitoring a Pipeline*

Additionally, some of the other key components include Change Data Capture, Data Flows and Power Query which are explained below:

- **Change Data Capture:** A feature designed to monitor and record changes in your primary data allows incremental updates to your target location. This tool helps to avoid complete data re-loads, boosting the efficiency and performance of your data synchronization efforts.

To activate change data capture, you need to set up both source and sink datasets, defining the watermark column while determining the start and end times for the changes being tracked. Additionally, the copy activity or mapping data flow activity can be utilized to execute the change data capture operation.

- **Data Flows:** A visual interface enabling the construction of data transformation processes through a simple drag-and-drop mechanism. With data flows, you can execute a variety of data manipulation tasks such as filtration, sorting, aggregation, combining, pivoting, and purification. Expressions and functions are also available to tailor your data transformations to fit specific business requirements.

Setting up a data flow involves specifying a source, adding multiple transformations, and designating one or more sinks. Parameters, variables, and conditional splits provide further customization of the data flow structure. Before deployment, data flows can be previewed and refined within the data factory framework.

- **Power Query:** A versatile query language designed for seamless connection to an array of data sources supports comprehensive data transformation operations through an intuitive interface. Power Query facilitates the retrieval, merging, and configuration of data from diverse origins such as files, databases, web pages, and APIs. Custom transformation of data is achievable through a range of formulas and functions.

Utilization of Power Query necessitates creating data flow and choosing Power Query as the source type. The Power Query editor links to your data source and applies the necessary transformation steps. For custom code, the advanced editor offers additional capabilities. Preliminary previews and validations of Power Query are possible before integration into your data flow.

Designing a Data Warehouse to Store Data

An effective data warehouse design is one of the most critical aspects of the data engineering solution which should cater to our business requirements and be able to hold the data that we have acquired from the source and parallelly ensure that the data warehouse meets the end goals of the project and the solution which could vary for multiple analytics and data processing presentation to the customers building reports for decision making for senior leadership, or could be used for other downstream systems.

Although a data warehouse system can be designed in multiple ways, at a high level it can be categorized into three different ways in which we can choose to design a data warehouse system based on the business requirements as described here:

- The single-tier architecture represents the most rudimentary and aged structure of data warehouse frameworks. It incorporates a single server that houses all the elements of the warehouse, proving to be an effective model for small entities with minimal data volumes.
- There are distinct layers in the two-tier data warehouse architecture: one back-end server dedicated to data storage and a front-end server responsible for presenting the user interface. This is more suitable for larger bodies with substantial data quantities.
- The three-tier architecture delineates the data warehouse into three separate sections: a back-end for data storage, a middle-tier for performing analytics and processing tasks, and a front-end for displaying the user interface. Such a framework accommodates organizations with intricate data requirements.

We can have the following components as part of a typical data warehouse solution that caters to almost the majority of the requirements of any data engineering solution and business needs:

- First, define the schema(s) we need in our target data warehouse, for example, to maintain the consistency and sanity of the source data which we have pulled into our data systems, it is preferred to have a staging schema as an industry best practice which holds the daily data pulled from the source system to target system as it is, and this staging data is usually a truncate and load basis.
- Once the data is loaded into staging tables, we should have some auditing mechanism in place to record how many tables were pulled from source to target, what the record count for each table in source as well as in target to ensure that we are not missing any data from source.
- Additionally, error logging should be in place while designing our ETL solutions to ensure that any sort of partial loads or error data is captured separately and then, have a remediation mechanism in place, either automatically or with some manual intervention.
- There should be a sequenced approach while designing an ETL solution, which ensures that the data load from staging to the main tables are only triggered when a successful flag or indicator is captured or notified for our staging set of tables.
- Once the staging tables are populated then the next set of ETL solutions that is taking care of loading the data from staging tables to our main tables should capture the incremental data logic that is either new data is getting inserted, existing records are being updated, or unrequired data is being deleted to be in sync with the source systems.

- Usually, any set of data transformations that are required while transforming the data from staging to the main data warehouse tables should be a part of the separate ETL packages or data pipelines to ensure easy debugging or look for any data inconsistencies later.
- When the final tables are loaded into the data warehouse as per the business logic, either we can use these tables directly for any downstream systems or analytics purposes or we can create additional tables specifically for analysis as a subset of these tables to avoid locking on the tables due to concurrent use.
- If our data engineering solution requires any reporting to be done on top of this data with additional business logic, then it is recommended to create another set of tables under RPT or reporting schema with the sole purpose of providing input to the reports for decision making.

Deciding the Data Refresh Methodology (Full vs. Incremental)

Depending on the data source and the business requirements, you may need to choose between full and incremental data refresh methods. A full refresh means that all the data in the source is reloaded into the data warehouse, regardless of whether it has changed or not. An incremental refresh means that only the new or modified data in the source is loaded into the data warehouse, saving time and resources.

The pros and cons of each method are as follows:

Full refresh

- **Pros**: Simpler to implement and maintain as it ensures data consistency and accuracy; avoids data duplication or corruption.
- **Cons**: Takes longer to execute as it consumes more resources and bandwidth; may affect the availability and performance of the source and the data warehouse.

Incremental refresh

- **Pros**: Faster and more efficient as it reduces the load on the source and the data warehouse; enables near real-time data analysis and reporting.
- **Cons**: More complex to implement and maintain as it requires tracking and storing changes in the source; may introduce data quality issues or errors.

Some factors that may influence your choice of data refresh method are as follows:

- The dimensions and capacity of the data origin
- The regularity and variety of modifications in the originating data

- The demands for promptness and speediness in data evaluation and reporting
- The accessibility and capability of both the origin and the data repository

Make sure the data is loaded into the data warehouse quickly and correctly by planning the loading process. This means deciding the loading order, dealing with incremental updates, and improving data flows and load performances.

You may have to pick between the ETL processes below:

- **Batch processing**: This common ETL process takes raw data from many sources, if required, changes it, and loads data into the data warehouse in groups.
- **Real-time processing**: This more complicated ETL process takes data from real-time data streams, changes it, and loads it into the data warehouse right away.

Pick the ETL processes that suit your business needs for correct data and be confident that you are doing well.

Automating the Process and Scheduling Jobs

Once we are done with the aforementioned steps successfully, the individual components are tested successfully in terms of the designing, execution, business logic, log metrics, and reporting purpose. We must ensure that the same process runs seamlessly without any issues daily.

To achieve the same, we need to design an automated approach which takes care of the same requirement without any manual intervention and runs automatically on the server; it could be either on-premises servers in case of an on-premises solution, or on any public cloud in case of a public cloud-based solution.

Let's discuss the two major approaches to achieve the same:

- **On-Premises:** We can achieve this by creating an **SQL Agent Job** in the SQL database engine:
    1. The Server Agent Job is a process to perform a certain set of operations step-by-step with the flexibility to start and stop at certain steps.
    2. The above can be tested or triggered manually in an ad hoc manner or be scheduled regularly.
    3. The SQL Agent Job Step can be a simple SQL Query statement, a Stored Procedure, an SSIS Package, a PowerShell command or any custom script as well.

Following is the step-by-step process to create a SQL Server Agent Job:

Step 1: Explore the SQL *Server Agent* Tab, right click and then select "`New Job`":

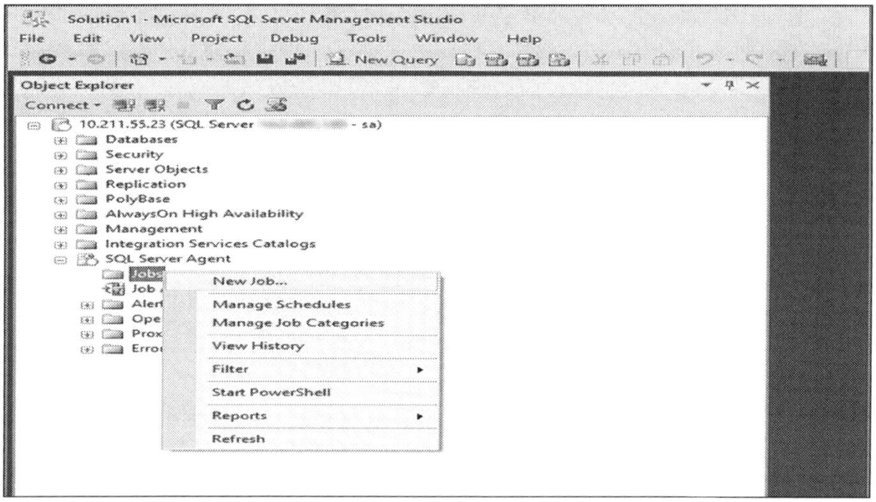

Figure 3.13: *SQL Server Agent Job - Create New Job*

Step 2: The following screen shows how to setup a Job Step that includes a Step name of your choice to identify this easily, what is the type of action we are doing in the step, for example, running a T-SQL, executing a SSIS Package, and so on; then in case of a T-SQL, which database it will run and what command to be executed.

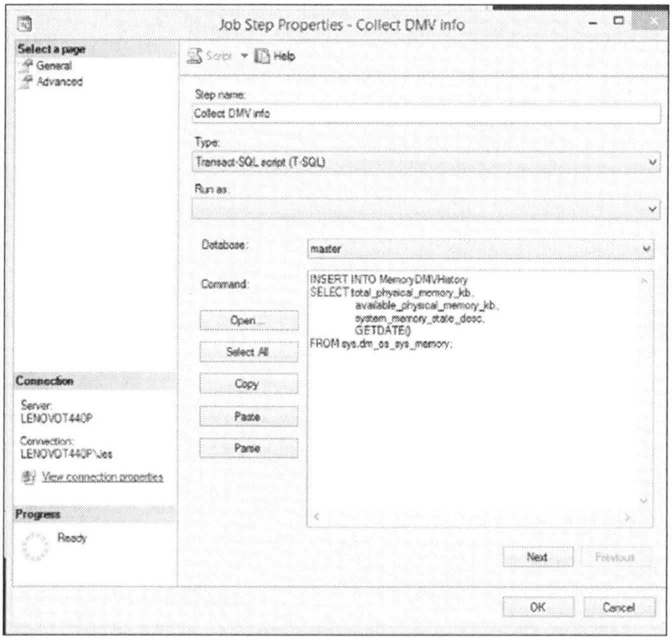

Figure 3.14: *SQL Server Agent Job - Create New Job Step*

Step 3: The following screen shows how we can explore the configuration and properties of an already created Job and modify the same, in case of any change request or debugging.

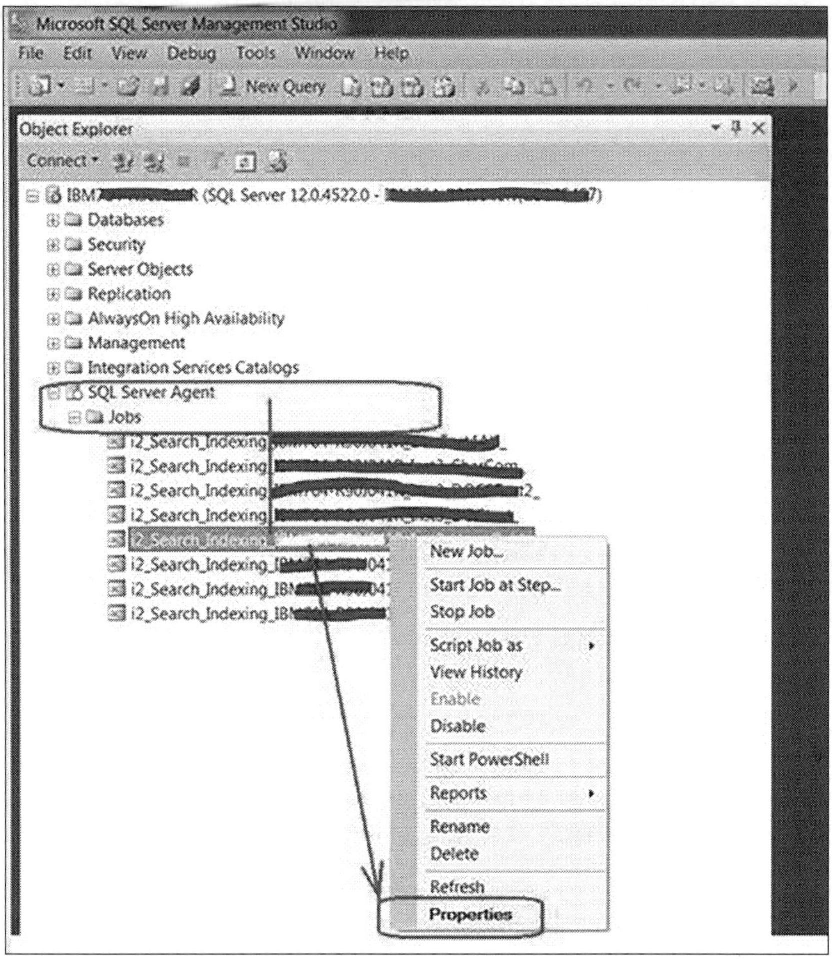

***Figure 3.15:** SQL Server Agent Job - View or Edit a Job*

Step 4: The following screen shows how we can start a job to perform the set of actions needed on an ad-hoc basis. This step is the execution of the Job.

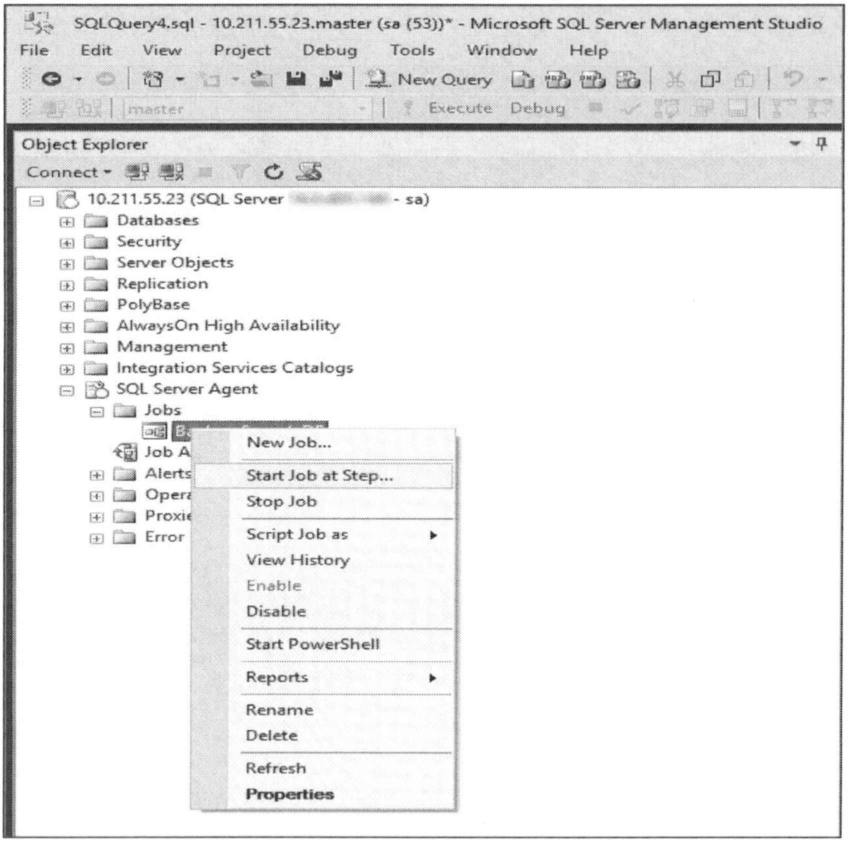

Figure 3.16: *SQL Server Agent Job - Starting a Job*

- **Azure Cloud:** We can achieve scheduling of the ADF pipeline by creating a **Schedule** in Azure Data Factory and attaching the schedule(s) to the required pipelines.
  - Have one pipeline that runs on a multiple scheduled basis on business needs.
  - Use a single schedule across multiple pipelines if suits the respective pipelines.

Step 1: The following screen shows how we can add a new trigger or edit an existing trigger.

Figure 3.17: *ADF v2 - Creating a Trigger to add an Automated Schedule - Step 1*

Step 2: Select the type of trigger, either schedule-based or action-based. Specify the frequency of the trigger if the trigger type is schedule-based.

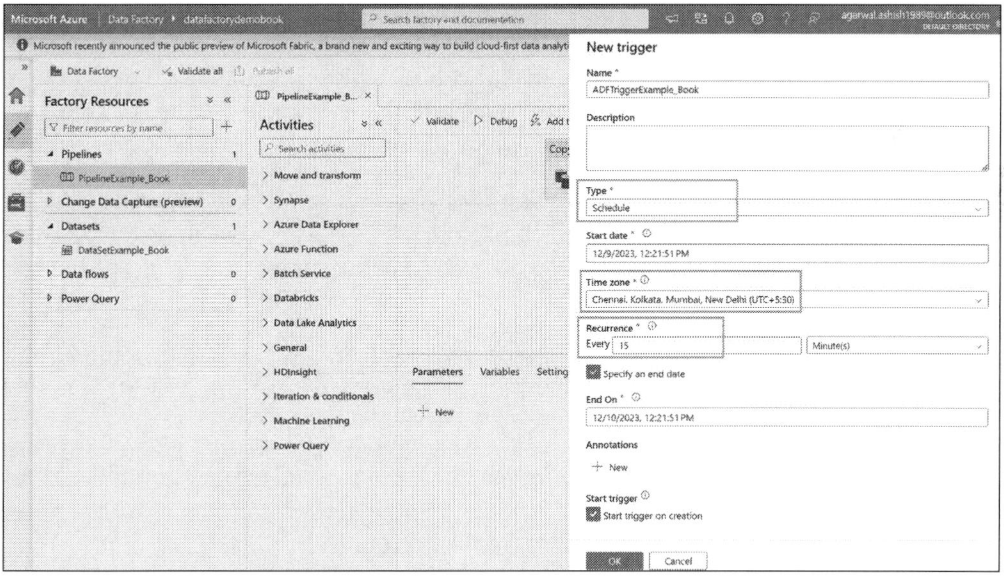

Figure 3.18: *ADF v2 - Creating a Trigger to add an Automated Schedule - Step 2*

Step 3: Monitor the history of all the executions and triggers by clicking on the monitor pipelines tab as shown.

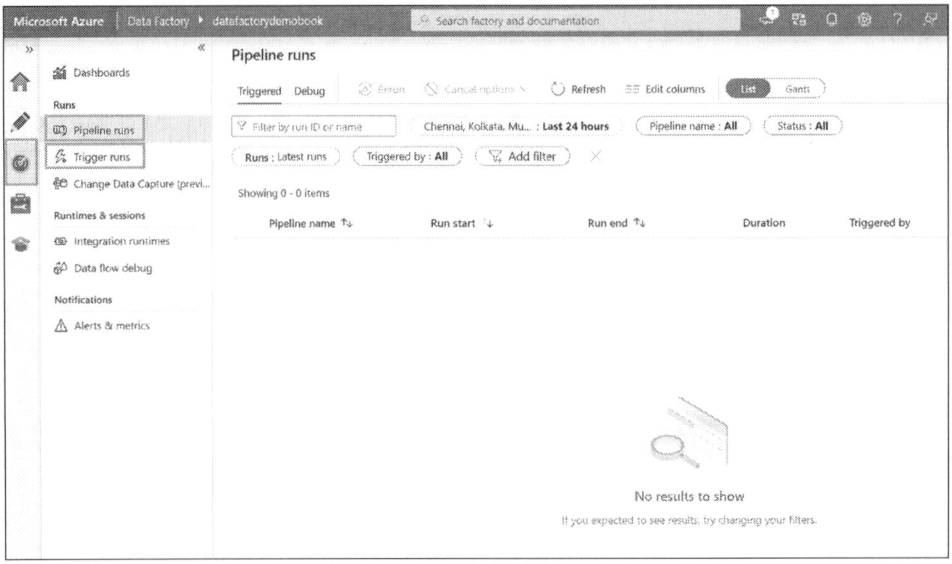

Figure 3.19: *ADF v2 - Monitoring Azure Data Factory Pipelines*

Building Reporting Systems for End-user Data Access

Business intelligence reporting involves collecting and examining data. BI enables businesses to present their data using visualizations and derive valuable insights that guide their key strategies and foster growth. Online reporting and business intelligence are intimately linked.

You must effectively analyze and present the data you collect, regardless of the industry or sector you work in. This requires involving every pertinent stakeholder in the process and adopting a cooperative data-driven approach that transcends background or location.

As a result, you can devise a more strategic approach to your various organizational decisions and discover insights that would have otherwise gone unnoticed.

- **SSRS:** SQL Server Reporting Services is a part of Microsoft's Business Intelligence suite that comes as a part of a 3-part package, including SSIS and SSAS. It is a reporting platform that runs on a server and has a programming and coding interface to create, test, and deploy reports that allow you to produce, share, and view reports. It requires manual intervention because of its programming basis. It also works with Visual Studio and SQL Formatting. The different types of reports that SSRS can generate are cached, linked, parameterized, ad-hoc, snapshot, click-through, and drill-down & drill-through reports.

- **Power BI:** Power BI is a popular choice for many professionals, such as Data Engineers, Database Administrators, Data Analysts and Business Intelligence Professionals, because of its superior capabilities, which include:
  - Real-time updates of reports and dashboards supported by Artificial Intelligence, Machine Learning, NLP, and Microsoft Digital Assistant, Cortana.
  - Data for Power BI can be obtained from various sources like Excel, SQL, CSV, Web files, Java APIs, and more.
  - The SaaS solution offers ready-made reports and dashboards.
  - Data Cleaning, data transmission, data modelling, and data visualization capabilities are all available on one platform.
  - Power BI allows you to securely connect (Row-level Security) on-premises or in the cloud.
  - Power BI easily integrates with other tools like Dynamics 365, SharePoint, Office 365, Hadoop, SAP, MailChimp, Salesforce, Spark, and so on.
  - Interactive reporting and easy-to-drag-and-drop visuals, live dashboarding, and quick insights can be embedded with other custom Apps.

We will discuss both SSRS and Power BI in detail in the later chapters of the book.

Conclusion

In this chapter, we have learned about the major aspects of data engineering in the on-premises world versus Azure and its related concepts and tools. This will help us to effectively design the solution architecture and the actual solutions at each of the stages of data engineering at the component level in both the on-premises world as well as Azure Cloud.

In the next chapter, we will be focusing on the Azure Cloud concepts in detail. This will help you understand how the Azure Cloud concepts uplift data engineering practices and help large enterprises in terms of effectively designing, developing, and managing data across the organization.

Points to Remember

- **Data Sources**: These are the systems that act as the key input and the originator for building any new data engineering solution.
- **ETL**: Extract, Transform and Load. This is one of the most important stages in any data engineering solution which takes care of dealing with connection between source and target systems.
- **SQL Server Agent**: It is a scheduling tool provided with an SQL Database engine that helps in the automation of any process be it SSIS Package, SQL Code, PowerShell code, and more.

CHAPTER 4
Azure Cloud Concepts

Introduction

This chapter will cover the concepts of Azure Cloud, how data systems are changing and how these changes influence data professionals. You will also investigate the distinctions between on-premises and cloud data solutions, as well as sample business cases that employ cloud technologies. You will learn about the roles and responsibilities of a data engineer and how they relate to other data and AI professions. You will look at common data engineering practices as well as a high-level architecting methodology for a data-engineering project designed and developed on Azure or in a hybrid model (on-premises with Azure).

Structure

In this chapter, we will discuss the following topics:

- Azure Cloud Overview
  - Microsoft Azure Cloud Working Fundamentals
  - IaaS vs. PaaS vs. SaaS in Azure
  - Azure Key Concepts and Components
- Basic Concepts of Azure
  - Azure Portal and Subscription Management
  - Resources and Resource Group
  - Azure Resource Manager (ARM)
  - Roles and Access
  - Pricing Calculator
- Azure SQL Databases
  - Azure SQL Database

  - Azure SQL-Managed Instance
  - Azure SQL Virtual Machine
- Database Migration from On-Premises to Azure
  - Target Readiness Assessment
  - Target SKU Assessment
  - Azure Migrate (Lift and Shift) to SQL Server on VM

Azure Cloud Overview

Azure is a cloud computing service by Microsoft. It is a versatile and adaptable cloud service that assists with development, data storage, service hosting, and service management. The Azure platform runs web applications online using Microsoft data centers.

Cloud computing means using the internet to store and access data. It does not save any data on your personal computer's hard disk. In cloud computing, you get data from a different server.

It is a platform that lets us access Microsoft's resources. For instance, to create a big server, we would need a lot of money, work, space, and so on. Microsoft Azure helps us in such cases. Microsoft Azure plays a pivotal role by offering robust computing capabilities for data storage, rapid data processing, advanced analysis, and comprehensive monitoring tools. This multifaceted support greatly simplifies our workflow and optimizes efficiency. The price of Azure is also easy and affordable. It is commonly known as "*Pay as You Go*," which means you only pay for what you use.

Microsoft Azure Cloud Working Fundamentals

It is a cloud platform that works for both private and public use. It helps developers and IT professionals to create, deploy, and manage applications and uses virtualization technology. Virtualization breaks the strong link between the hardware and the operating system with a layer of abstraction called a hypervisor. A hypervisor in cloud computing, also known as a virtualization manager, is a crucial component that enables the efficient sharing of physical hardware resources among multiple virtual machines (VMs). It sits between the underlying hardware and the VMs, managing and allocating resources such as CPU, memory, and storage. By abstracting the physical infrastructure, the hypervisor allows multiple operating systems to run concurrently on a single physical server, optimizing resource utilization and providing isolation between VMs. This virtualization technology is fundamental to the flexibility, scalability, and cost-effectiveness of cloud computing, as it allows for the dynamic provisioning and management of virtualized resources to meet varying workloads and demands. Azure uses this virtualization method and applies it on a large scale in the data center owned by Microsoft. Each data center has many racks with servers and each server has a hypervisor to run several virtual machines. The network switch connects all those servers.

IaaS vs. PaaS vs. SaaS on Azure SQL

The offering of Azure Cloud comes as follows:

- Infrastructure as a service (IaaS)
- Platform as a service (PaaS)
- Software as a service (SaaS)

Infrastructure as a service (IaaS): This category of infrastructure as a service includes virtual machines, storage, and networking. The users must build and deploy the applications manually. Azure can support many operating systems because of its Hyper-hypervisor. It is the basic cloud platform layer. This Azure service helps IT administrators with processing, storage, networks, and other essential computer tasks. It is one of the Azure topics to learn that lets users run any software.

Advantages of IaaS:

- Allows for effective design time flexibility
- Suitable for the application that requires full control
- Enables fast migration of services to clouds
- Saves you from the worries of creating many physical or virtual machines
- Helps you to access, monitor, and manage data centers.

Disadvantages of IaaS:

- Many security threats from unpatched servers.
- Some companies have specific processes for testing and updating on-premises servers' vulnerabilities, which is not possible with Azure.

Platform as a service (PaaS): Some of the services that Azure offers under the platform as a service are Azure app service, Azure functions, and logic apps. This service has autoscaling and load-balancing features and a ready-made environment for the application.

Advantages of PaaS:

- The overall cost is cheap as the resources are assigned as needed and servers are automatically increased or decreased.
- Azure is more secure because servers are automatically scanned for all known security problems.

- The entire process is hidden from the developer so that there is no chance for data breach.

Disadvantages of PaaS:

- Portability problems can happen when you use PaaS services.
- There may be different environments at Azure, so the application needs to adapt accordingly.

Software as a service (SaaS): It is software that is centrally run and controlled. It has one version of the application for all customers. You can expand to many instances and guarantee the best performance everywhere. The software is licensed through monthly or annual payment. MS Exchange, Office, and Dynamics are a few examples of SaaS. Microsoft Azure manages the entire application including deploying, scaling, and load balancing.

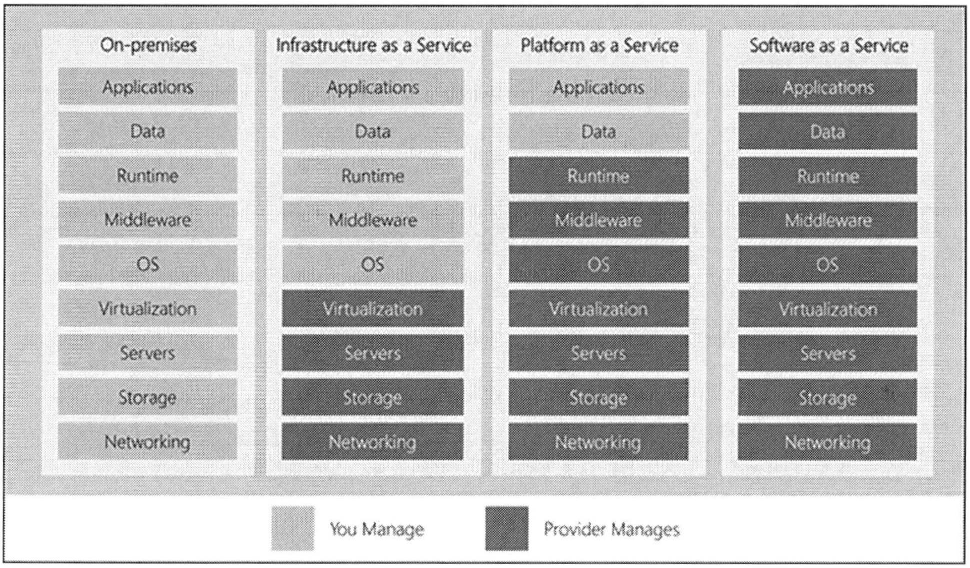

Figure 4.1: *On-Premises vs. IaaS vs. PaaS vs. SaaS*

Advantages of SaaS:

- Decision-makers are attracted by the convenience and ease of setting up SaaS.
- SaaS helps save money on servers, which are expensive and need constant attention and upkeep from your IT staff.
- SaaS enables you to scale up access as your business grows, instead of spending on software licenses and internal server resources.
- SaaS is based on the idea that it can be used anytime and anywhere.
- The provider handles the update so that you don't have to deal with endless downloads and installations of patches.

Disadvantages of SaaS:

- The provider's servers usually store data of the client company, which can raise privacy concerns.
- SaaS is a web-based service that depends on a reliable internet connection. Therefore, connectivity is a disadvantage as you need a stable network for the system to function properly. Network issues can result in frustrating delays in downloading, which can affect your productivity.
- The main reason why some companies are still hesitant to use SaaS is the lack of security and transparency. Some SaaS owners are not clear about the methods they use and only give assurance that data protection is inherent to the service.

Azure Key Concepts and Components

Azure is a cloud computing platform that provides various services and solutions for different situations and requirements. In this section, we will explain some of the main concepts and components that you need to understand to use Azure efficiently. These include:

- **Azure portal:** The Azure portal is a web-based application that you can use to make, manage, and delete Azure resources and services. You can find it at https://portal.azure.com.
- **Regions:** Azure is a cloud platform that operates in different regions around the world. When you ask for a service, application, or VM in Azure, you need to choose a region first. The chosen region is the data center where your application runs.
- **Datacenter:** You can deploy your applications in various data centers across the world in Azure. Choose a region that is near to most of your customers. It helps you to lower latency in network requests.
- **Resources:** An Azure resource is a single computer, networking data, or app hosting service that is charged separately. Some common resources are virtual machines (VM), storage accounts, or SQL databases.
- **Resource groups:** An Azure resource group is a container that keeps related resources for an Azure solution. It can have all the resources or just the ones that you want to manage.
- **Resource Manager:** It is a JSON that specifies one or more resources to deploy to a resource group. It also sets dependencies between the deployed resources.
- **Automation:** Azure lets you automate the processes of making, managing, and deleting resources by using PowerShell or the Azure command-line Interface (CLI).

- **Azure PowerShell:** Azure PowerShell is a set of modules that provide cmdlets to manage Azure. In most cases, you can use the cmdlets command for the same tasks you do in the Azure portal.
- **Azure command-line interface (CLI):** The Azure CLI helps you to make, manage, and delete Azure resources from the command line.
- **REST APIs:** Azure is based on a set of REST APIs that help you do the same operation you do in the Azure portal User Interface. It allows Azure resources and apps to be controlled via any third-party software application.
- **Azure Cloud Key Components:** The following are the key cloud components of the Azure Cloud that comprise the overall structure and design of Azure Cloud and form the underlying architecture for any cloud deployment and implementation.

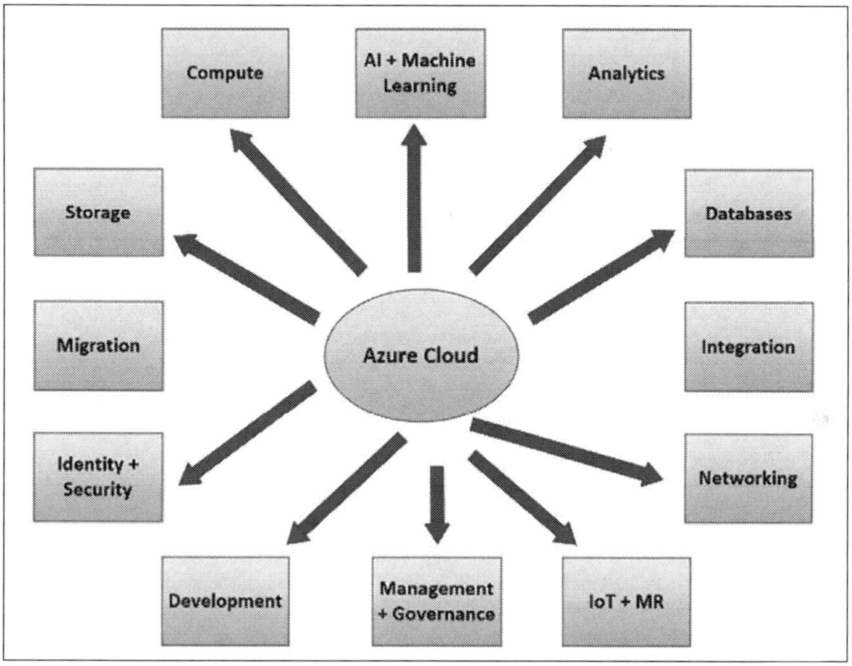

Figure 4.2: *Azure Cloud Key Components*

Azure Compute

It provides computing services, such as app hosting, development, and deployment on the Azure Platform. Its components include:

- **Virtual Machine**: Enables you to run any language and workload in any operating system
- **Virtual Machine Scale Sets**: Enables you to launch thousands of identical virtual machines in minutes

- **Azure Container Service**: Builds a container hosting solution that is tailored for Azure. Scales and orchestrates applications using Kube, DC/OS, Swarm, or Docker
- **Azure Container Registry**: Stores and manages container images across all kinds of Azure deployments
- **Functions**: Allows you to write code without worrying about infrastructure and server provisioning. Automatically scales up when your functions are called more frequently
- **Batch**: Helps you scale to tens, hundreds, or thousands of virtual machines and run computer pipelines
- **Service Fabric**: Simplifies microservice-based application creation and management. Supports JAVA, PHP, Node.js, Python, and Ruby

Azure Storage

Azure Storage is a cloud storage service for modern applications designed to satisfy the scalability needs of their customers. It enables you to store and process hundreds of terabytes of data. Its components are:

- **Blob Storage**: Stores unstructured data in the Cloud as objects/blobs and stores any kind of text or binary data, such as a document, media file, or application installer.
- **Queue Storage**: Offers cloud messaging between application components and provides asynchronous messaging to create communication between application components.
- **File Storage**: Helps you to migrate legacy applications. It depends on file shares to Azure quickly and without expensive rewrites.
- **Table Storage**: Stores semi-structured NoSQL data in the cloud and offers a key/attribute store with a schema-less design.

Azure Databases

This category includes Database as a Service (DBaaS) which offers SQL and NoSQL services. It also includes databases like Azure SQL, Azure Cosmos DB and Azure Database for PostgreSQL. It has the following components:

- **SQL Database**: A relational database service in the Microsoft Cloud based on the market-leading Microsoft SQL Server engine.
- **SQL Managed Instance**: A fully managed platform as a service (PaaS) database engine that does most database management tasks such as upgrading, patching, backups, and monitoring without user involvement.

- **Redis Cache**: A secure and highly advanced key-value store that stores data structures like strings, hashes, lists, and so on.

Azure Networking

Azure Networking comprises a suite of services designed to connect, safeguard, and oversee your Cloud and hybrid resources. The features offered by Azure Networking include:

- **Virtual Network**: A Virtual Network in Azure provides a logically isolated space within the Cloud, enabling the creation and control of a private network environment. One can set up custom IP address ranges, subnets, routing tables, security groups, and network interfaces. It also allows connections between your virtual network and other virtual networks, on-site networks, or even the internet.
- **LoadBalancer**: The Load Balancer efficiently manages incoming network traffic by dispersing it across several servers or instances within your virtual network. It accommodates TCP and UDP protocols and ensures consistent high availability and scalability. This tool is utilized for various cases, including internal and external setups, for web applications, database servers, or VPN gateways.
- **ApplicationGateway**: This web traffic load balancer operates at the application layer (Layer 7) of the OS model and includes features such as SSL offloading, cookie-based session affinity, route-based on URL path, a web application firewall, and the ability to host multiple sites. It utilizes Application Gateway to enhance the performance and security of your web applications.
- **ExpressRoute**: ExpressRoute establishes a direct private connection from your local network to Azure, circumventing the public internet for enhanced reliability, speed, lower latency, and increased security. Use it for direct access to Azure services like virtual machines, storage solutions, SQL databases, and Azure Active Directory.
- **AzureDNS**: The Azure DNS service offers DNS domain hosting, utilizing Microsoft Azure infrastructure for name resolution. With integrated management tools compatible with other Azure services, manage your DNS records easily. Azure DNS can also be paired seamlessly with services like Traffic Manager, Web Apps, and Cloud Services.

Azure Security and Identify Management

It offers the ability to recognize and address risks to cloud security. You can also manage sensitive assets like encryption keys. It consists of the following parts:

- **Azure Key Vault**: Azure Key Vault generates secrets that are utilized by Cloud services and apps while also protecting cryptographic keys.

- **Azure Active Directory**: Identity management and Azure Active Directory services covers device registration and multi-factor authentication.
- **Azure AD B2C**: This cloud identity management solution is designed for your mobile and online applications that are used by consumers. You can scale hundreds of millions of customer identities using it.
- **Azure Service Bus**: Service Bus is a third-party communication system-based information delivery service.
- **Azure AD Domain Services**: Provides managed domain services, including LDAP, group policy, and domain join. This authentication works with Active Directory on Windows Server.
- **Azure Multi-Factor Authentication (MFA)**: This two-step verification method that uses two factors provides an easy sign-in process and facilitates your access to data and apps.

Azure Management and Governance Services

Some other Azure Management and Governance Services that allow easy management of Azure deployment are:

- **AzureAdvisor:** Offers customized suggestions for enhancing your Azure resources in terms of cost-efficiency, performance, reliability, and security. Examines the recommended best practices and implement them on your resources effortlessly.
- **AzureMonitor:** Helps to gather, scrutinize, and respond to telemetry data from both your Azure and on-site environments. Allows monitoring the well-being and performance of your applications, infrastructure, and network, delivering immediate alerts and insights.
- **AzurePolicy:** Assists in applying and maintaining compliance standards throughout your Azure resources. Helps to set policies that control how resources are created and configured, as well as evaluate the compliance status of your current resources.
- **AzureBackup:** Offering an uncomplicated and dependable method for backing up your information to the Cloud, this service ensures your data is protected against unintended loss, corruption, or ransomware with the capability to recover it as necessary. Additionally, it facilitates the administration and surveillance of your backups from a unified platform.

Azure Analytics

This platform offers an all-encompassing solution for data analysis, business intelligence, and machine learning. It allows you to collect, keep, work on, and present data from different origins while utilizing sophisticated analytics and AI solutions to extract insights and prompt decisions. Key components of Azure Analytics include:

- **AzureSynapse Analytics:** This comprehensive service offers data warehousing, big data analytics, and data integration within a single cloud-native framework. Users can utilize SQL, Spark, or Python for queries and develop full-scale data pipelines through either code-free or code-first choices.
- **AzureData Lake Storage:** Tailored for scalability and security, this cloud storage solution accommodates, both structured and unstructured data. It is designed for analytic operations and integrates with Azure Synapse Analytics among other Azure offerings fluently.
- **AzureDatabricks:** Built on Apache Spark, this swift, cooperative platform addresses data engineering, data sciences, and scalable machine learning. It provides an interactive workspace, access to a wealth of libraries and frameworks, and compatibility with Azure tools and services.
- **AzureHDInsight:** A completely managed cloud service that operates various open-source frameworks including Hadoop, Spark, Hive, Kafka, and Storm. The service simplifies the process and analysis of expansive data volumes using prevalent open-source instruments and programming languages.
- **AzureMachine Learning:** This cloud service supports the creation, training, deployment, and management of machine learning models via diverse methodologies and frameworks. It features automated machine learning, a user-friendly drag-and-drop interface, as well as coding options, and capitalizes on Azure's infrastructure and accelerators to boost experiments and operational scaling.
- **DataFactory:** As a cloud-based orchestrator, this service facilitates data migration and transformation across multiple platforms. It provides a visual approach as well as scripting capabilities for pipeline formation and maintenance while ensuring thorough monitoring and auditing of data processes.
- **PowerBI:** Providing business intelligence solutions at both a self-service and enterprise level, this cloud platform allows connection to an array of data sources, facilitating transformation, modeling, and the creation of dynamic dashboards and reports. Additionally, it enables simplified sharing and collaboration among users.

Integration

Azure provides an assortment of services and tools designed for the smooth integration of applications and data across various platforms and environments. It also offers a visual designer to help you construct and automate your workflow, which is a set of steps in your process.

Below are some prominent features offered by Azure for integration purposes:

- **LogicApps**: Enables building and orchestrating business processes through a visual designer or coding. With Logic Apps, you can link up an array of data sources, such as SQL Server, Office 365, Salesforce, or Twitter, initiating actions based on triggers and conditions. This service also grants access to over 200 ready-to-use APIs and services through connectors.
- **ServiceBus**: This robust and secure communication infrastructure supports messaging between applications and services within Azure and beyond. It caters to different messaging architectures, including queues, topics, and subscriptions, allowing asynchronous and isolated data transfer.
- **APIManagement**: It provides functionalities to create, publish, administer, and safeguard your application's APIs. The service facilitates the exposure of APIs to both internal and external users, implementing policy controls, tracking activity and output, as well as offering monetization opportunities for your APIs.
- **Notification Hubs**: An intuitive, cross-platform, scalable push engine provided by Azure Notification Hubs.
- **Azure Event Hubs**: This platform for data streaming has the capacity to handle millions of events every second. Any real-time analytics solution that supports batching and storage adapters can be used to transform and store data that is provided to an event hub.
- **Azure Search**: This cloud-based search-as-a-service tool provides infrastructure and server management. It provides a service that is ready to use once your data is entered. You may use this to incorporate search into your mobile or online application.

The detailed list of components can be viewed here - https://azurecharts.com/overview/

Basic Concepts of Azure

Azure Cloud enables users to manage compute, storage, network, and application resources through an online portal.

A key aspect of Azure is its capacity for on-demand provisioning of different resource types or services via the Azure portal. A resource refers to a service instance that you initiate, which could range from a virtual machine to a database or a storage account.

To allocate a resource on the Azure portal, specific steps must be executed as follows:

1. Access the Azure portal by entering your credentials.
2. Navigate to and select '`Create a resource`' in the top left corner of the portal.

3. From the list of available services, pick the type of resource you wish to create—options include **`Compute`**, **`Database`**, **`Networking`**, and so on. Alternatively, locate a service by name or category using the search function.
4. Enter all necessary details for your resource including name, subscription, resource group, location, and other configurations unique to the resource type. Review the projected cost for the resource prior to creation.
5. Initiate the deployment by clicking on **`'Create'`**. The **`Notifications`** panel or **`Deployment`** center allows you to track the deployment progress.
6. Upon completion, manage the new resource directly from the portal or employ tools such as Azure CLI, PowerShell, or SDKs for further interaction.

By utilizing templates, which are defined as JSON files that describe the attributes and connections of the resources, you can deploy multiple resources concurrently. You can either utilize prebuilt templates from the Azure Marketplace or develop custom templates tailored to your needs. Implementing templates streamlines and regulates the deployment methodology, guaranteeing a uniform setup across various platforms.

Furthermore, if we take examples of a specific resource, let's say a Virtual Machine, a user can set up a virtual machine (VM) configuration with the following options: the VM size (in terms of CPU, RAM, and local disks), the operating system, any preinstalled software, the network configuration, and the location of the VM. The user can then launch the VM based on that configuration and access the deployed VM in a few minutes. Microsoft Azure is more advantageous than the previous method of deploying a physical machine, which could take weeks for the procurement process alone. Besides the public clouds described earlier, there are also private and hybrid clouds. In a private cloud, you build a cloud environment in your own datacenter and offer self-service access to compute resources to users in your organization. This simulates a public cloud for your users, but you still have full responsibility for the purchase and maintenance of the hardware and software services you offer. A hybrid cloud combines public and private clouds, allowing you to host workloads in the best-suited location. For example, you could host a high-traffic website in the public cloud and connect it to a highly secure database hosted in your private cloud (or on-premises datacenter).

Microsoft supports public, private, and hybrid clouds. Microsoft Azure is a public cloud. Microsoft Azure lets you deploy many essential Azure services via Azure Portal on your Azure Subscription in your preferred Azure datacenter and gives a self-service portal experience to your users.

Let us talk now about some of these basic concepts of Azure in detail.

Azure Portal and Subscription Management

Azure Portal is an online management portal which is the most convenient way to manage the resources you launch into Azure.

You can use this to set up virtual networks, configure Web Apps, create VMs, specify storage accounts, and more, as mentioned in the previous section. It can be accessed using the URL - https://portal.azure.com/.

All the resources that use the Resource Manager deployment model can only be reached in the Azure portal.

Let's explore the Azure portal and how you navigate through it.

Figure 4.3 shows an overview of an Azure Portal dashboard. Here you can see all the resources that have been provisioned or recently used. For example, we have a SQL Server. We have an Azure Data Factory. We have a few more services like SQL databases, storage accounts, Key Vault, and many more.

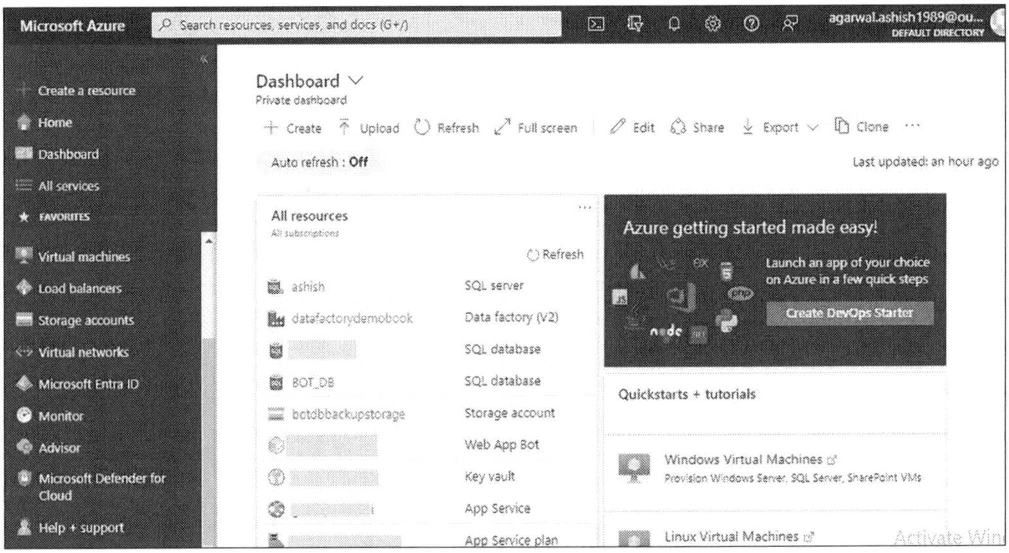

Figure 4.3: *Azure Portal Dashboard Overview*

The left navigation pane helps you to navigate through various other available options like provisioning a new resource "**`Create a resource`**" and other options like going to the home page to explore the list of resources or a particular type of resource, for example, Virtual Machines, Storage accounts, virtual networks or if you want to reach out to support using the "**`Help + support`**" option.

Some of the default tiles on the Dashboard are useful:

- **`All Resources`**: Displays all your resources in a list when you click it.
- **`Service Health`**: Shows the status of the regions across the globe. You can click this to see a list of the regions and choose one to get more information.
- **`Marketplace`**: Takes you straight to the Marketplace blade where you can find and add resources.

- **Subscriptions:** Shows the subscriptions that you can manage with the account you are using. You can choose a subscription and see the billing details for the current month. If you have a starting credit, this will show the remaining credit. Accounts with starting credit include MSDN accounts and BizSpark accounts.
- **Help + support**: Takes you to the blade, where you can create a new support ticket and manage the ones you have already submitted. It also provides links to the MSDN forums where you can ask questions.

Figure 4.4: *Azure Portal Top Menu Bar*

The icons from left to right have these meanings:

- **The Shell icon** initiates the cloud shell to be able to select either **Bash** or **PowerShell** as the options to perform the cloud shell activities using the portal. The most recently used environment will be the default for your next session.
- **The Directory Icon** allows you to navigate to other sets of subscriptions or directories you have access to and put a filter to view resource groups, resources or services under the particularly filtered subscription.
- **The bell icon** shows the notifications from this session. For instance, if you create a new VM, you will see a notification here when it is done.
- **The gear icon** opens the Settings screen for the portal, where you can do things like turn on or off toast notifications, choose the default language, and so on.
- The options to choose and select directories and subscriptions have also been recently moved under the gear icon, and you can now view and toggle between the directories and subscriptions using the gear button.
- **The question mark icon** shows a drop-down menu that lets you create a new support request, view your current support requests, and so on.
- **The Feedback icon** allows the users to provide any feedback related to the portal.
- **The profile icon** shows the account you have used to log into the portal. If you manage more than one subscription, this will show the list of Azure ADs the user belongs to. You can click this to sign out, change your password, or suggest an idea.

Resources and Resource Groups

Resource Groups

A *resource* group is a collection of *resources* that belong to an Azure solution. You can include all or some of the resources for the solution in the resource group, depending on how you want to organize them. You have the flexibility to choose how to assign resources to resource groups based on your organization's needs. Usually, you should group resources with the same lifecycle so that you can manage them more easily as a unit.

The resource group keeps metadata about the resources. This means that the location of the resource group determines where that metadata is stored. For legal purposes, you may have to ensure that your data is stored in a specific region.

The following are the steps to be followed to create a new resource group:

1. Click on the **`Resource Groups`** section on the portal dashboard on the left navigation pane.
2. Click on "**`Create`**" (*Figure* 4.5).

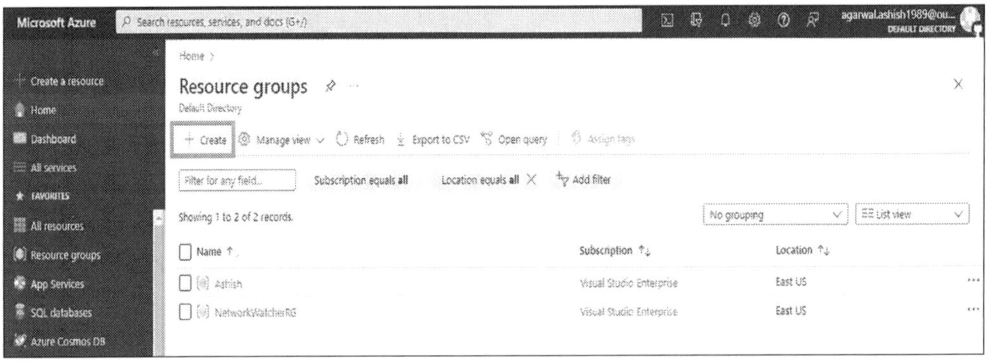

Figure 4.5: *Creating a Resource Group*

3. On the next window, fill in the required details, as depicted in *Figure* 4.6.
4. Once all the details are filled, click "**`Review + Create`**".
5. Once the validation is passed, it will allow us to create as the last step.
6. Look for notifications for the successful creation.

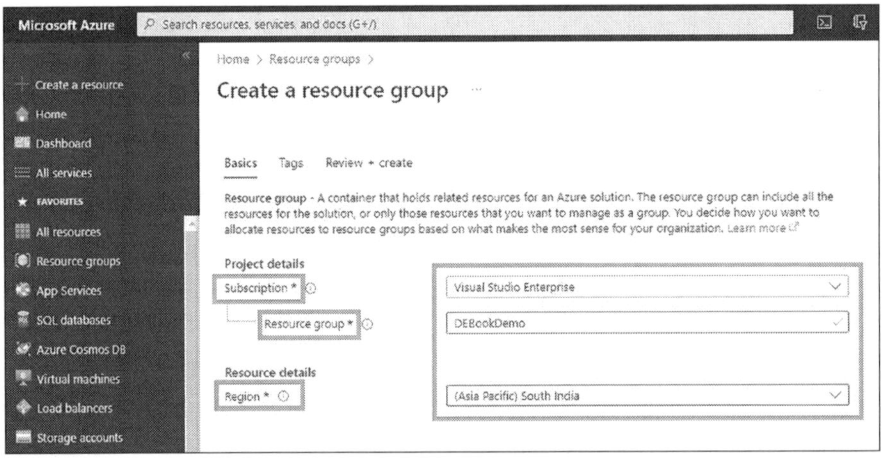

Figure 4.6: *Resource Group Details and Review*

Creation and Management of Resources

Once we have created a Resource Group, you can use the Azure portal to provide various Azure resources as per your requirement and categorize or distribute them across one or many resource groups based on the business needs.

We can also manage these Azure resources once they are provisioned by clicking on each resource and viewing their properties, as well as managing them using the portal.

The following are the steps to be followed to create a new resource group:

1. Click on the "**`Create a resource`**" section on the portal dashboard on the left navigation pane.
2. Click on "**`Create`**" (*Figure* 4.7).

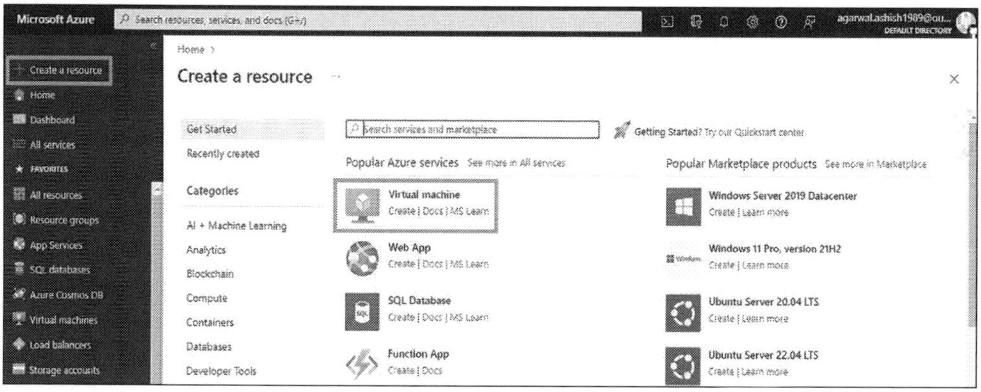

Figure 4.7: *Creating a Resource using Portal*

3. On the next window, fill in the required details, as depicted in *Figure* 4.8.
4. Once all the details are filled, click "**`Review + Create`**".
5. Once the validation is passed, it will allow us to create as the last step.
6. Look for notifications for the successful creation.

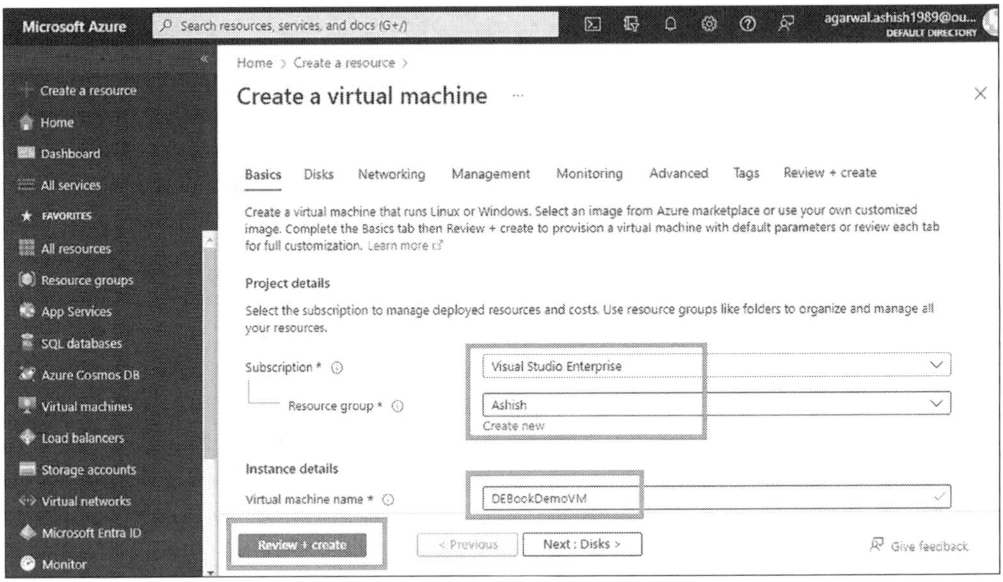

Figure 4.8: *Creating a Virtual Machine Resource*

Azure Resource Manager (ARM)

Azure Resource Manager (ARM) is a vital component of Azure that enables you to manage and deploy resources in a simple, consistent, and automated way. Azure Resource Manager lets you organize and control your cloud infrastructure with ease and efficiency. For enterprise IT managers and MSPs, learning how to use the Azure Resource Manager is essential to leverage the full capabilities of the Azure platform.

It also provides a management layer that enables you to create, update, and delete resources in your Azure account. You use management features, like access control, locks, and tags, to secure and organize your resources after deployment.

In this section, we will learn what ARM is, how it works, and what advantages it provides. This will help us improve your cloud performance and prepare you for a more flexible, scalable, and agile future.

Azure Resource Manager is Microsoft's solution for controlling and arranging resources in the Azure Cloud. Its reliable management layer provides a systematic and effective way to build, launch, handle, and track Azure resources. These resources range from virtual machines, databases, storage accounts, web apps, and more.

How ARM links to Resource Groups

Azure Resource Manager (ARM) has a core concept called a "*resource group*." A resource group is a logical group that contains resources related to an application or a specific workload. ARM lets you create and manage these resource groups, simplifying the process of organizing, deploying, and monitoring your resources in a consistent and controlled way.

Basic functioning of ARM

ARM uses a declarative, JSON-based language to specify the infrastructure and configuration of your resources. This means you state what you want your Azure resources to be like, and ARM handles the underlying provisioning and management details, ensuring that your desired state is preserved.

This Jason-based ARM template can be exported once we have the resources provisioned in the portal by going to the resource and clicking on the export template option.

The following is one of the sample ARM templates generated from the Azure Blob Storage.

JSON

```json
"resources": [
  {
    "type": "Microsoft.Storage/storageAccounts",
    "apiVersion": "2022-09-01",
    "name": "mystorageaccount",
    "location": "centralus",
    "sku": {
      "name": "Standard_LRS"
    },
    "kind": "StorageV2"
  },
]
```

***Figure 4.9**: Sample ARM template JSON Code Format*

Importance of ARM in Azure

Azure Resource Manager (ARM) is a crucial component of centralized management in the Azure ecosystem. It acts as a centralized control hub that enables smooth monitoring and governance of Azure resources. This integrated control panel lets users create, change, and remove resources simultaneously. This method simplifies the management of complex applications and varied environments, making the overall operational process more efficient.

Azure Resource Manager also works with Azure's Role-Based Access Control (RBAC) system. This integration allows organizations to have granular control over resource management within their Azure subscription. RBAC's capabilities are important for maintaining ARM security measures and ensuring compliance, especially in multi-user, multi-resource scenarios.

Resource dependencies are common when dealing with complex, multi-tier applications in Azure. Azure Resource Manager pays attention to these dependencies. It makes sure that resources are provisioned and updated in the right order, thus reducing deployment errors and improving resource consistency. This careful handling of resource dependencies is useful to ARM's functionality.

Advantages of Azure Resource Manager

- Azure Resource Manager acts as a central orchestration engine, offering a unified control plane for creating, modifying, and deleting resources in a consistent and simple way.
- ARM templates let you define infrastructure as a code to achieve the desired state of resources, ensuring reliability and consistency in deployments across different environments and project stages.
- ARM integrates smoothly with Azure's Role-Based Access Control (RBAC) system, giving you fine-grained access control for security and compliance, following the principle of least privilege.
- Azure Resource Manager makes resource dependency management easy, ensuring that resources are created and updated in the right order, reducing errors, and improving resource consistency when dealing with interconnected resources.
- ARM templates support infrastructure as a code practice, allowing collaboration, version control, and repeatability. Templates stored in version control systems like Git enable you to track changes over time and work with your team, resulting in well-documented configurations.
- Templates are also scalable and efficient, enabling resource creation, updates, and deletion across projects and environments. This scalability enhances resource utilization and cost-effectiveness.

Roles and Access

Managing access to cloud resources is essential for any organization that uses the Cloud. Azure role-based access control (Azure RBAC) lets you control who can access Azure resources, what actions they can perform on those resources, and what scopes they can access.

Azure RBAC is an authorization system that uses Azure Resource Manager to give you granular access control to Azure resources.

Attribute-based access control (ABAC) is an authorization system that determines access using attributes related to security principles, resources, and the context of an access request. With ABAC, you can allow a security principal to access a resource based on attributes. Azure ABAC is the application of ABAC for Azure.

The following diagram is a high-level view of how the roles of Azure, Microsoft Entra, and classic subscription administrator are related.

Azure RBAC is a recent authorization system that gives you detailed access control to Azure resources. Azure RBAC with many predefined roles can be applied at various scopes, allowing you to make your own custom roles. To manage resources in Microsoft Entra ID, such as users, groups, and domains, you need to use some Microsoft Entra roles.

- Azure roles
- Microsoft Entra roles

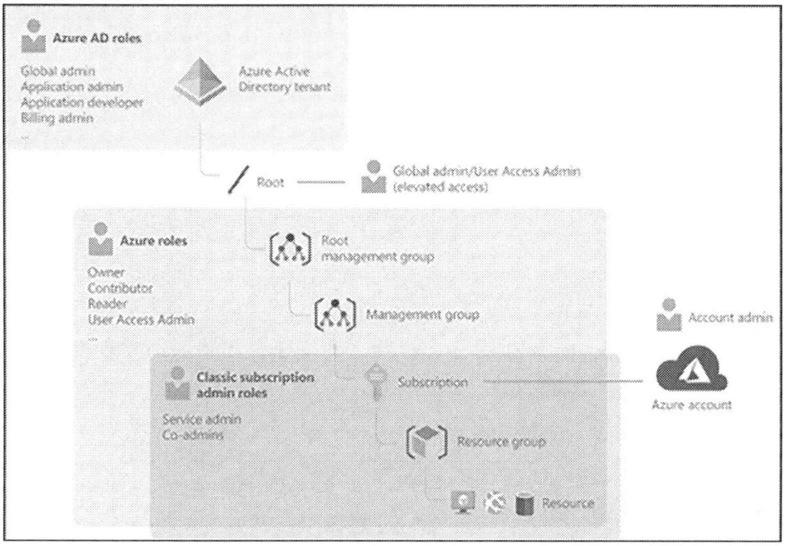

***Figure 4.10**: High-Level Azure Roles Overview*

The following are the fundamental Azure roles:

Role Name	**Role Permission**	**Are All Resource Types Applicable?**
Owner	• Grants full access to manage all resources • Assign roles in Azure RBAC	Yes
Contributor	• Grants full access to manage all resources • Cannot assign roles in Azure RBAC • Cannot manage assignments in Azure Blueprints or share image galleries	Yes
Reader	• View Azure resources	Yes

RBAC Admin	• Manage user access to Azure resources • Assign roles in Azure RBAC • Assign themselves or others the Owner role • Cannot manage access using other ways, such as Azure Policy	No
User Access Administrator	• Manage user access to Azure resources • Assign roles in Azure RBAC • Assign themselves or others the Owner role	No

Table 4.1: *Fundamental Azure Roles*

Pricing Calculator

With the Azure pricing calculator, you can estimate how much your Azure usage will cost based on your expected usage. This helps you plan and budget your cloud expenses more easily. Whether you run a small business or a large corporation, the online tool helps you make smart choices about your cloud investment. When you sign in, the calculator also shows you how much you can save on your Azure usage with your special or reduced prices.

The following is the URL to visit the Pricing Calculator on Azure

https://azure.microsoft.com/pricing/calculator/

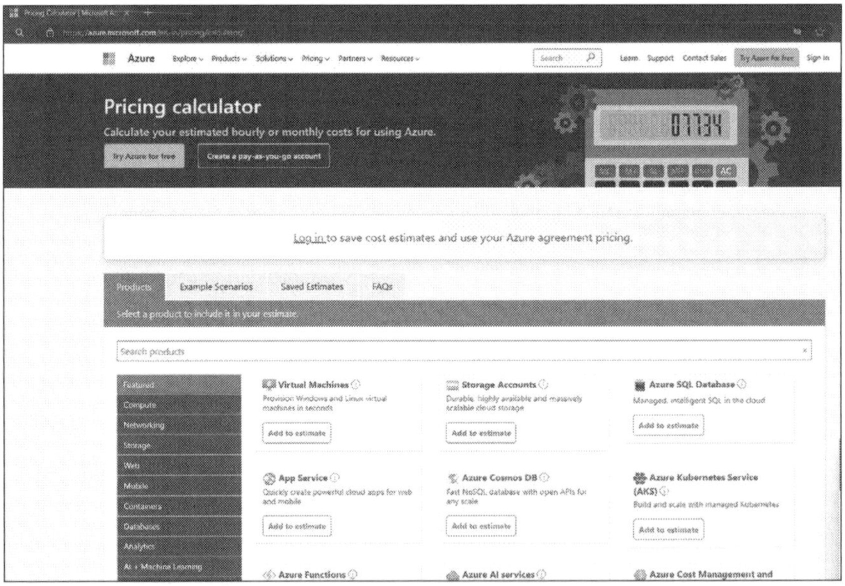

Figure 4.11: *Azure Pricing Calculator Overview Page*

Steps to calculate the price for a particular product and build estimates

1. As a first step, pick the required product you want to calculate the price for and build your estimate. There are multiple categories of products present on the pricing calculator page, and we can choose from that category of the required products as per our needs.

2. Once you have added the required product or products to the page, we need to select the specifications for that product. These specifications vary from product to product and have some common specifications, for example, region, savings plan, reservations, and so on.

3. A few examples of product-wise specifications include features like the instance type for SQL virtual machine or a virtual machine, compute capacity and storage capacity in case of the PaaS offerings of SQL, for example, SQL database or SQL managed instance.

4. The pricing calculator also gives us the flexibility to choose the usage or capacity on which we will be utilizing our resources, for example, the number of hours per month to enable us to create an optimized and accurate estimate based on our needs.

Azure SQL Databases

Azure SQL is a collection of smart, secure, and managed products that run on the SQL Server database engine in the Azure cloud. Azure SQL is based on the SQL Server engine you know, so you can easily move your applications and use the same tools, languages, and resources you are familiar with. You can leverage your existing skills and experience in the cloud and do more with what you have.

The Azure SQL family consists of three products as follows.

Azure SQL Database

Azure SQL Database is a relational database service that is fully managed and smart, and that runs on the newest stable version of the SQL Server database engine.

You can select from various deployment options, such as single databases, elastic pools, or hyperscale, to achieve the best performance, scalability, and cost for your workloads.

Some of the features offered are -

- Builds modern cloud applications with a smart, managed database service that offers serverless computing.

- A cloud-based relational database service (DBaaS) that runs on Azure and belongs to the industry category of Platform-as-a-Service (PaaS).
- Ideal for modern cloud applications that need the latest stable SQL Server features and have tight deadlines in development and marketing.
- A fully managed SQL Server database engine, based on the latest stable version of the SQL Server.

SQL Database runs on standardized hardware and software that is owned, hosted, and maintained by Microsoft. With SQL Server, built-in features and functionality often need extensive configuration (either on-premises or in an Azure virtual machine). When using SQL Database, you pay only for what you use with options to scale up or out for more power with no interruption. SQL Database has some extra features that are not available in SQL Server, such as built-in high availability, intelligence, and management.

Azure SQL Database has the following deployment options:

- As a single database with its own set of resources managed by a logical server. A single database is like a contained database in the SQL Server. This option is optimized for modern application development of new cloud-native applications. *Hyperscale* and *serverless* options are available.
- An *elastic pool* is a group of databases with a shared set of resources managed by a logical server. A single database can be moved in and out of an elastic pool. This option is optimized for modern application development of new cloud-native applications using the multi-tenant SaaS application pattern. Elastic pools offer a cost-effective solution for managing the performance of multiple databases that have variable usage patterns. Elastic pools for Hyperscale are currently being previewed.

Azure SQL Database always keeps the SQL Server database engine, and the OS updated and secure, with 99.99% uptime. You can use the PaaS features of Azure SQL Database to concentrate on the database administration and optimization tasks that matter to your business. Azure SQL Database lets you build a reliable and fast data storage layer for your applications and solutions in Azure. SQL Database is suitable for many modern cloud applications, as it can handle both relational and nonrelational data types, such as graphs, JSON, spatial, and XML.

One of the unique features that Azure SQL Database offers to support modern cloud applications is ***ledger table support***. Ledger tables are a type of system-versioned temporal table that provides cryptographic verification of the data history in the table. Ledger tables can help you achieve regulatory compliance, data security, and auditability by ensuring your data is tamper-evident and immutable.

When setting up a ledger table, include the **`SYSTEM_VERSIONING`** clause with **`LEDGER = ON`** in the **`CREATE TABLE`** command. This activates system versioning and stores historical data in a history table, mirroring the main table's schema plus two extra columns for row and chain signatures. These signatures connect each row to adjacent ones cryptographically, allowing detection of unauthorized changes or deletions.

Ledger tables offer robust functionality that guarantees the security and unchangeability of your data within Azure SQL Database. They are suitable for use in various situations, including monetary transactions, audit trails, medical documentation, or any data needing cryptographic validation. Ledger tables are currently accessible for public preview and can be found across all Azure regions.

SQL Database has two purchasing models:

The vCore-based purchasing option enables customization of your database core count, memory allocation, and storage specifications. It also incorporates Azure Hybrid Benefit, allowing cost savings using existing licenses. Conversely, the DTU-based model groups compute power, memory, and input/output resources into three distinct packages catered to varying operational demands. This model offers flexibility to scale storage capacity according to necessity.

- With the vCore approach, you have the freedom to tailor the number of virtual cores and the amount of memory and select the storage options that best fit your database's needs. The Azure Hybrid Benefit is also applicable, offering an opportunity for cost efficiency by applying your existing SQL Server licenses. The DTU model simplifies resource allocation by presenting fixed combinations of computational power, memory, and I/O capabilities across three service tiers aligned with different workload profiles while allowing separate scalability for storage.
- Opting for the vCore-based model grants liberty in setting the number of virtual cores, adjusting memory size, and choosing the type and extent of storage for your database. Additionally, it embraces Azure Hybrid Benefit, enabling cost-effective use of your SQL Server licenses. On the other hand, the DTU-based model delineates a trio of service levels that merge set proportions of computing, memory, and I/O capacities, tailored to suit various database operations. Its design also permits incremental enhancements to storage as the need emerges.

SQL Database has two purchasing models with different service tiers:

- The vCore-based purchasing model has three service tiers:
    - The ***General-Purpose*** service tier is for common workloads. It has balanced computing and storage options that are budget-friendly.
    - The ***Business-Critical*** service tier is for OLTP applications that need high transaction rates and low latency I/O. It has the best failure protection by using multiple isolated replicas.

- The ***Hyperscale*** service tier is for most business workloads. Hyperscale has high flexibility and performance with compute and storage resources that can scale independently. It has better failure resilience by letting you set up more than one isolated database replica. The Hyperscale service tier enables you to scale to 100 TB, with fast backup and restore capabilities.

- The DTU-based purchasing model has two service tiers:
  - The ***Standard*** service tier is for common workloads. It has balanced compute and storage options that are budget-friendly.
  - The ***Premium*** service tier is for OLTP applications that need high transaction rates and low latency I/O. It has the best failure protection by using multiple isolated replicas.

Azure SQL-Managed Instance

Update your SQL Server applications at a scale with a smart, fully managed instance as a service, with nearly 100% compatibility with the SQL Server database engine. It is ideal for most cloud migrations.

Azure SQL Managed Instance is a Platform-as-a-Service (PaaS) product ideal for most cloud migrations. SQL Managed Instance is a group of system and user databases with a shared set of resources that is ready to move.

- Best for new applications or existing on-premises applications that need the latest stable SQL Server features and that are moved to the Cloud with little changes. An instance of SQL Managed Instance is like an instance of the Microsoft SQL Server database engine that offers shared resources for databases and more instance-scoped features.
- SQL Managed Instance enables database migration from on-premises with little to no database changes. This option gives all the PaaS benefits of Azure SQL Database but also has extra capabilities, such as a native virtual network. SQL Managed Instance gives full SQL Server access and feature compatibility to move your SQL Server instances to Azure.

SQL Managed Instance supports vCore-based purchasing model

SQL Managed Instance lets you use the vCore-based purchasing model to get flexibility, control, and transparency, and an easy way to move your on-premises workload requirements to the cloud. This model lets you adjust compute, memory, and storage based on your workload needs. The vCore model also saves up to 55 percent with the Azure Hybrid Benefit for SQL Server.

You can pick hardware configurations in the vCore model as follows:

- **Standard Series** (Gen5) logical CPUs with 5.1 GB of RAM per CPU vCore and compute sizes from 4 to 80 cores.

- **Premium Series** logical CPUs with 7 GB of RAM per CPU vCore and compute sizes from 4 to 80 cores.
- **Premium Series Memory-Optimized** logical CPUs with 13.6 GB of RAM per CPU vCore and compute sizes from 4 to 64 cores.

SQL Managed Instance is available in two service tiers:

- **General Purpose:** Designed for applications with typical performance and I/O latency requirements.
- **Business Critical:** Designed for applications with low I/O latency requirements and minimal impact of underlying maintenance operations on the workload.

SQL Server on Azure VMs

Move your SQL Server workload without hassle and keep 100% SQL Server compatibility and operating system-level control.

SQL Server on Azure VMs is an Infrastructure-as-a-Service (IaaS) product that lets you run SQL Server in a fully managed virtual machine (VM) on Azure.

- SQL Server hosted and running in the Cloud on Windows Server or Linux virtual machines on Azure. You can install any supported version and edition of SQL Server on an IaaS virtual machine.
- Best for migrations and applications that need OS-level access. SQL virtual machines on Azure are ready to move for existing applications that need quick migration to the Cloud with little or no changes. SQL virtual machines give full administrative control over the SQL Server instance and underlying OS for migration to Azure.
- The primary distinction between SQL Server on Azure Virtual Machine and Azure SQL Platform as a Service (PaaS), encompassing SQL Database and SQL Managed Instance, lies in the level of control provided. SQL Server on Azure Virtual Machines grants comprehensive control over both the database engine and the underlying Operating System, offering a more hands-on approach to configuration and management. You can decide when to start maintenance activities, including system updates, change the recovery model to simple or bulk-logged, pause or start the service as needed, and fully customize the SQL Server database engine.
- With this extra control comes the extra responsibility of managing the virtual machine. Fast development and test scenarios when you don't want to purchase on-premises hardware for the SQL Server. SQL virtual machines also work on standardized hardware that is owned, hosted, and maintained by Microsoft.

- When using SQL virtual machines, you can either pay only for what you use for a SQL Server license already included in a SQL Server image or easily use an existing license. You can also stop or resume the VM as needed.
- Optimized for moving existing applications to Azure or extending existing on-premises applications to the cloud in hybrid deployments. Also, you can use the SQL Server in a virtual machine to develop and test traditional SQL Server applications. With SQL virtual machines, you have full administrative rights over a dedicated SQL Server instance and a cloud-based VM.
- It's a great choice when an organization already has IT resources available to maintain virtual machines. These capabilities let you build a highly customized system to address your application's specific performance and availability needs.

With **SQL Database** and **SQL Managed Instance**, you can still manage your database without worrying about the database engine, operating system, or hardware. You can still handle things, such as databases and logins, index and query tuning, and auditing and security. Also, setting up high availability to another data center is easy and simple.

With **SQL Server on Azure VMs**, you have full control over the operating system and SQL Server instance settings. With a VM, you can choose when to update/upgrade the operating system and database software and when to add any extra software, such as anti-virus. Some automated features are available to make patching, backup, and high availability much easier. Moreover, you can adjust the size of the VM, the number of disks, and their storage settings. Azure lets you change the size of a VM as you need.

Database Migration From On-Premises to Azure

Database migration from SQL on-premises environment or SQL hosted on any other non-Azure cloud environment to Azure SQL requires a planned approach as migrating large enterprise estates and data centers from on-premises to Azure can be tricky sometimes and is considered a bit complicated process if not done with proper planning. Sustainability challenges may arise after migration if the process does not adhere to Microsoft's recommended best practices and guidance. It is essential to incorporate these guidelines thoroughly, starting from the planning phase and extending through the actual migration and deployment on Azure, ensuring a seamless and sustainable transition.

Azure migration is a three-phased approach that involves a pre-migration, migration phase, and post-migration phase.

- Pre-Migration (Assessment of SQL Server deployed on on-Premises or customer data centers or third party cloud providers)

- Migration (Planning the migration activities and actual migration)
- Post-migration (Sustainability and successful migration)

The various available methods of migration are as follows:

- **Database Migration Assistant (DMA):** This method helps you to assess the target readiness of an on-premises SQL Server Instance and databases to move to a current data platform by finding compatibility issues and the right sized SKU for the proposed target (SQL Database or SQL-Managed Instance)

    1. Upgrade to a newer version of SQL Server
    2. Migrate to Azure SQL Database
    3. Migrate to Azure SQL Managed Instance

    DMA suggests performance and reliability enhancements for your target environment and allows you to transfer your schema, data, and uncontained objects from your source server to your target server.

    To make your database migration smoother, Database Migration Assistant (DMA) offers SKU suggestions in a clear and simple way. Based on performance data, DMA also advises you on the best Azure SQL SKU for your target database and explain why.

The SKU recommendations feature empowers you to gather performance data from your source SQL Server instances hosting databases and subsequently suggests suitable Azure SQL Database, Azure SQL Managed Instance, or SQL Server on Azure VM right-sized SKU recommendations based on the collected data. This feature delivers insightful recommendations pertaining to pricing tier, compute level, and data size.

- **Azure SQL migration extension for Azure Data Studio:** This extension helps you assess your database requirements, get the right-sized SKU recommendations for Azure resources, and migrate your SQL Server database to Azure.

    1. A flexible UI for a complete migration process. The extension begins with a migration readiness assessment and SKU suggestion (preview) (using performance data).
    2. A better assessment tool that can check SQL Server instances. The extension finds databases that are set to migrate to Azure SQL targets.
    3. An SKU suggestion engine that gathers performance data from the local source SQL Server instance and then creates right-sized SKU suggestions based on your Azure SQL target.

4. A dependable Azure service powered by Azure Database Migration Service that manages data movement tasks to provide a smooth migration experience.
5. You can do your migration online (for migrations that need little downtime) or offline (for migrations that have downtime throughout the migration) based on your business needs.
6. You can set up a self-hosted integration runtime to use your own compute resources to reach the source SQL Server instance backup files in your local environment.

- **Azure Migrate (Lift and Shift) to SQL Server on VM:**
    1. Assessment and Target Readiness in terms of Readiness and SKU
    2. Existing SQL Server to be moved as-is to an instance of SQL Server on an Azure VM using Azure Migrate
- **Distributed availability group:** A distributed AG is used to move a single SQL Server instance or an Always on AG to SQL Server on Azure VMs. It is a special availability group that spans two separate availability groups. A DAG allows you to synchronize data between SQL Server instances in different locations, such as on-premises and Azure, or between Azure regions. A DAG is used to migrate an existing SQL Server instance or an Always On availability group to SQL Server on Azure virtual machines (VMs) with minimal downtime and data loss.

To use a DAG for SQL PaaS migration, you need to perform the following steps:

1. Ensure that the source and target SQL Server instances are prepared. It's essential to have matching versions and editions of SQL Server on both ends and to have the Distributed AG feature activated. Network connectivity and firewall settings between the instances must also be established.
2. Construct an availability group for each side, incorporating the database you wish to transfer. The availability groups can share the same name or have distinct ones, as preferred. Each availability group should include at least one synchronous replica to safeguard data.
3. Establish a Distributed Availability Group (DAG) linking the two availability groups, utilizing either the `New-SqlAvailabilityGroup` cmdlet or the New Availability Group Wizard in SQL Server Management Studio. A unique DAG name, the names of the constituent availability group, and the endpoints for the availability replicas must be outlined. Additionally, provide a certificate for secure authentication and encryption.

4. Keep tabs on the data synchronization process across the availability groups. To assess the status and performance of the DAG and its components, employ the dashboard within SQL Server Management Studio or utilize the `Get-SqlDistributedAvailabilityGroup` cmdlet. Monitoring tools like Performance Monitor or Extended Events are useful for observing latency and throughput metrics for data transmission.

5. Execute the cut-over to transition to the target SQL Server instance when appropriate. Halt the data movement from the source to the target by pausing the DAG or by excluding the target availability group from the DAG. Subsequently, it prompts a failover to the target availability group, rendering it the primary and adjusting your applications' connection strings to the new instance. Post-migration, you may opt to dismantle the source availability group and the DAG.

- **Backup to a file:**
    1. Do a complete backup of your database to a local site.
    2. Transfer your local backup files to your VM with a remote desktop, Azure Data Explorer, or the AzCopy tool (Backups over 2 TB are suggested.)
    3. Restore the full database backups on the SQL Server on Azure VMs.

- **Backup to URL:** Backing up to a URL enables the execution of either full or differential backups for on-premises databases, which are then stored within an Azure Blob storage container. This procedure is beneficial when dealing with substantial databases that prove challenging to detach or replicate effortlessly. To use this process, consider adhering to these essential instructions:
    1. Initiate an Azure storage account and establish a container designated for the backup files.
    2. Produce a shared access signature (SAS) token for the said container, ensuring secure entry.
    3. Set up credentials on your local SQL Server instance by utilizing the SAS token as the confidential key.
    4. Execute a complete or differential database backup to the Azure Blob storage container via the BACKUP DATABASE Transact-SQL command or by utilizing SQL Server Management Studio, leveraging the configured credential.
    5. Create identical credentials on your Azure VM with the previously used SAS token as the secret element.

6. Employ the **RESTORE DATABASE** Transact-SQL command or SQL Server Management Studio to recover the databases from the Azure Blob storage container by accessing through the established credential.

- **Log shipping:** Log shipping copies transactional log files from local to an instance of SQL Server on an Azure VM. This option has low downtime during the failover and is easier to configure than an Always on Availability group.
- Convert on-premises machine to Hyper-V VHDs, upload to Azure Blob storage, and then deploy a new virtual machine using uploaded VHD:

  This method lets you move all system and user databases from a local SQL Server instance to an Azure VM. Follow these general steps to migrate a whole SQL Server instance with this manual method:

  1. Transform physical or virtual machines into Hyper-V VHDs.
  2. Load VHD files to Azure Storage using the Add-AzureVHD cmdlet.
  3. Create a new virtual machine with the loaded VHD.

- **Ship hard drive using Windows Import/Export Service:** Use the Windows Import/Export Service method to move big amounts of file data to Azure Blob storage when network upload is too costly or impossible. With this service, you mail one or more hard drives with that data to an Azure data center where your data will be loaded to your storage account.

Conclusion

In this chapter, we have learned about the Azure Cloud concepts in detail related to the basics of Azure overview from Portal experience to resources deployment and major components of Azure related to data engineering and architecture.

We also learned about various types of Azure Cloud and their features, that is, IaaS, PaaS, and SaaS and how it is similar/different compared to on-premises.

We also understood the Azure SQL options and basics of how we plan the migration of our SQL databases from on-premises to Azure SQL and available migration tooling offerings from Microsoft Azure.

With this chapter, we are concluding the understanding section(s) of the book and will now be entering into the implementation section where we will learn some interesting case studies and examples of real-world implementations we have learned so far.

Key Terms

- **IaaS/PaaS/SaaS**: These are types of cloud services offered where we have key differences related to services managed by cloud providers and self-managed.

- **Azure SQL:** How Azure SQL services work and their benefits, various services are Azure SQL DB, Managed Instance, Elastic Pools, and so on.
- **DMA:** Database Migrate Assistant is a first-party migration tool offered by Microsoft for the assessment and migration of SQL on-premises to Azure.

References

- https://docs.microsoft.com/en-us/learn/modules/principles-cloud-computing/5-types-of-cloud-services
- https://learn.microsoft.com/en-us/azure/role-based-access-control/rbac-and-directory-admin-roles
- https://learn.microsoft.com/en-us/azure/cost-management-billing/costs/pricing-calculator
- https://learn.microsoft.com/en-us/azure/azure-sql/azure-sql-iaas-vs-paas-what-is-overview?view=azuresql
- https://learn.microsoft.com/en-us/sql/dma/dma-sku-recommend-sql-db?view=sql-server-ver16
- https://azurecharts.com/overview/

CHAPTER 5
Working with Heterogenous Data Sources

Introduction

This chapter will deal with one of the key aspects of data engineering, which is to deal with a variety of different data sources where the company might have their data residing and on top of which we try to build a centralized and single source of data which will act as a "*Single Source of Truth*" while dealing with a Datawarehouse solution. These data sources can be as different as some of the legacy systems, custom Applications, third-party software, files (Excel, CSV, XML, JSON, Parque, and so on), and other parallel database systems, for example, Oracle, PostgreSQL, Mainframe datasets or even on-premises SQL Server or heterogeneous cloud database engines.

This chapter will cover how we can deal with such a variety of source systems while designing and developing an end-to-end data engineering solution. What are the best practices and complexities that occur while doing the same? How can we maintain the data quality and checks in place to ensure that the data is not manipulated or altered while moving across various pipelines?

Structure

In this chapter, we will discuss the following topics:

- Heterogeneous Data Sources
    - Types of Source Systems and its Impact on Data Engineering Solutions
- Connectivity Challenges Between Source and Target Systems
- Case Study: Data Engineering Solution Source Data Analysis

Heterogeneous Data Sources

Dealing with multiple types of data sources is one of the key aspects as well as challenges of working with data engineering projects. Whether it's on-premises setup or cloud environment, each type of enterprise architecture has its own set of difficulties or challenges in managing these various data sources and then generating a single source of truth of meaningful data which can be then leveraged to build large data warehouses and data marts to serve or cater to the needs of their specific business.

In this chapter, we will learn in detail about the different or common data sources that usually come across while designing or dealing with any data warehouse or data engineering solution and how we deal with these data sources.

Dealing with source systems is the first and foremost part of architecture, yes it lays the foundation for an effective and optimal solution.

Types of Source Systems and its Impact on Data Engineering Solutions

The phrase "*source systems*" should not be applied universally to some systems and not to others. A specific data warehouse serves as our beginning point when we refer to source systems as the data sources upon which the data warehouse is built. Numerous businesses have multiple data warehouses that are essentially connected so that they can also serve as source systems for one another.

However, we can distinguish between systems that generate data for the first time and those that don't when discussing data-generating systems. For instance, a checkout register is a data-generating system because, in addition to scanning products, it creates data files that inform the business about which things are leaving the store at what time and for what amount. The store has the option to erase the data in the register when the day is finished, the customer has left, and the register is balanced. However, since this data can be utilized for a variety of purposes, we don't always want to do so.

The system that creates the data becomes a source system for one or more data warehouses once the data is saved. We may conduct a wide range of studies and business initiatives using the data from this data warehouse, for example, inventory management, supply chain management, earnings analysis, multi-purchase analytics, and so on.

Source System Categories that Generate Data

We will now discuss the various types of source systems most prominently used or available across the industry to store the data or provide the data for other downstream systems to build meaningful insights, dashboards, data pipelines or raw processing as well.

- **Invoicing schemes Bills** are printed by these systems to specific clients. We can perform value-based segmentations, behavior-based segmentations, and other similar analyses by examining this data.
- **Data from social media**: This information can be used to gauge how people and groups feel. Employees handling corporate social relationship management may find it extremely useful to gain insights into how the organization is perceived by the public and important influencers. For this type of market monitoring, text mining that examines the positive and negative terms that an organization is linked to is a good place to start. Utilizing this data, the marketing department may also assess how successfully "*above-the-media-line*" efforts perform in the short term, that is, within days as opposed to months. The method is based on curves that display the past correlation between actual sales and social media attention. Thus we can predict the future campaign outcome early on by monitoring the campaign's position on a curve.

  Social media data can be used by HR to monitor applicants' and employees' public perceptions of the company.

  To target influencers, social network analysis can also be utilized to determine who impacts whom on the public view of the company.
- Information from Wikipedia and related databases. These databases can aid intelligent robots in conducting client conversations by helping them comprehend intricate relationships.
- **Geodata:** This information, when paired with an app user's location, can provide the groundwork for several new services. For example, we can notify a user when they are approaching one of the cafes and get a special discount in exchange. In the banking industry, as most people always carry both their phones and credit cards with them, a notification to the consumer may also be issued if a credit card is used more than 30 miles from the phone's location.

Flat Files

The flat file (txt, csv, and so on) sources are the most used and easiest to deal with reading or extracting data from them as they are simple, have a non-complex data structure, and are compatible with most of the ETL data tools available across the industry.

Like any other source data type or source system, flat files also have a certain set of structures or concept which we should know while dealing with them.

The flat files follow a structured two-dimensional data structure with rows and columns as the main components of it. Another important component of a flat file is a column delimiter which is used to differentiate between the data of one column to another. The most used column delimiter is a comma (,) and that is the reason when we have a separated flat file, we call it a CSV file. They can also use other delimiters like a semi-colon (;) or pipe-separated delimiter (|), or we can also define our custom delimiter which could be a combination of multiple characters.

A line terminator, otherwise called a row terminator helps us identify when to start reading from column one for a new row instead of continuing for the same row and looking for a new column in the same row.

The following figure shows a sample CSV file with columns as state ID country region and so on in the first row which call the header row and then from the second row onward, the actual data follows in the same order as the headers, delineated by separator.

Additionally, whenever two commas come together that means the value is not provided by the source itself and is considered null in our downstream systems.

```
ID,StateProvinceCode,CountryRegionCode,IsOnlyStateProvinceFlag,Name,TerritoryID
1,AS ,AS,1,American Samoa,1
2,BS,IN,1,Indian,1
3,ZS,CH,1,Japanse,1
4,CS,GR,1,Germany,1
5,MS,UA,1,UAE,1
6,JF,MK,2,Macau,1
7,KD,KF,3,Kolar,1
8,GF,LD,1,,1
9,DS,RD,1,,1
```

***Figure 5.1**: Source Type: Flat Files*

TXT File

- It is the simplest way to store data in a system using plain text format.
- Plain text files are the basic and universal storage formats; they may not be the best or most advanced solution, but they are effective and reliable.
- The data are organized in rows, with multiple values in each row.
- Almost all software applications can read and write text files, and they can be used across different computer systems.
- The low-level format of storing everything as characters, with one byte per character, is not wise in terms of the amount of computer memory needed.
- It is used to store unstructured data like log files or structured data with delimiters.

CSV File

- The Comma-Separated Value (CSV) format is a specific type of plain text format.

- CSV files are popular and are a consistent plain text delimited format that can identify the fields in each row in the file.
- There can be a single header line with the names of the fields or even a file with no headers, and we need to map it accordingly.
- CSV files are a common way to transfer data from a spreadsheet to other software.
- The most preferred file format by data scientists, data analysts, and business owners or professionals.

Excel Files

Microsoft Excel has become an essential source of data in most organizations and is one of the most widely used data sources since it is highly used across multiple departments and teams at various levels, be it at organizational leadership level or department leads level to analyze and visualize data at several fronts.

Also, most source systems and custom applications do have an option to export the data or extract the data in form or an Excel file which is then used for downstream systems to use it for multiple purposes. Hence, it becomes a crucial part of any data engineering solution architecture to ensure that it is capable of handling these files as source systems, and also the ETL tools that are chosen as a part of the system architecture, support it seamlessly.

An Excel file is a document which is also called a workbook and that contains multiple tabs also known as sheets; each Excel sheet is a source of data with columns and rows in it.

The workbook(s) below has two different sheets as shown and here is how we can interpret the structure of these two different sheets for using the data as a source.

- **Sheet1 - "`dataset`":** The sheet dataset contains 4 columns which are "**`first_name`**", "**`last_name`**", "**`country`**" and "**`car`**" with 20 data rows.
- **Sheet2 - "`users`":** The sheet data has only a single column with the name "**`users`**" with 19+ rows of data.

Both the sheets have the first row as the column names and is very important to highlight or note while designing data engineering or an ETL solution for considering the Excel sheets as a data input source.

If you don't have the column names coming in as input from the Excel file then we should uncheck the property as the first line contains the column names and by default, the Excel file will generate columns on its own as "**`F1`**", "**`F2`**", "**`F3`**", "**`F4`**", and so on, as the default format.

If the Excel file has some vacant rows or rows with no meaningful data, then we can skip some of the top rows before reading the Excel file to make sure the ETL tool reads the data from the right place in the document. We will learn this concept in detail in the coming chapters.

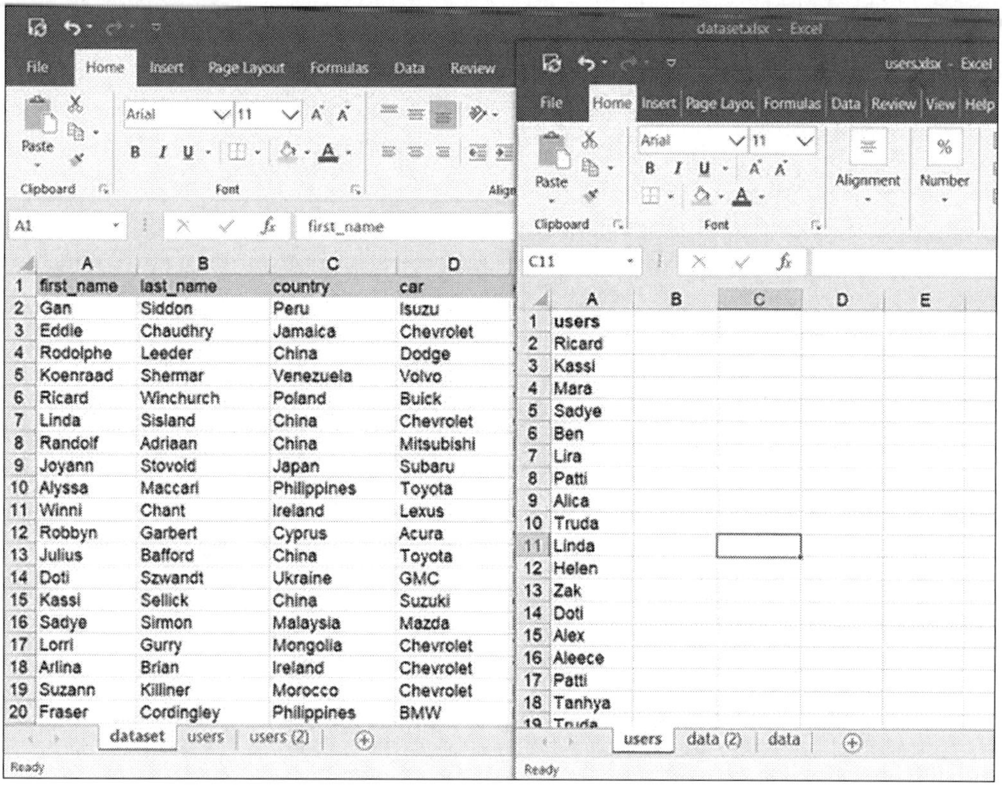

***Figure 5.2**: Source Type: Excel Workbook*

There are multiple ways of importing the data of an Excel file or an Excel sheet into the Azure SQL database or SQL Server database which are listed as follows:

- The SQL Server import and export wizard comes as a part of the SQL Server management studio client.
- The SQL Server integration services ETL tool known as SSIS comes with a source type connector where you can choose Excel as a source.
- The Azure data factory or ADF v2, which supports the linked service or data to connect to an Excel file that is placed in any of the cloud storage like Azure BLOB storage container or Azure data leak Gen 2.
- You can also create custom functions called Azure functions or logic apps to read data from Excel files.

We will understand each of these methods and tools in detail in our next chapter about the ETL technologies to deal with Excel files as a source system for any data engineering project or solution.

XML Files

eXtensible Markup Language or XML is a markup language that stores and transports data online or even in the files which are stored offline in file systems or even in local servers or machines.

- XML is a data format that uses text to represent data in a way that humans can easily read and manipulate. XML is widely used for data exchange and storage on the web and in databases.
- XML can handle different kinds of data, such as numerical values, text strings and code snippets. This makes XML a versatile option for web applications that need to store and transmit various types of data.
- XML data format works using tags to identify different types of data and define the structure of the stored data.

Following is the example of a sample XML file:

```
<company>
  <name>Microsoft</name>
  <sector>Information Technology</sector>
  <Headquarters>Redmond</Headquarters>
  <Founded>1975</Founded>
</company>
```

Figure 5.3: *Source Type: XML File*

The XML tags are defined by the developer of the application to reflect the data in a way that suits the application. For instance, the XML in the above example begins with a "**company**" tag, followed by tags like name, sector, Headquarters, and Founded. This could be the data for a recruitment firm.

The advantage of the XML format is that it allows developers to express and organize data in a way that is easy to send over the web, easy for humans to read, and comprehensible by machines.

XML Schema Definition (XSD) is a language that describes the structure of an XML document. It defines the rules for all the attributes and elements in an XML document, including the number of child elements, data types for elements and attributes, default and fixed values for elements and attributes, and more.

XSD is used to formally describe the elements in an XML document and can be used by programmers to verify each piece of item content in a document, to ensure that it adheres to the description of the element it is placed in XSD is an XML-based language and is also referred to as XML Schema.

Below is an example of a XSD File for a particular defined XML file:

```
XML File
<class>
  <standard>Fourth</standard>
  <teacher>Ashish</teacher>
</class>

XSD File (For the Above XML File)
<xs:element name="class">
  <xs:complexType>
    <xs:sequence>
      <xs:element name="standard" type="xs:string"/>
      <xs:element name="teacher" type="xs:string"/>
    </xs:sequence>
  </xs:complexType>
</xs:element>
```

***Figure 5.4**: Source Type: XSD File*

There are other data formats besides XML that we can use for online data transfer. In fact, **JSON** is the most common and preferred data format for this task.

- **JSON (JavaScript Object Notation):** JSON is a text-based format that resembles XML. However, JSON does not use tags to label the data. Rather, it uses key-value pairs (such as "**`company`**":"**`Microsoft`**"). JSON is the most widely used data format for sending data over the web.

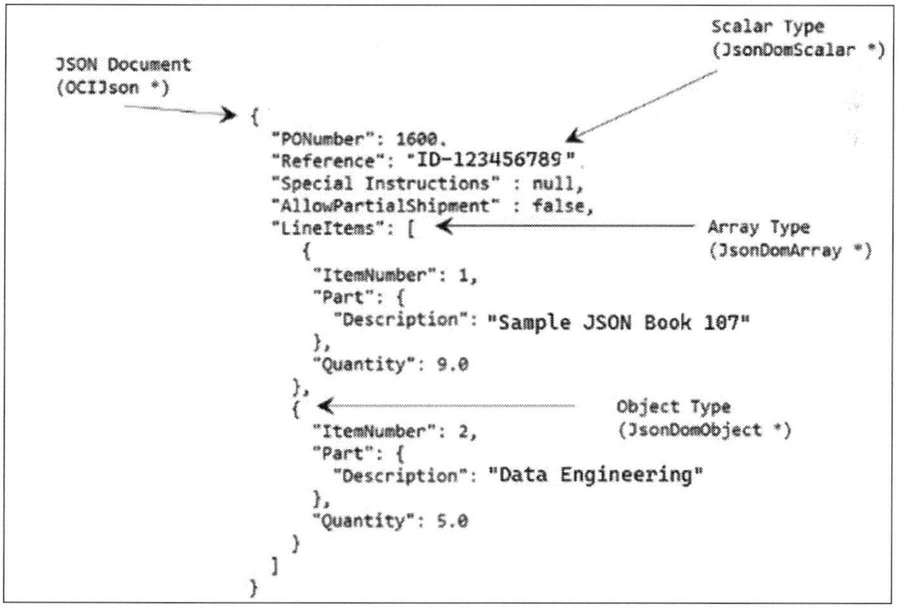

***Figure 5.5**: Source Type: JSON File*

Online Data Sources

Online data sources (Web API, SharePoint List, SharePoint Folder, and so on) are websites or web services that provide data in a structured/semi-structured format, such as XML or JSON. Online data sources can be accessed through APIs (application programming interfaces) or URLs (uniform resource locators). Online data sources offer various data, such as weather information, stock prices, news articles, social media posts, or product reviews. Online data sources can be useful for data analysis, visualization, or integration with other applications.

SharePoint List

A SharePoint list is a web-based way of storing data, like a database or a spreadsheet. It has three main parts:

- **Fields:** These are similar to the columns in a spreadsheet or database where different types of information or metadata can be stored.
- **Items:** These are the actual pieces of data or records in the list.
- **Views:** These are the different ways of showing the list of items

A SharePoint list can hold any kind of data you need and let you choose what kind of data goes in each column.

The connection string to a SharePoint list is the URL to the SharePoint site or subsite, for example –

- https://YourSharePointFarm/YourSharePointSite
- https://YourSharePointFarm/YourSharePointSite/Subsite/

SharePoint list displays a list of all the SharePoint lists on the site for this data source. Select a list and then select the fields that you want in your query. The names of fields in this panel are the SharePoint-friendly names, also known as display names. Hover over an item to display the following properties in the tooltip:

- **Name:** The unique name of the field.
- **Identifier:** The unique identifier of the field.
- **Field Type:** The data type of the field.
- **Hidden:** Whether the field displays in the SharePoint list view.

Selecting fields from multiple lists is not supported. You can create a dataset for each list and select fields from each dataset.

If you want to migrate data from a SharePoint list to SQL Server or Azure SQL, you need to follow these steps:

- Connect to the SharePoint site that contains the list as a data source in Azure Data Factory using the Logic Apps as an interim solution or using a dataset connection.
- Select the fields you want to include in the dataset. You can use the reference for the field type and hidden properties.
- Export the report data to a CSV file and save it to your local drive or a cloud storage service.
- Import the CSV file into SQL Server or Azure cloud SQL using the appropriate tools, such as SQL Server Import and Export Wizard or Azure Data Factory.

Alternatively, you can use a third-party tool or service that can directly transfer data from SharePoint lists to SQL Server or Azure SQL, such as Layer2 Cloud Connector, Skyvia, or CData Sync. However, these solutions may have different costs, features, and limitations, so you should compare them before choosing one.

Legacy Systems

Legacy data is information that is kept in old or outdated systems, formats, or technologies that are hard to access. Though this data was produced a long time ago and may not be in active use by an organization, it is often important for legal, regulatory/compliance, or historical purposes.

Handling legacy data can be difficult, but it is essential for meeting compliance, enhancing data management, and making smarter business choices.

Legacy data refers to data that is stored in old or obsolete formats, such as paper documents, magnetic tapes, floppy disks, or early versions of software (for example, Microsoft Excel). These formats can pose challenges for accessing and using the data, especially if the systems and technologies that created them are no longer available or compatible with modern technology. Sometimes, newer technology cannot even open or read legacy data files. Therefore, it is important to manage legacy data effectively, as it can have implications for compliance, data management, and business decisions.

Forms of Legacy Systems

Legacy systems can have different shapes. Here are the four main ones:

- **End of life (EOL):** An EOL system is one that the vendor does not support anymore. These are usually software products that the supplier has made better, so the original is not sold by the developer anymore.

  EOL systems do not get any updates, making them open to cybersecurity problems. They often do not work well with other software or hardware too.

  An example of an EOL system is Windows XP, an old version of Windows that is outdated now.

- **Extensive software patching:** Most software products have a life cycle of five years.

  Like any technology, software has a short lifecycle. Software patches can make the life cycle longer, but systems that need a lot of patches can have cybersecurity weaknesses.

  When software needs more and more patches to run, the chances of a bad patch go up. This means that, when you can, you should always change from software that needs a lot of patches.

- **Outdated system knowledge:** Think of technology as a language. If people stop using a language, it will soon disappear. The same is true of legacy systems. As software or hardware gets old, the number of people who can work well with technology goes down.

  This means you may have only a few people in your company who can make the software that is important to your organization, leaving you with no choice but to change it.

- **Limited scalability:** A piece of technology can also be a legacy system if it does not fit the needs of a business anymore. Even if the software is still updated and used by other companies, if your needs are bigger, then it will have the same problems as other legacy systems. Companies can outgrow systems if their data gets bigger or they go into a new area. Software needs to grow with you, or it will become old.

  If legacy systems are on physical, on-site servers, they may also have limited scalability. This is because of the price of the new hardware and the space needed to run it. With limited scalability, it can be hard to meet changing customer or market needs.

Organizations may have to deal with different kinds of legacy data, such as

- **Structured data:** This data has a clear structure, like in a database or spreadsheet. It contains various types of information, such as customer data, financial data, inventory data, employee data, sales data, medical data, website data, and more.
- **Semi-structured data:** This data has some structure but is not as rigid as in a database or spreadsheet. It contains elements of both structured and unstructured data, such as XML files, JSON files, web pages, and emails with attachments. It is stored in different ways and may need special tools to parse and extract the relevant information.
- **Unstructured data:** This data does not have a clear structure, like emails, documents, images, and videos. It can be stored in different ways and may need special tools to manage and analyze.

- **Applications-generated data:** This data comes from machines, like log files, sensor data, and machine-generated reports. It is very large and may need special tools to process and analyze.
- **Manual data:** This data is generated manually, and it includes emails, chat logs, documents, spreadsheets, presentations, and social media posts. It is stored in different ways and may need specific software to access, review and update.

Legacy Data Migration

Legacy data migration is the act of moving data from a system that is old or outdated to a new one. It is often needed when organizations change their technology platforms or use new systems that need data from earlier systems.

The migration process includes taking the legacy data out of the old system, changing it into a format that works for the new system, and putting (sometimes known as importing or ingesting) it into the new system. It also often includes many other steps besides just moving the data.

Legacy data migrations can be of different kinds, such as:

- **Platform migration:** Moves data from one software platform to another, like moving data from a legacy system to a cloud-based system.
- **Database migration:** Moves data from one database to another, like changing from an old database system to a newer one.
- **Application migration:** Moves data from one application to another, like moving from a legacy CRM system to a new one.
- **Storage migration:** Moves data from one storage system to another, like moving data from tape backups to a disk-based system.
- **Server migration:** Moves data from one server to another, like moving data from an old server to a new one.
- **Format migration:** Changes data from one format to another, like changing data from an old file format to a newer one.
- **Cloud migration:** Moves data from on-site servers to cloud-based systems, like moving from a legacy data center to a cloud infrastructure. Cloud migration often has many extra benefits (around data accessibility) but also comes with its own challenges.

Each kind of data migration needs good planning and execution to make sure the data moves well from the legacy system to the new system.

Legacy data migration is the act of moving data from an old or outdated system to a new one. It can be hard and tricky, as the data may be in different formats and structures and may be spread across many systems. It needs good planning, testing, and execution to ensure the data moves well and safely, and that the new system can use it well.

Legacy data migration is good for organizations as it lets them use new technology platforms and systems, while keeping useful data from earlier systems. It also helps to lower the risks of data loss, damage, or unavailability, and ensure that business operations can go on without problems.

Custom Apps

Custom applications may use different programming languages, frameworks, or databases, depending on the requirements and preferences of the developers. Therefore, it is important to understand the structure, format, and quality of the data stored in these applications, as well as the methods and protocols to access and extract the data. This will help to design a data engineering solution architecture that can effectively migrate the data from the custom applications to the target systems, such as database systems, data warehouses, or data lakes.

Below are the various types of custom application types:

- **Web applications** that handle user interactions, transactions, or online services.
- **Mobile applications** that provide access to information, entertainment, or communication on smartphones or tablets.
- **Desktop applications** that run on personal computers and perform various tasks, such as word processing, spreadsheet, or presentation.
- **Embedded applications** that control hardware devices, such as sensors, cameras, or robots.

Database Systems

Database systems (SQL, Mainframe, Oracle, Sybase, Teradata, SAP, and more) are software applications that manage the storage, retrieval, and manipulation of data in a structured and organized way. Database systems can be categorized into distinct types based on several factors, including the data model they use, the query languages they support, their architectural design, or the specific application domains they serve.

Mainframe Systems

Some of the common types of database systems are Mainframe systems which are widely used by large enterprises to store and process large amounts of structured data.

However, migrating data from mainframe to Azure cloud can pose several challenges, such as:

- **Data volume and complexity:** Mainframe data can be stored in various formats, such as VSAM, IMS, DB2, or flat files and may have complex data structures, such as hierarchical or network models. Moreover, the data size can be very large, ranging from terabytes to petabytes, which can make migration time-consuming and costly.
- **Data quality and integrity:** Mainframe data may have inconsistent or missing values, duplicates, or errors that need to be cleaned and validated before migration. Additionally, the data may have complex dependencies and relationships that need to be preserved during migration to ensure data integrity and consistency.
- **Data security and compliance:** Mainframe data may contain sensitive or confidential information, such as personal or financial data, that need to be protected and encrypted during the migration process. Moreover, the data may be subjected to various regulatory and legal requirements, such as GDPR, HIPAA, or PCI-DSS, that need to be complied with in the target environment.
- **Assess and plan the migration:** Identify the scope, objectives, and requirements of the migration project, such as the data sources, formats, sizes, types, dependencies, and quality issues. Evaluate the costs, benefits, and risks of migration and select the appropriate tools, methods, and resources for migration. Define the migration strategy, timeline, and milestones and communicate them to the stakeholders.
- **Prepare and extract the data:** Perform data profiling and cleansing to identify and resolve any data quality and integrity issues in the source data. Convert the data to a common format, such as CSV, XML, or JSON, that can be easily transferred and loaded to the target environment. Use efficient and scalable tools, such as Azure Data Factory, SSIS, or Informatica, to extract the data from the mainframe and transfer it to a staging area, such as Azure Blob Storage or Azure Data Lake Storage, where it can be further processed and transformed.
- **Transform and load the data:** Apply any necessary data transformations, such as mapping, filtering, aggregation, or enrichment, to the data in the staging area using tools, such as Azure Databricks, Azure Synapse Analytics, or Azure Data Lake Analytics, to make the data compatible and optimized for the target environment. Load the data to the target destination, such as Azure SQL Database, Azure Cosmos DB, or Azure SQL Data Warehouse using tools, such as Azure Data Factory, SSIS, or Informatica, and verify the data accuracy and completeness.
- **Secure and comply with the data:** Implement data encryption, masking, or anonymization techniques to protect the data from unauthorized access or

leakage during the migration process. Use tools, such as Azure Key Vault, Azure Security Centre, or Azure Sentinel, to manage and monitor the data security and compliance policies and standards in the target environment. Document and audit the data migration process and results and report any issues or deviations to the stakeholders.

Oracle as Source Data Systems

To use Oracle as a source data system while migrating data to Azure cloud, you need to install and configure the Oracle client software on the machine where the data extraction tool is running. You also need to create an Oracle connection manager in the tool that specifies the Oracle server name, database name, username, password, and other connection properties.

Following are some of the considerations while dealing with Oracle data source:

1. You can use Azure Data Factory, SSIS, or Informatica as the data extraction tool to connect to the Oracle source and extract the data in a common format, such as CSV, XML, or JSON. You can also use Azure Data Factory Copy Activity or SSIS Oracle Source component to perform incremental data extraction based on a timestamp or an ID column in the Oracle source tables.

2. You can transfer the extracted data to a staging area in Azure Blob Storage or Azure Data Lake Storage using Azure Data Factory Copy Activity, SSIS Azure Blob Destination component, or Informatica Cloud Data Integration service. You can also compress and encrypt the data during the transfer process to reduce the size and enhance the security of the data.

3. You can follow the same steps as described to transform and load the data from the staging area to the target destination in the Azure cloud. You can also use Azure Data Factory Data Flow or SSIS Data Flow to perform complex data transformations on the fly without using a staging area.

4. Another method to move data from Oracle to Azure cloud involves using SQL Server Migration Assistant (SSMA) for Oracle, a tool designed to simplify the Oracle to SQL Server and Azure SQL Database migration.

Using SSMA for Oracle includes several key activities:

- Evaluate the source database for compatibility problems or unsupported features that could impact the migration or functionality of the destination database.
- Translate schema objects from Oracle to their equivalents in SQL Server or Azure SQL Database, including tables, views, indexes, stored procedures, functions, and triggers, with custom options to adjust mappings for data types, identifiers, sequences, and synonyms as required.

- Transfer data from the source Oracle database to the target SQL Server or Azure SQL Database using the SSMA for Oracle Data Migration Wizard. You have choices regarding bulk mode versus online mode and can configure settings for identity insert, logging, and encryption during the transfer.
- Conduct tests to ensure the functionality and performance of the new database to meet expectations, also addressing any errors or issues found.

Sybase or Teradata as Source Data Systems

If you want to use **Sybase or Teradata** as a source data system while migrating data to Azure cloud, you can follow these steps:

1. Install and configure the appropriate ODBC drivers for Sybase or Teradata on your on-premises machine that will connect to the source database.
2. Use Azure Data Factory or SSIS to create a linked service that connects to the source database using the ODBC drivers. You can also use Informatica Cloud Data Integration service to create a connection to the source database using the native connectors for Sybase or Teradata.
3. Use Azure Data Factory Copy Activity, SSIS ODBC Source component, or Informatica Cloud Data Integration task to extract the data from the source database and transfer it to a staging area in Azure Blob Storage or Azure Data Lake Storage. You can also compress and encrypt the data during the transfer process to reduce the size and enhance the security of the data.
4. Use SQL Server Migration Assistant (SSMA) for Sybase to migrate the schema and data from the source database to Azure SQL Database or Azure SQL Managed Instance.

SAP as Source Data Systems

If you are using SAP as a source data system while migrating data to Azure cloud, you need to follow these steps:

1. Install and configure the appropriate SAP drivers or libraries on your on-premises machine that will connect to the SAP system. You can use either SAP NetWeaver RFC SDK or SAP Java Connector to enable communication between SAP and other systems.
2. Use Azure Data Factory or SSIS to create a linked service that connects to the SAP system using the SAP drivers or libraries. You can also use Informatica Cloud Data Integration service to create a connection to the SAP system using the native connector for SAP.
3. Use Azure Data Factory SAP Table connector, SSIS SAP BI Source component, or Informatica Cloud Data Integration task to extract the data from the SAP tables or views and transfer it to a staging area in Azure Blob Storage or Azure

Data Lake Storage. You can also apply filters, transformations, and validations on the data during the extraction process to optimize the data quality and performance.

SQL Server On-Premises as Source Data Systems

- **Using Azure Data Factory or SSIS**: Use Azure Data Factory or SSIS to create a data source that connects to the SQL On-Premises database using the ODBC or OLE DB drivers. You can also use Informatica Cloud Data Integration service to create a connection to the SQL On-Premises database using the native connector for SQL Server.
- **Using Copy Data or Data Flow**: Use Azure Data Factory Copy activity SSIS Data Flow task, or Informatica Cloud Data Integration mapping to load the data from the SQL On-Premises tables or views and transfer it to a destination in Azure, such as Azure SQL Database, Azure SQL Data Warehouse, or Azure Synapse Analytics. You can also apply transformations, mappings, and validations on the data during the loading process to optimize the data quality and performance.
- **Using Azure Data Factory Data Flow activity**: SSIS Control Flow task, or Informatica Cloud Data Integration workflow to orchestrate and schedule the data migration process from SQL On-Premises to Azure. You can also monitor and troubleshoot the data migration process using the Azure portal, SSIS Catalog, or Informatica Cloud Monitor.
- **Using native backup and restore for SQL**: A straightforward approach to transfer data from SQL On-Premises to Azure is utilizing the built-in backup and restore feature of SQL Server. You back up the source database to a file, move that file to Azure storage, and then restore it to an Azure database. The pros include retaining the source database's schema, data, and permissions and compatibility with most SQL Server versions and editions. The cons involve the need for downtime during backup and restoration and possible incompatibility with certain SQL Server features or settings not supported by Azure.
- **Distributed Availability Group**: A different strategy to transfer data from SQL On-Premises to Azure utilizes a distributed availability group. This feature is available in SQL Server 2016 and later versions, enabling the establishment of an availability group that spans platforms and domains. It is composed of two interconnected availability groups, with one situated on-premises and the other in Azure, capable of synchronizing data in both directions and just one. Its benefits include minimal downtime during migration and the feasibility of maintaining both source and target databases, operational and reachable. However, it necessitates the use of SQL Server Enterprise Edition for both instances and may face certain restrictions or compatibility issues with specific SQL Server features or configurations.

- **Replication in SQL Migration**: Using replication, a feature of SQL Server that lets you copy and spread data between databases, is another approach to shift data from SQL On-Premises to Azure. This method, which can be set up using modes like snapshot, transactional, or merge, supports ongoing updates, minimal downtime, and two-way sync. However, it demands more resources and setup and may clash with specific SQL Server features or configurations.
- **Azure DMS and Azure Migrate for SQL Migration**: An alternative method to move data from SQL On-Premises to Azure is the use of Azure Data Migration Service (DMS) or Azure Migrate, Microsoft's migration tools. These applications facilitate the evaluation of your source database's migration suitability, pinpointing potential compatibility or efficiency issues, and carrying out the actual migration either online or offline. Benefits of using these tools include support for a range of SQL Server versions and features, control over the migration process, and harmony with other Azure services, though they also need extra preparation and configuration and might entail more costs for accessing DMS and Azure Migrate solutions.

Connectivity Challenges Between Source and Target Systems

Connecting the source and target systems securely and reliably can be a challenge when moving data from Source to target data systems. Different methods and tools have different needs and limits for the connection. This also changes depending on the kinds of source systems as follows.

Excel File as a Source System

Working with Excel files as a source system is not as easy as compared to flat file systems because of the underlying architecture of the Excel files. It does have internal metadata where data types are stored and could have formulas embedded or scripting as well in some of the cases when we receive these files as source systems.

Following are some of the common issues that can occur or some of the best practices we can follow while considering Excel files as source systems.

Issues with data types in Excel Source

- **Data types**

  The Excel driver recognizes only a limited set of data types. For example, all numeric columns are interpreted as doubles (`DT_R8`), and all string columns (other than memo columns) are interpreted as 255-character Unicode strings (`DT_WSTR`). SSIS maps the Excel data types as follows:

- **Numeric:** double-precision float (DT_R8)
- **Currency:** currency (DT_CY)
- **Boolean**: Boolean (DT_BOOL)
- **Date/time:** datetime (DT_DATE)
- **String**: Unicode string, length 255 (DT_WSTR)
- **Memo:** Unicode text stream (DT_NTEXT)

- **Issues with data type and length conversions in Excel Source**

  Most ETL tools do not implicitly convert data types. As a result, you may have to use Derived Column or Data Conversion transformations to convert Excel data explicitly before loading it into a destination other than Excel, or to convert data from a source other than Excel before loading it into an Excel destination.

  Here are some examples of the data conversions that may be required:

  - Conversion between Unicode Excel string columns and non-Unicode string columns with specific codepage.
  - Conversion between 255-character Excel string columns and string columns of different lengths.
  - Conversion between double-precision Excel numeric columns and numeric columns of other types.

- **Issues with data import in Excel Source**

  - **Empty rows:** The driver reads the cells that are next to each other, starting from the first cell that is not empty in the top-left corner of the worksheet or range. This means that your data can start from any row, but there should not be any empty rows in between. For example, you cannot have a blank row between the column names and the data rows, or a title with blank rows below it at the beginning of the worksheet.
  - *Solution:* If your data has empty rows above it, you cannot query it as a worksheet. You need to select the data range and give it a name in Excel, and then query the name instead of the worksheet.
  - **Missing values:** The Excel driver scans a certain number of rows (eight rows by default) in the source to guess the data type of each column. When a column has different data types, especially numbers and text, the driver chooses the data type that has more values and returns null values for the cells that have a different type. (If there is a tie, the number type wins.) The data type is not affected by most of the formatting options in the Excel worksheet.

  Solution: You can change this behavior of the Excel driver by specifying Import Mode to import all values as text. To do this, add IMEX=1 to the value of

Extended Properties in the connection string of the Excel connection manager in the Properties window.

- **Truncated text:** When the driver finds that an Excel column has text data, the driver picks the data type (string or memo) based on the longest value that it scans. If the driver does not find any values longer than 255 characters in the scanned rows, it treats the column as a 255-character string column instead of a memo column. So, values longer than 255 characters may be cut off.

  Solution: To import data from a memo column without cutting off, you have two options:

  - Make sure that the memo column has a value longer than 255 characters in at least one of the scanned rows
  - Increase the number of rows scanned by the driver to have such a row. You can do this by increasing the value of `TypeGuessRows` under this registry key.

Legacy Data as a Source System

Legacy data can pose many challenges for organizations, and these challenges may differ depending on the organization and its location.

Some of the main challenges are as follows:

- **Compatibility:** Legacy data may be in old formats (such as Lotus 1-2-3 spreadsheets) or systems that do not work with current technologies (such as CDROM data). This makes it hard to use, view, or move the data.
- **Accessibility:** Even if the data can be accessed, it may be hard to locate or extract specific data points within the data. This makes it inefficient and costly to use the data well.
- **Data quality:** Legacy data may have spelling mistakes, gaps, or errors that can make it less reliable for analysis or decision-making. Improving data quality may need a lot of work and resources.
- **Security:** Legacy data may have sensitive or private information that needs to be kept safe from unauthorized access or attacks. As security risks change over time, keeping the legacy data secure can be a big challenge, especially if some of the old systems or software are no longer updated by the original maker.
- **Cost:** Managing legacy data can be pricey, especially if it involves moving data to new systems or technologies. The cost of keeping old systems or finding special tools, or skilled staff to manage the data can also be high.

- **Complexity:** Managing legacy data can be complicated, especially if the data is in different formats or places.
- **Legal and regulatory compliance:** Legacy data may have to follow legal and regulatory rules that say how it should be stored, managed, protected, and deleted. Following these rules can be hard.

To deal with these challenges, organizations may need to spend money on special tools and skills to manage legacy data well. Both can be very expensive. However, by doing this, you can ensure that the data stays usable, correct, and safe over time and can discover useful insights and information that can help your business work better and succeed. It can also help you plan how to move the right legacy data to a newer, more accessible system.

Legacy systems can have many complexities for organizations and these complexities may vary depending on the organization and its location.

Some of the main reasons are as follows:

- **Technical debt:** Legacy systems can build up technical debt over time, which means the cost of keeping outdated software, hardware, and other technologies. This can make it hard to update or move legacy systems to newer technologies.
- **Integration challenges:** Legacy systems may not work well with newer technologies or systems. This can make it hard to connect legacy systems with newer tools and technologies, which may cause compatibility problems and mistakes. The common issue is the drives becoming out of support and hence unavailability of the drivers for modern tools, software, and services.
- **Customization:** Legacy systems may be very customized to fit the specific needs of an organization, but those needs may have changed over time. This makes it hard to move the system to a new setting, as the organization may need to copy customizations in the new setting or do a long (and expensive) mapping process between legacy and more modern systems.
- **Documentation:** Legacy systems may have old or incomplete documentation, which can make it hard to know how the system works and how it should be handled. If the legacy system is not supported by the original maker anymore, then fixing the issues with the documentation will be hard.
- **Knowledge transfer:** Employees who know how to use legacy systems may leave or change roles in your organization or go to a different organization. This makes it hard to pass on knowledge about how the legacy system works and how it should be handled by new employees.
- **Security risks:** Legacy systems may be less safe than newer systems, as they may not have been made with modern security risks in mind and the legacy system may not get security updates anymore. This makes it hard to protect

the system and the data it has. In some organizations, this may lead to more limited access to valuable legacy data.

Some of the key security risks associated with the legacy data are as follows:

- Outdated security protocols
- Vulnerabilities
- Increased attack surface
- Access controls
- Data integrity

Non-SQL (Heterogeneous) Source Systems

Another challenge that data engineers face is the connectivity between non-SQL sources and Azure SQL databases. Non-SQL sources, such as NoSQL databases or flat files, may have different data formats, schemas, and structures than relational databases. To transfer data from these sources to Azure SQL, data engineers need to use appropriate tools and techniques, such as Azure Data Factory, PolyBase, or Bulk Copy Program (BCP). These tools can help with data extraction, transformation, and loading (ETL) processes, but they also introduce some potential issues, such as

- **Data quality:** ETL tools may not preserve the original data quality or integrity of the source data, especially if there are inconsistencies or errors in the data. Data engineers need to verify and validate the data before and after the ETL process and apply data cleansing and standardization techniques if necessary.
- **Performance:** ETL tools may incur high costs and latency when transferring large volumes of data from non-SQL sources to Azure SQL. Data engineers need to optimize the ETL process by choosing the right tool, format, and method for each data source and by applying compression, partitioning, and indexing techniques if possible.
- **Security:** ETL tools may expose sensitive data to unauthorized access or modification during the data transfer. Data engineers need to ensure that the data is encrypted both in transit and at rest and that the ETL tools comply with the security policies and regulations of the organization and the Azure SQL service.

Case Study: Data Engineering Solution Source Data Analysis

Let us consider a case study where we will first analyze the various source systems which we have to build a data engineering solution architecture. We will start by defining our data sources first and then how they can impact the overall system architecture and other factors.

The following are some considerations for designing a source data pipeline with multiple source types:

- **Data Format:** The data format refers to the way the data is stored and represented in the source system. For example, flat files can have different formats, such as CSV, JSON, XML, and so on. Excel files can have multiple worksheets, macros, formulas, and so on. Heterogeneous data sources can have different data models, such as relational, non-relational, hierarchical, and so on. The source data pipeline should be able to read and parse the data format of each source and convert it into a common format that can be loaded into the target data store.
- **Data Structure:** The data structure refers to the way the data is organized and related to the source system. For example, flat files can have different structures, such as fixed width, delimited, nested, and so on. Excel files can have different structures, such as tables, ranges, pivot tables, and so on. Heterogeneous data sources can have different structures, such as schemas, keys, indexes, constraints, and so on. The source data pipeline should be able to understand and transform the data structure of each source and map it to the data structure of the target data store.
- **Data Quality:** The data quality refers to the accuracy, completeness, consistency, and validity of the data in the source system. For example, flat files can have missing, incorrect, or inconsistent values. Excel files can have errors, duplicates, or outliers. Heterogeneous data sources can have inconsistent or incompatible data types, formats, or standards. The source data pipeline should be able to validate, clean, and enrich the data quality of each source and ensure that the data meets the quality requirements of the target data store.
- **Data Volume:** The data volume refers to the size and frequency of the data in the source system. For example, flat files can have large or small sizes and can be generated or updated at different intervals. Excel files can have varying sizes and complexities and can be modified or appended by different users. Heterogeneous data sources can have different volumes and velocities and can be streamed or batched. The source data pipeline should be able to handle the data volume of each source and optimize the data transfer performance and scalability.

To implement a source data pipeline with multiple source types, one possible approach is to use Azure Data Factory as the orchestration and integration service and use different connectors, activities, and transformations to handle each source type.

Some of the examples to perform the most common data operations using Azure Data Factory are as follows:

- To extract data from flat files, one can use the Copy Activity with File System connector or Blob Storage connector.

- To extract data from Excel files, one can use the Copy Activity with Excel connector or Office 365 connector.
- To extract data from heterogeneous data sources, one can use the Copy Activity with SQL Server connector, Cosmos DB connector, MongoDB connector, and so on.
- To transform the data format, structure, quality, and volume, one can use the Data Flow Activity with Mapping Data Flows or Wrangling Data Flows.
- To load the data into the target data store, one can use the Copy Activity with Azure SQL connector, Azure Synapse connector, Azure Data Lake Storage connector, and so on.

Alternatively, one can also use other services, such as Azure Logic Apps, Azure Functions, Azure Databricks, and so on to implement custom logic and functionality for the source data pipeline.

The case study with a combination of multiple data files as source is as follows:

Problem Statement:

- Flat files (CSV) with multiple extensions defining each category.
- Excel files with multiple tabs and have data for various departments per tab.

Challenges:

One of the challenges of migrating data from multiple data files with different formats and structures is to ensure the consistency and quality of the data.

Proposed Solution:

1. Construct a universal schema capable of incorporating data from various source files, like CSV and Excel, mapping columns or fields as needed. If CSV files contain extensions reflecting data categories, such as **`sales.csv`** or **`inventory.csv`**, introduce a new column in the schema for category information. Likewise, if Excel files feature different tabs per department, including **`Finance`**, **`HR`**, and **`Marketing`**, establish a separate column for departmental data.

2. Utilize the Data Factory UI or Copy Data tool to assemble a pipeline that imports source files from storage services, including Azure Blob Storage or Azure Data Lake Storage, implementing schema mapping and data type transformation rules. Alternatively, the Azure Data Factory SDK or REST API is available for programmatically constructing pipelines and related processes.

3. Adjust the configurations and attributes of both source and target connectors, like Azure SQL, Azure Synapse, or compatible data stores, to enhance data transfer efficiency and dependability. Techniques like parallel copies, staging,

compression, partitioning, or leveraging PolyBase can significantly accelerate and streamline the copy process.

4. Ensure the pipeline and its activities are functioning correctly by validating and overseeing their execution through the Azure Data Factory Monitoring and Management app or the Azure portal. Implement alerts, metrics, and logs to oversee the migration's progression, including any issues or errors.

Conclusion

In this chapter, we have learned about the various source data systems in detail and how each of them impacts the design of any data engineering solution and its architecture.

We also learned about importance of each source system in detail while assessing the migration of the data from a particular source to a target due to various reasons that could be related to the systems being obsolete, security and compliance requirements, end-of-life or support for older systems, lack of resources for obsolete technology in terms of managing the legacy data systems, and so on.

In the next chapter, we will understanding in detail how we can design an effective ETL (extract, transform, and load) strategy while dealing with the variety of source systems and making sure that data migration is seamless, reliable, efficient, and fast enough to have a minimal business impact while migration as well as post-migration sustainability.

Key Terms

- **Heterogeneous Data Sources**: A data from multiple, dissimilar sources. These sources may include different types of databases, such as relational databases (like Oracle, Sybase, and so on.), NoSQL databases (like Mongo, CosmosDB, and so on), and flat files, as well as different platforms and operating systems.
- **Legacy Systems**: These are outdated or obsolete software or hardware systems that are still in use, often because they are difficult or costly to replace.
- **Custom Applications**: These are software applications that are specifically designed and developed for a particular purpose, client, or function. Custom applications are tailored to the specific requirements and preferences of the users or the organization and may offer features or capabilities that are not available in off-the-shelf software.
- **Azure Data Factory**: This is an online data migration and orchestration tool provided by Microsoft Azure.

References

- https://learn.microsoft.com/en-us/sql/integration-services/load-data-to-from-excel-with-ssis?view=sql-server-ver16
- https://support.microsoft.com/en-us/office/import-data-from-data-sources-power-query-be4330b3-5356-486c-a168-b68e9e616f5a
- https://learn.microsoft.com/en-us/sql/reporting-services/report-data/sharepoint-list-connection-type-ssrs?view=sql-server-ver16

CHAPTER 6
ETL Concepts

Introduction

In this chapter, we will cover the core tasks of data engineering which is to perform ETL (Extract, Transform, Load) operations on data from various sources. ETL is a process of extracting data from one or more source systems, transforming it according to some business rules and requirements, and loading it into a target system, such as a data warehouse or a data lake. ETL enables businesses to integrate, consolidate, and analyse data from disparate sources and gain insights or decision-making.

ETL can be done in various ways, depending on the complexity, volume, and frequency of the data, as well as the tools and technologies available. In this chapter, we will explore some of the methods that SQL Server provides to perform ETL operations, such as:

- **Import and Export Data Wizard:** A graphical tool that allows you to quickly copy data between different sources and destinations, such as flat files, relational databases, or Azure Blob Storage.
- **BCP Command-line Utility:** A command-line tool that allows you to bulk import or export large amounts of data in or out of SQL Server tables or views. This command only performs a bulk load of the source data into the target without applying any transformation.
- **Stored Procedures:** An approach using code that enables the crafting of specific SQL queries or scripts to carry out ETL tasks on SQL Server information. With stored procedures, you're able to set parameters, variables, processing logic, iterations, error management, and more to improve the ETL workflow. These stored procedures can be carried out by hand, programmed on a timeline, or activated by events or other stored procedures.
- **SQL Server Integration Services (SSIS):** A powerful and flexible platform that allows you to create complex ETL workflows with graphical and code-based components, such as data sources, transformations, destinations, control flows, and data flows.
- **Azure Data Factory:** A cloud-based service that allows you to create scalable and reliable ETL pipelines using a drag-and-drop interface or code and

orchestrate data movement and transformation across on-premises and cloud sources and destinations.

Structure

In this chapter, we will discuss the following topics:

- Import and Export Data Wizard
- Stored Procedures
- SQL Server Integration Services
- Azure Data Factory
- Data migration strategies using Microsoft Azure Tools (DMA, ADS Migration Extensions, DMS, SSMA, BCP, and so on)
- Case Study: Data Engineering ETL Solutions

Import and Export Data Wizard

One of the simplest and most convenient tools for migrating data between different sources is the Import and Export Data Wizard, which is included in SQL Server Management Studio (SSMS). This wizard allows you to copy data from and to various data sources, such as SQL Server, Oracle, MySQL, Excel, Access, flat files, and more. You can also perform basic transformations and mappings on the data, such as changing data types, column names, or table names. The wizard also generates an SSIS package that can be saved and executed later or modified in Visual Studio.

To launch the wizard, you can either right-click on a database in SSMS and select **`Tasks`** > **`Import Data or Tasks`** > **`Export Data`** or use the dtswizard.exe command-line utility.

The wizard will guide you through the following steps:

- **Choose the database where you want to import:** The first step is to select the database where you want to import the data from any source system. If you want to import from a Flat file, then you should select "**`Import Flat File`**" else "**`Import Data`**" as shown in *Figure* 6.1.
- **Choose a data source and a data destination:** You can select from a list of common providers or use an ODBC or OleDB connection. Also, you need to specify the server's name, authentication method, and database name for each source and destination.
- **Specify the tables and views to copy:** You can either copy all the tables and views or select specific ones. You can also write a query to specify the data to copy.

- **Review and edit the column mappings and transformations:** You can change the destination table name, column name, data type, and length for each column. You can also apply some basic transformations, such as converting null values, trimming spaces, or handling errors.
- **Save and run the package:** You can choose to run the package immediately or save it as an SSIS package file (`.dtsx`) or as a SQL Server Agent job. Also, you can schedule the package to run later or repeatedly.

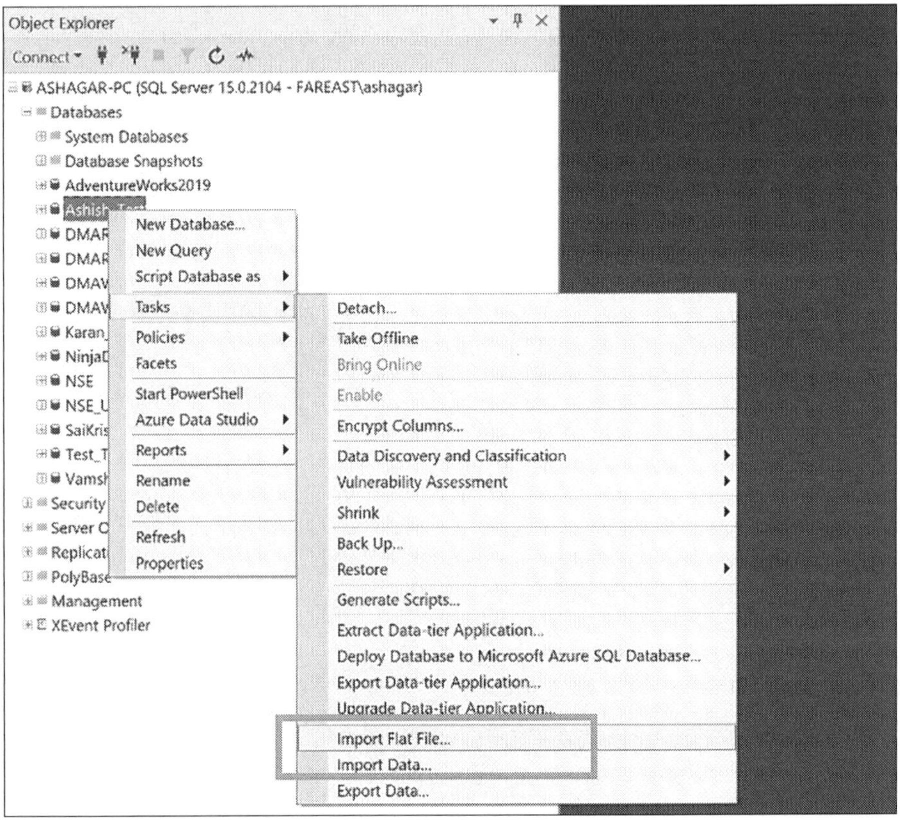

***Figure 6.1:** Import Flat File or Data using SSMS*

- **Export the data from one system to another:** You can also choose to export the data from the current database as selected in the above figure and then export it to any preferred target (be it another database in the same server or a different server or database system or even to a file).

Stored Procedures

Stored Procedures are a powerful feature of SQL that allows you to define and execute complex queries or tasks on the database server. They are useful for performing repetitive operations, enforcing business logic, enhancing security, and improving performance. Stored procedures can be written in various languages, such as T-SQL, PL/SQL, or Java, depending on the database system.

- They reduce network traffic by sending only the procedure name and parameters, instead of the entire query, to the server.
- They improve performance by caching the execution plan and reusing it for subsequent calls.
- They increase security by restricting the access and permissions of the users who can execute them.
- They simplify maintenance by centralizing the logic in one place and avoiding code duplication.

The Stored procedure can be used to write a code to import data using BCP command or select data from Excel or XML files using the necessary OleDB drivers, and then this can be used as a packaged code which can be triggered as one statement for ETL at regular intervals.

To create a stored procedure, you need to use the **CREATE PROCEDURE** statement and specify the name, parameters, and body of the procedure. For example, the following code creates a stored procedure named **usp_get_book_details** that returns the details of all books from the Northwind database:

```
CREATE PROCEDURE usp_get_book_details

AS

BEGIN

SELECT * FROM Book_Details

END
```

To execute a stored procedure, you need to use the **EXECUTE** or **EXEC** statement and provide the name and any required parameters. For example, the following code executes the **usp_get_book_details** procedure and displays the result set:

```
EXECUTE usp_get_book_details
```

You can also modify or delete a stored procedure by using **the ALTER PROCEDURE** or **DROP PROCEDURE** statements respectively.

SQL Server Integration Services

SQL Server Integration Services (SSIS) is a data integration tool that allows you to create and manage data transformation workflows, such as extracting data from various sources, transforming it to meet business rules and loading it into destination systems. SSIS can also perform tasks, such as data cleansing, data profiling, data conversion, and data quality assessment.

SSIS is used to migrate data from on-premises SQL Server databases to Azure SQL Database or Azure SQL Managed Instance, or vice versa. You can use the Azure Feature Pack for SSIS to connect to Azure services, such as Azure Blob Storage, Azure Data Lake Store, Azure SQL Database, Azure SQL Data Warehouse and Azure HDInsight. You can also use the Azure Data Factory Migration Assistant to convert your existing SSIS packages to Azure Data Factory pipelines, which can run on Azure-SSIS Integration Runtime in Azure Data Factory.

Below are the major components of SSIS:

SSIS Designer

A graphical tool that allows you to create, edit and debug SSIS packages using drag-and-drop components. You can use the SSIS Designer to configure data sources, transformations, destinations, control flow elements, variables, parameters, expressions, and logging.

Let's understand each of the designer items in detail:

- **SSIS Control Flow:** A graphical tool that allows you to define the workflow and logic of your SSIS package. You can use the control flow to orchestrate the execution of tasks and containers, such as data flow tasks, script tasks, execute SQL tasks, for-loop containers, or sequence containers. You can also use the control flow to implement branching, looping, and error-handling logic using precedence constraints, expressions, breakpoints, and event handlers. The control flow is the main entry point and the highest level of abstraction in an SSIS package.

  Below are the most used control flow tasks:

  - **Execute SQL Task:** Allows you to execute SQL statements or stored procedures against a relational database. You can use the execute SQL task to perform various database operations, such as creating tables, inserting data, updating data, deleting data, or truncating tables. You can also use the execute SQL task to return result sets or scalar values that can be stored in variables or parameters. The execute SQL task is configured using a connection manager, a SQL statement or stored procedure name, and input and output parameters.
  - **Script Task:** Allows you to write custom code using Visual Basic or C# to perform any operation that is not supported by other built-in tasks. You can use the script task to access file system, registry, web services, or external applications. You can also use the script task to manipulate variables, parameters, or expressions. The script task is configured using a script editor, where you can write and debug your code, and a script project, where you can reference assemblies and add project items.

- **File System Task:** Allows you to perform file and directory operations, such as copying, moving, renaming, deleting, or creating files and directories. You can use the file system task to manage your files and directories as part of your data integration process. The file system task is configured using an operation type, source and destination connection managers, file, and directory names, overwrite options, and error-handling options.
- **FTP Task:** Allows you to perform file transfer protocol (FTP) operations, such as sending or receiving files, creating or deleting remote directories, or listing remote files. You can use the FTP task to transfer files between your local machine and a remote FTP server as part of your data integration process. The FTP task is configured by using an operation type, an FTP connection manager, local and remote paths, file masks, overwrite options, and error-handling options.
- **Send Mail Task:** Allows you to send email messages with optional attachments. You can use the send mail task to notify users or administrators about the status or results of your SSIS package execution. The send mail task is configured by using an SMTP connection manager, message properties, such as from, to, subject, and body, and attachment options.
- **SSIS Sequence Container:** Groups and executes a set of tasks in a specific order. You can use the sequence container to organize your control flow into logical units, such as phases or modules. The sequence container is configured using precedence constraints, which define the execution logic and conditions for the tasks inside the container.
- **SSIS For Loop Container:** Repeats a set of tasks for a specified number of iterations. You can use the for-loop container to implement looping logic based on a counter variable, such as processing a fixed number of files or records. The for-loop container is configured using an initialization expression, an evaluation expression, and an assign expression, which defines the initial value, the termination condition, and the increment value of the counter variable.
- **SSIS Foreach Loop Container:** Repeats a set of tasks for each element in a collection. You can use the foreach loop container to implement looping logic based on a collection of objects, such as files in a folder, rows in a table, or nodes in an XML document. The foreach loop container is configured using a collection enumerator, which defines the type and source of the collection, and a variable mapping, which defines the variable that stores the current element of the collection.

- **SSIS Data Flow Task:** A graphical tool that allows you to perform data extraction, transformation, and loading (ETL) operations using data flow components. You can use the data flow task to connect to various data sources and destinations, such as relational databases, flat files, Excel files, XML files, or web services. You can also use the data flow task to apply transformations to the data, such as sorting, filtering, aggregating, merging, splitting, converting, or validating. The data flow task is one of the most used tasks in SSIS packages, as it enables you to implement complex data integration scenarios with minimal coding.

- **SSIS Source and Destination:** Data flow components that allow you to read data from or write data to a specific data source or destination. You can use SSIS sources and destinations to connect to various data, such as relational databases, flat files, Excel files, XML files, or web services. SSIS provides built-in sources and destinations for common data formats, and you can also create your own custom sources and destinations using the SSIS object model or scripting. SSIS sources and destinations are configured using connection managers, which define the connection properties and credentials for accessing the data.
- **SSIS Transformations:** Data flow components that allow you to modify, enhance, or enrich the data that flows through your data flow task. You can use SSIS transformations to perform various operations on the data, such as sorting, filtering, aggregating, merging, splitting, converting, or validating. SSIS provides built-in transformations for common data manipulation tasks, and you can also create your own custom transformations using the SSIS object model or scripting. SSIS transformations are configured using transformation editors, which define the input and output columns, the transformation logic, and the error-handling options.
- **SSIS Connection Managers:** Objects that define the connection properties and credentials for accessing various data sources and destinations in your SSIS packages. You can use SSIS connection managers to create reusable connections shared by multiple data flow components or to configure dynamic connections that can be modified at run time. SSIS provides built-in connection managers for common types of data, such as OLE DB, flat files, Excel files, XML files, or web services. You can also create your own custom connection managers using the SSIS object model or scripting. SSIS connection managers are configured using connection manager editors, which allow you to specify the connection string, the provider, the authentication method, and other connection options.
- **SSIS Variables and Parameters:** Objects that store values that can be used in your SSIS packages. You can use SSIS variables and parameters to make your packages more dynamic, flexible, and reusable. SSIS variables are scoped to a package, a container, or a task, and their values can change during package execution. SSIS parameters are scoped to a project or a package, and their

values can be set by the user or by an environment reference at run time. SSIS variables and parameters are configured using the Variables window or the Parameters window in SSDT, or by T-SQL commands or stored procedures in the SSIS Catalog.

- **SSIS Expressions:** A language that allows you to write formulas or expressions to assign values, perform calculations, or make decisions in your SSIS packages. You can use SSIS expressions to set the properties of data flow components, control flow elements, variables, or parameters at run time or to create dynamic connections, queries, or file names. SSIS expressions are based on the syntax and data types of Visual Basic .NET, and support common functions such as string manipulation, date and time operations, mathematical calculations, and logical comparisons. SSIS expressions are configured by using expression builders, which provide a graphical interface for creating and testing expressions.
- **SSIS Logging:** Allows you to capture and record information about the events, status, and performance of your SSIS packages. You can use SSIS logging to track progress, diagnose problems, measure performance, or audit the execution of your SSIS packages. SSIS logging supports different levels of granularity, from the package level to the individual component level, and different types of information, such as errors, warnings, informational messages, or custom messages. SSIS logging also supports different log providers, such as text files, XML files, SQL Server tables, or Windows Event Logs. SSIS logging is configured using the SSIS Designer or the SSIS object model, and the log entries can be viewed using various tools, such as the SSIS log viewer, SQL Server Management Studio, or the Windows Event Viewer.
- **SSIS Event Handlers:** Allows you to execute custom tasks or workflows in response to specific events that occur during SSIS package execution. You can use SSIS event handlers to perform actions, such as sending notifications, logging additional information, cleaning up resources, or recovering from errors. SSIS event handlers are configured by using the SSIS Designer or the SSIS object model, and they can be scoped to a package, a container, or a task. SSIS event handlers support different types of events, such as **`OnError`**, **`OnWarning`**, **`OnPreExecute`**, **`OnPostExecute`**, or **`OnVariableValueChanged`**. SSIS event handlers can also use SSIS variables, parameters, expressions, and logging to customize their behavior.

SSIS Service

A Windows service that manages the storage and execution of SSIS packages. You can use the SSIS Service to monitor and administer SSIS projects and environments, and to deploy SSIS packages to the SSIS Catalog.

SSIS Catalog

A centralized database that stores SSIS projects, packages, parameters, environments, and operational history. You can use the SSIS Catalog to manage the security, configuration, execution, and troubleshooting of SSIS packages.

SSIS Runtime Engine

The component that executes SSIS packages on a local or remote machine. The SSIS Runtime Engine handles tasks such as loading and unloading packages, creating connections, managing transactions, logging events, and handling errors.

SSIS Data Flow Engine

The component that performs the data movement and transformation tasks within a data flow task in an SSIS package. The SSIS Data Flow Engine optimizes the performance of data flow operations by using parallelism, buffering, and caching.

SSIS Toolbox

A window that displays the built-in and custom SSIS components that you use in your SSIS packages. You can drag and drop components from the SSIS Toolbox to the SSIS Designer to create data and control flows.

SSIS Object Model

A set of classes and interfaces that expose the SSIS functionality programmatically. You can use the SSIS Object Model to create, modify, and execute SSIS packages in code or to create custom SSIS components and extensions.

Methods of deployment of SSIS Packages

- **Deploying to the SSIS Catalog:** The SSIS Catalog is a centralized database that stores SSIS projects, packages, parameters, environments, and execution logs. You can deploy SSIS packages to the SSIS Catalog using the Project Deployment Wizard in Visual Studio or by using the Integration Services Deployment Wizard in SQL Server Management Studio (SSMS). You can also use the `catalog.deploy_project` stored procedure to deploy SSIS packages programmatically.
- **Deploying to the SSIS Server:** The SSIS Server is a service that runs SSIS packages stored in the `msdb` database or the file system. You can deploy SSIS packages to the SSIS Server using the `Package Installation Wizard` in SSMS or using the `dtutil` command-line utility. You can also use the `sp_add_jobstep` stored procedure to create a SQL Server Agent job that executes an SSIS package on the SSIS Server.

- **Deploying to Azure Data Factory:** Azure Data Factory is a cloud-based service that orchestrates data integration and transformation workflows. You can deploy SSIS packages to Azure Data Factory by using the Azure-SSIS Integration Runtime, which is a managed cluster of virtual machines that can run SSIS packages in the cloud. You can create and configure the Azure-SSIS Integration Runtime by using the Azure portal, Azure PowerShell, or Azure CLI. You can also use the Azure Data Factory UI to upload, download, and execute SSIS packages in the cloud.

Azure Data Factory

Azure Data Factory is a cloud-based service that orchestrates data integration and transformation workflows. You can use Azure Data Factory to create data pipelines that move and process data from various sources and destinations, such as Azure Blob Storage, Azure SQL Database, Azure Synapse Analytics, on-premises SQL Server, and so on. Azure Data Factory supports both code-based and code-free authoring of data pipelines, as well as hybrid scenarios that combine cloud and on-premises data sources. You can also monitor and manage your data pipelines using the Azure portal, Azure PowerShell, Azure CLI, or REST API.

Benefits of Azure Data Factory

Azure data factory comes with a lot of benefits including orchestration of data integration and transformation workflows across various sources and destinations, both in the cloud and on-premises. It supports both code-based and code-free authoring of data pipelines, as well as hybrid scenarios that combine Cloud and on-premises data sources.

It leverages the power and elasticity of the Azure Cloud to run your data pipelines at scale and with great speed, using different runtime environments and engines.

- **Flexible and extensible:** Azure Data Factory supports a wide range of data sources and destinations, both in the Cloud and on-premises. You can also use custom activities to execute your own code or scripts or use Azure Functions to run serverless code in response to data pipeline events. You can also integrate with other Azure services, such as Azure Data Lake Analytics, Azure Machine Learning, or Azure Databricks, to perform advanced analytics and machine learning on your data.
- **Ease of use and productivity:** Azure Data Factory provides a code-free graphical user interface (GUI) for creating and debugging data pipelines, as well as a code-based editor for writing and deploying JSON or ARM templates. You can also use Azure Data Factory tools for Visual Studio or Visual Code to design and deploy data pipelines from within your familiar development

environment. Additionally, you can use built-in templates, samples, and guides to get started quickly and learn best practices.

- **Performance and scalability:** Azure Data Factory leverages the power and elasticity of the Azure cloud to run your data pipelines at scale and speed. You can use Azure Integration Runtime to move and transform data across different network environments, as well as Azure-SSIS Integration Runtime to run SSIS packages in the cloud. You can also use Azure Data Factory Mapping Data Flows to perform data transformations using a scalable Spark-based engine, without writing any code.
- **Security and compliance:** Azure Data Factory ensures your data is secure and compliant throughout the data integration process. You can use Azure Active Directory (AAD) to authenticate and authorize users and applications, as well as encrypt your data at rest and in transit using encryption keys managed by Azure Key Vault. You can also use Azure Data Factory Data Flow Debug mode to test and debug your data transformations in an isolated and private environment, without affecting your production data. Furthermore, you can use Azure Data Factory Data Lineage to track the origin and movement of your data across data pipelines and data sources, as well as Azure Data Factory Data Protection to mask or hash sensitive data elements.

Below are the major components of Azure Data Factory:

- **Pipelines:** A pipeline is a logical grouping of activities that perform a unit of work. For example, a pipeline can copy data from one source to another or transform data using a Mapping Data Flow or a notebook. You can schedule pipelines to run at a specific time or interval or trigger them based on an event or condition.
- **Activities:** An activity is a task that the pipeline performs. There are different types of activities; data movement, data transformation, control , and custom . Each activity has a set of properties that define its configuration and behavior.

  Below are a few commonly used activities to build pipeline:

  - **Copy activity:** This activity copies data from a source to a sink. It supports various data sources and destinations, such as Azure Blob Storage, Azure Data Lake Storage, Azure SQL Database, Azure Synapse Analytics, and so on. You can configure the copy performance, fault tolerance, and data consistency options for this activity.
  - **Data flow activity:** This activity executes a Mapping Data Flow that transforms data using a graphical interface. You can use various transformations, such as filter, join, aggregate, derive column, pivot, and more to manipulate the data. You can also integrate with Azure Machine Learning and Azure Cognitive Services to perform advanced analytics and AI tasks.

- **Lookup activity:** This operation fetches a dataset from any compatible source and prepares it for further use in the following activities. It's useful for conducting lookup operations on reference data, including configuration tables, dimension tables, mapping tables, and so on. Additionally, you can define the query or filter conditions for the lookup. The outcome of this activity may either be saved to a variable or used as an input parameter for subsequent activities.
- **Stored Procedure activity:** This operation carries out a stored procedure on a SQL server database. Utilize this to handle data manipulation or conduct operations encapsulated in the stored procedure's business logic. It also allows for the passage of parameters and variables to the stored procedure from the pipeline.
- **For Loop activity:** Through this activity, it cycles through a collection, performing a designated action for each element. Ideal for batch data processing, executing parallel tasks, or implementing conditional operations tied to the iteration value. The collection may originate from a static array, dynamic expression, or output from another activity. Actions include any singular activity or a sequence integrated within the loop with configurable concurrency and termination conditions detailed.
- **Conditional activity:** By evaluating an expression, this activity dictates one of two possible alternatives depending on the outcome. It is appropriate for directing pipeline routes or crafting logical constructs, such as **`if-then-else`**, **`switch-case`** scenarios, and so on. This activity is also employable with any parameters, variables, or functions based Boolean expressions. This is designed to accommodate any activity or chain of activities set within the consequential true or false branches.
- **Notebook activity:** This activity runs a notebook in Azure Databricks or Azure Synapse Analytics. You can use notebooks to write code in Python, Scala, SQL, or R and perform complex data processing and machine learning operations. You can also pass parameters and secrets to the notebook from the pipeline.
- **Web activity:** This activity calls a REST endpoint using HTTP or HTTPS method. You can use this activity to trigger a webhook, invoke a function, or start another pipeline. You can also specify the request headers, body, and authentication for this activity.
- **Execute pipeline activity:** This activity executes another pipeline within the same data factory. You can use this activity to create modular pipelines and reuse them across different scenarios. You can also pass parameters and variables to the child pipeline from the parent pipeline.
- **Data flow activity:** This activity executes a data flow in Azure Data Factory or Azure Synapse Analytics. A data flow is a graphical interface that lets

you transform and manipulate data using a Spark-based engine. You can use data flows to perform complex data transformations, such as join, merge, union, pivot, aggregate, filter, window, and lookup operations. You can also configure the settings and performance of the data flow execution, such as the integration runtime, the debug mode, and the fault tolerance.

- **Datasets:** A dataset is a named reference to a data source or a data destination. It defines the structure and format of the data and the connection information to access the data. You can use datasets as inputs or outputs for activities in a pipeline.
- **Linked services:** A linked service is a connection string that links the data factory to an external data source or destination. It contains the authentication and configuration information required to access the data. You can use linked services to define the connection properties for datasets.
- **Integration runtimes:** An integration runtime is the compute infrastructure that executes the activities in a pipeline. It defines the location, network, performance, and scalability of the data integration. There are three types of integration runtimes: Azure, self-hosted, and Azure-SSIS. You can use the Azure integration runtime to move and transform data across cloud data sources, the self-hosted integration runtime to move and transform data across on-premises and cloud data sources, and the Azure-SSIS integration runtime to run SSIS packages in the Cloud.
- **Power Query and Change data capture in ADF:** Power Query serves as a data transformation and combination tool, allowing connections to various data sources, execution of transformations, and loading of transformed data into a designated location. In Azure Data Factory, Power Query is utilized to develop and oversee data flows that modify and enrich data through a visual interface.

  Change data capture (CDC) is a method to monitor modifications within a source database and implement those alterations in a target database or data warehouse. CDC facilitates incremental data updates, curtailing the amount of data transferred, and enhancing the efficacy of your data integration processes. Within Azure Data Factory, CDC is employed to track and manage updates from databases like SQL Server, Oracle, MySQL, PostgreSQL, and MongoDB, as well as for data synchronization across different regions or cloud environments.

Some of the benefits of using Power Query and CDC with Azure Data Factory are as follows:

- Utilizing the user-friendly Power Query interface, you can orchestrate and maintain data flows without coding.

- Built-in connectors and transformations are available to retrieve and alter data from a multitude of sources, including relational databases, files, web services, and more.
- Each step of the data flow allows preview and verification of your data and its modifications.
- Your data flows can be expanded through Azure integration runtime, which offers parallel processing, error resilience, and workload distribution.
- The Azure Data Factory portal or employing PowerShell commands are used for monitoring and troubleshooting data flows.
- The CDC feature enables incremental data loading from various sources, enhancing the timeliness and currency of the data.
- The CDC feature can also manage complex situations such as alterations to the schema, deletions, updates, and insertions.
- Furthermore, the CDC feature facilitates the data synchronization across different locations or cloud platforms like Azure SQL Database, Azure Synapse Analytics, and Azure Cosmos DB.

Data Migration Strategies Using Microsoft Azure Tools

Migrate your data from SQL Server to Azure SQL using one of the available methods, such as Azure Database Migration Service (DMS), bulk copy program (BCP), SQL Server Management Studio (SSMS), SQL Server Integration Services (SSIS) or Azure Data Factory (ADF). You can choose the method that best suits your data size, migration speed, and downtime tolerance. You can use tools such as DMA to automate the schema and data migration.

- Test your migrated database and verify its functionality and performance in Azure. Tools such as Azure Data Studio or SSMS to connect to and query your database are used. Also, Azure Monitor or Query Performance Insight are used to monitor and optimize your database performance.
- Switch your application to use the Azure SQL database as the data source and decommission your SQL Server database on-premises. Tools such as Azure App Service Migration Assistant or Azure Migrate are used to migrate your web applications to Azure while Azure DevOps or GitHub are used to manage your code and deployment pipelines.

If you want to migrate from SQL on-premises to Azure SQL, you need to plan and execute the following steps:

The migration from on-premises to the Cloud is majorly segregated into two categories or phases which are explained below.

Pre-Migration Phase

- Assess your current SQL Server database and identify any compatibility issues or unsupported features that might affect the migration. Tools such as Data Migration Assistant (DMA) or Azure Migrate are used to perform the assessment and generate reports.
- Choose a suitable service tier and performance level for your Azure SQL database based on your workload requirements and budget. Tools such as Azure SQL Database DTU Calculator or Azure SQL Database vCore Calculator are used to estimate the resource consumption and cost of your database in Azure.
- Select a migration method that suits your scenario and minimizes downtime and data loss. You can use different methods depending on the size and complexity of your database, such as backup and restore, transactional replication, Azure Database Migration Service (DMS), bulk copy (BCP), SSIS, ADF, and so on.
- Prepare your source and target databases for the migration by configuring the network settings, firewall rules, authentication methods, and permissions. You can use tools such as Azure portal, PowerShell, or Azure CLI to manage your Azure SQL database.

Cut-Over and Migration Phase

- Perform the migration by following the steps of the chosen method and monitor the progress and status of the migration. You can use tools such as DMA, SSMA (for Heterogenous Sources like DB2, Sybase, Oracle, and so on), DMS, BCP, or SSIS to execute and track the migration process.
- Schema and data migration scenarios from on-premises to Azure are dependent on the source and target databases, the complexity and duration of the migration, and the downtime requirements, you can choose from different schema and data migration scenarios to move your on-premises database to Azure SQL database.

Some of the common scenarios are as follows:

- **Offline migration** involves transferring schema and data from the original database to a new one as a single task, with the original database being offline or read-only. Though it ensures data consistency, it can lead to extensive downtime and demands ample storage on the new database.
- **Online migration** implies gradually syncing the schema and data from the original to the new database while keeping the original one operational for regular use. This approach keeps downtime low but could result in data delays and needs constant internet access.

- **The hybrid migration** strategy combines elements of both offline and online migrations, starting with an offline transfer of schema and data, followed by ongoing online updates reflecting any changes in the original database. It strikes a balance between reducing downtime and data latency but entails increased supervision and planning.

Each method offers different benefits and drawbacks that should be weighed against your business needs and technology constraints when deciding on the most suitable approach for your data migration.

Post-Migration Phase

- Validate the migration by verifying data integrity, functionality, and performance of Azure SQL database. You can use tools such as Query Performance Insight, Automatic Tuning, Query Store, or Azure Monitor to analyze and optimize the database in Azure.
- Validate the actual data using the database compare utility or schema compare using the SSDT or any other tools available or by writing custom scripts to compare schema and data.

Migration Tools for Homogenous and Heterogenous Migrations

Depending on the source and target data platforms, you may use different tools and methods to migrate data. For homogenous migrations, where the source and target platforms are the same or compatible, you can use tools such as Azure Database Migration Service (DMS), which supports migration from SQL Server, MySQL, PostgreSQL, and MongoDB to their corresponding Azure services. DMS simplifies the migration processes by automating many tasks and providing a guided experience.

For heterogenous migrations, where the source and target platforms are different or incompatible, you can use additional tools or steps to convert the schema, data types, queries, and stored procedures to the target platform. For example, if you want to migrate from Oracle or Sybase to Azure SQL Database, then you can use the SQL Server Migration Assistant (SSMA), which helps you assess the migration feasibility, convert the schema and code, and migrate the data using DMS or other methods.

In both cases, you should also test and validate the migration before switching to the Azure database for production. Tools such as Data Migration Assistant (DMA) are used to detect compatibility issues, perform assessment checks, and generate migration reports. You can also use Azure Data Studio or SQL Server Management Studio to compare and sync the schema and data between the source and target databases. Finally, you should monitor and optimize the performance of your Azure database using tools such as Query Performance Insight, Automatic Tuning, or Azure Monitor.

Database Migration Assistant (DMA)

Database Migration Assistant (DMA) is a tool that helps you migrate your on-premises SQL Server databases and AWS – RDS SQL Server to Azure SQL Database, Azure SQL Managed Instance, or SQL Server on Azure VMs. DMA can perform the following tasks:

- Assess your source database for potential compatibility issues and feature parity with the target platform. DMA provides a detailed report of the assessment results, which include breaking changes, behaviour changes, and unsupported features. You can use this report to plan and prepare for the migration.
- Migrate your schema and data from the source database to the target database using various methods, such as online, offline, or hybrid. DMA supports different migration scenarios, such as same-server migration, cross-server migration, or cross-cloud platform migration in case of migration from AWS RDS SQL to Azure PaaS services. You can monitor the progress and status of the migration using DMA's dashboard.
- Validate your migration by comparing the schema and data between the source and target databases. DMA can generate a validation report that shows the differences and discrepancies between the two databases. You can use this report to verify and troubleshoot the migration.
- A category of databases that can be transferred to Azure through the DMA includes SQL Server Integration Services (SSIS) packages. SSIS serves as a framework for creating data integration and conversion solutions, capable of pulling, modifying, and depositing data from different sources into desired destinations. These SSIS packages are typically utilized in areas, such as data warehousing, data migration, and business intelligence processes.

To assess and migrate your SSIS packages using DMA, you need to follow these steps:

- You need to set up and adjust the SSIS package extension for DMA. This tool allows DMA to identify, evaluate, and transfer SSIS packages from your local SQL Server instances to Azure Data Factory, a cloud-based solution for data integration.
- Use DMA to locate and examine your SSIS packages. DMA will search your SQL Server instances for SSIS packages stored in the file system, SSIS Catalog, or msdb database. It will analyse how compatible your SSIS packages are with Azure Data Factory and provide an analysis report explaining how ready they are for migration, any obstacles, and suggested steps for each package.
- Transfer your SSIS packages with DMA. The process involves transforming your SSIS packages into Azure Data Factory pipelines and moving them to your Azure subscription. You can either migrate the packages as they are or

modify them for better performance in your pipelines. You can also select the method of migration–online, offline, or hybrid–based on your network's bandwidth and availability.

- Verify your migration through DMA. It checks the consistency between the original and migrated SSIS packages and pipelines by comparing schema and data and creates a validation report. This report can help you confirm and fix any issues during migration to ensure the accuracy of your data integration and transformation within Azure Data Factory.

By adhering to these instructions, you can effectively shift your SSIS packages to Azure Data Factory using DMA, thus benefiting from its scalability, dependability, and heightened security for your data integration and processing requirements.

In summary, DMA is a comprehensive and integrated tool that simplifies and streamlines the database migration process to Azure. You can download and install DMA for free from the Microsoft Download Centre. For more information on how to use DMA, you can refer to the official documentation and tutorials at https://learn.microsoft.com/en-us/sql/dma/dma-overview?view=sql-server-ver16

Azure Migrate

Azure Migrate is a tool that helps you assess and migrate your on-premises servers, databases, applications, and virtual desktops to Azure. Azure Migrate provides a central hub that guides you through the discovery, assessment, and migration steps. Azure Migrate also integrates with other Azure services and tools, such as Azure Database Migration Service, Azure App Service Migration Assistant, and Azure Monitor, to provide a seamless and comprehensive migration experience.

Azure Migrate supports the migration of different types of workloads, such as Windows and Linux servers, SQL Server and other databases, web applications, and virtual desktop infrastructure (VDI). Azure Migrate uses agents or appliances to discover and collect data from your on-premises environment and then provides insights and recommendations on the readiness, sizing, and cost of migrating to Azure. Azure Migrate also allows you to perform agentless or agent-based migrations, depending on your needs and preferences. You can track the progress and status of your migrations from the Azure Migrate dashboard. You can download and install Azure Migrate for free from the Azure portal. For more information on how to use Azure Migrate, you can refer to the official documentation and tutorials at https://learn.microsoft.com/en-us/azure/migrate/

Azure SQL Migration Extension for Azure Data Studio

Azure SQL Migration extension for Azure Data Studio is a tool that helps to migrate your on-premises SQL Server databases to Azure SQL Database or Azure SQL

Managed Instance. Azure Data Studio is a cross-platform database tool that provides a modern and intuitive user interface for working with data sources. Azure SQL Migration extension is an extension of Azure Data Studio that enables you to perform the migration steps from within the same tool that you use to manage your databases.

Azure SQL Migration extension allows you to discover and assess your SQL Server databases, generate scripts to create the target Azure SQL databases and migrate the schema and data using online or offline methods. You can also monitor the migration progress and status from the Azure Data Studio dashboard. Azure SQL Migration extension leverages the existing Azure Database Migration Service (DMS) and Azure Database Migration Assistant (DMA) to perform the migration tasks. You can download and install Azure SQL Migration extension for free from the Azure Data Studio marketplace. For more information on how to use Azure SQL Migration extension, you can refer to the official documentation and tutorials at https://learn.microsoft.com/en-us/azure-data-studio/

SKU Recommendations SQL Server

Stock Keeping Unit (SKU) is a unique identifier for a product or service that is used to track inventory and pricing. Azure SQL Database offers different SKUs that vary in performance, availability, storage, and features. Choosing the right SKU for your migrated database depends on several factors, such as the size of your database, workload characteristics, service tier requirements, and budget constraints.

Azure SQL Database provides three service tiers: Basic, Standard, and Premium. Each tier has a range of SKUs that differ in compute units, memory, storage, backup retention, and read replicas. You can use the Azure portal, PowerShell, or REST API to create and configure your database with the desired SKU. You can also change the SKU of your database at any time to scale up or down as needed. Azure SQL Database also offers a serverless compute option that automatically scales the compute resources based on the workload demand and shuts down the database when it is not in use. Serverless is ideal for databases with unpredictable or intermittent usage patterns that want to optimize the cost and performance trade-off.

To select the best SKU for your database, you can use the Azure SQL Database Pricing Calculator, which estimates the monthly cost and performance level of the database based on the selected SKU and region. You can also use the DTU Calculator, which measures the database throughput units (DTUs) of your source database and recommends a corresponding SKU for Azure SQL Database. DTUs are a blended measure of CPU, memory, and I/O that represent the relative capacity of a database. Alternatively, you can use the vCore Calculator, which measures the virtual cores (vCores) of the source database and recommends a corresponding SKU for Azure SQL Database. vCores are a direct measure of the CPU cores and memory that are allocated to a database. You can choose between the DTU-based or the vCore-based purchasing model depending on your preference and compatibility.

DMA SKU Console Utility

The DMA SKU Console Utility is a command-line tool that helps you estimate the performance and cost of your database migration to Azure SQL Database. The tool uses the Data Migration Assistant (DMA) engine to assess your source database and recommend the optimal SKU for your target database based on the workload characteristics and service tier requirements. The tool also provides a detailed assessment report, including the estimated monthly cost, DTUs or vCores, storage size, backup retention, and availability SLA of the recommended SKU.

The DMA SKU Console Utility can be downloaded from GitHub and requires .NET Framework 4.7.2 or higher to run. To use the tool, you need to provide the connection string of your source database and the desired service tier of your target database as parameters. You can also specify other options, such as the assessment duration, the output format, the log level, and the region of the target database. The tool supports the migration of databases from SQL Server, AWS – RDS SQL to Azure SQL Database. For more information on using the DMA SKU Console Utility, refer to the README file and the samples folder in the GitHub repository.

There are two major steps involved in doing the SKU recommendation:

1. **Performance data collections**

   The collected data includes limited information about the hardware configuration of your server, and aggregated SQL-specific performance data from system Dynamic Management Views (DMVs) such as CPU, memory, storage usage, IO throughput, and IO latency. The collected data is stored locally on your machine for further aggregation and analysis. The performance characteristics of your source instance are analysed to enable SKU recommendations for Azure SQL offerings (including SQL Database, SQL Managed Instance, and SQL on Azure VM) that best suit your workload while being cost-effective.

2. **SKU Recommendations**

   The data points collected in the previous step are used as the input for the SKU recommendation process.

   For the single database option, DMA provides recommendations for the Azure SQL Database single database tier, the compute level, and the recommended storage configuration for each database on your SQL instance.

   For Azure SQL Managed Instance and SQL Server on Azure VM, the recommendations support a lift-and-shift scenario. As a result, the SKU recommendations console app can provide you with recommendations for the Azure SQL Managed Instance, or SQL Server on Azure VM tier, the compute level, and the recommended storage configuration for the set of databases on your SQL instance. You can also specify only a subset of databases to be included or excluded from the SKU recommendations.

The output of the SKU recommendation is saved as a detailed report in JSON format and a summarized easy-to-read HTML file.

The output covers the following sections:

- **Instance Name:** Name of the SQL Server instance.
- **Database Name:** Name of the SQL Server database.
- **SKU Recommendation:** The minimum cost-efficient SKU offering among all the performance-eligible SKUs that could accommodate your workloads.
- **Recommendation Reason:** For each tier recommended, we provide the reasons and collected data values driving the recommendations.

The final recommended tier and configuration values for that tier reflect the minimum SKU required for your queries to run in Azure with a success rate like your on-premises databases.

SQL Server Migration Assistant (SSMA)

SQL Server Migration Assistant (SSMA) is a tool that automates the conversion of database objects and data from other relational database management systems to Azure SQL Database. SSMA supports the migration of databases from Oracle, MySQL, DB2, Sybase, Access, and PostgreSQL to Azure SQL Database. SSMA can also migrate data from MongoDB to Azure Cosmos DB's API for MongoDB.

SSMA consists of two components: a graphical user interface (GUI) client application and an extension pack containing the providers and metadata to connect to the source and target databases. The GUI allows you to analyse the source database, map the source and target schemas, convert the schema, load the data, and test the migrated database. The extension pack enables the communication between the GUI and the databases and performs the schema and data conversion. You can download and install SSMA and the extension pack for free from the Microsoft Download Centre. For more information on how to use SSMA, you can refer to the official documentation and tutorials at https://learn.microsoft.com/en-us/sql/ssma/sql-server-migration-assistant?view=sql-server-ver16

Case Study: Data Engineering ETL Solutions

In this section, we will cover a few sample case studies that will help us understand how to use the tools and techniques studied in this chapter to build a database migration solution.

Case Study Objectives

- To transfer the data from the source database to the target database without losing any information or compromising the data quality.
- To transform the data according to the target schema, which follows a star schema design with fact and dimension tables.
- To automate the ETL process and schedule it to run periodically, so that the target database is always updated with the latest data from the source database.
- To monitor and troubleshoot the ETL process and ensure its performance and reliability.

The data engineering team follows these steps to achieve the objectives:

1. Install and configure SSMA and the extension pack on a Windows machine that connects the source and target databases.

2. Launch SSMA and create a new project. Select `MySQL` as the source database type and `SQL Server` as the target database type. Enter the connection details for both databases and test the connections.

3. In the SSMA GUI, expand the source database and select the tables to be migrated. Right-click and choose `Convert Schema`. SSMA will analyse the source schema and generate a conversion report, showing the issues and warnings that may arise during the conversion.

4. Review the conversion report and resolve any issues or warnings. For example, some data types may not be compatible between `MySQL` and `SQL Server`, or some constraints may not support the target database. SSMA provides suggestions and options to fix these issues, such as mapping the data types or modifying the constraints.

5. After resolving the issues, select the tables again and choose `Synchronize with Database`. SSMA will create the corresponding tables in the target database, with the same structure and data as the source tables. You can verify the results by querying the target database.

6. Next, create an SSIS project in Visual Studio and add a `Data Flow` task to the `Control Flow`. In the Data Flow, add an OLE DB source and an OLE DB destination. Configure the source to connect to the target database and select the tables created by SSMA. Configure the destination to connect to the target database and select the fact and dimension tables that match the star schema design.

7. Add the necessary transformation components between the source and the destination, such as **`Lookup`**, **`Derived Column`**, **`Sort`**, **`Aggregate`**, and so on to map and transform the data according to the target schema. For example, you can use Lookup to join the source tables and get the foreign key values for the dimension tables or use **`Derived Column`** to calculate the measures for the fact table.
8. Run the SSIS package and check the results. The data should be transferred and transformed from the source tables to the target tables, following the star schema design. Also, you can add logging and error-handling components to the SSIS package, such as **`Event Handlers`**, **`Checkpoints`**, or **`Data Viewers`** to monitor and troubleshoot the ETL process.
9. Finally, use the **`SQL Server Agent`** to schedule the SSIS package to run periodically–daily or weekly–depending on the business requirements. This will ensure that the target database is always updated with the latest data from the source database and support the data warehouse and business intelligence system.

This case study demonstrates how SSMA and SSIS can be used together to migrate and perform ETL operations on a relational database and how they can help the data engineering team achieve their objectives quickly and efficiently.

Conclusion

In this chapter, we have learned about the various ETL concepts and tools available in detail and how each of them impacts the design of any data engineering solution and its architecture.

We also learned about how the choice of an ETL tool is critical in assessing the migration of the data from a particular source to a target due to various reasons that could be related to the systems and how to design a solution that helps us in the effective and efficient transfer of the data from the source system to target.

In the next chapter, we will understand in detail how to design a database solution and do effective data modelling to support the business needs.

Key Terms

- **ETL**: Extract, Transform, and Load Operation from source to target databases with data transformation to support business needs.
- **Azure Data Factory**: This is an online data migration and orchestration tool provided by Microsoft Azure.

- **SSMA**: SQL Server Migration Assistant for heterogeneous database migration scenarios.
- **DMA**: Database Migration Assistant for database migration for homogenous systems (SQL Server to SQL as Target on cloud)
- **Azure Migrate**: An Azure service that helps you discover and assess your SQL data estate at scale on VMware, Hyper-V, and physical servers. It provides Azure SQL deployment recommendations, target sizing, and monthly estimates.

References

- https://learn.microsoft.com/en-us/sql/integration-services/load-data-to-from-excel-with-ssis?view=sql-server-ver16
- https://learn.microsoft.com/en-us/data-migration/
- https://learn.microsoft.com/en-us/azure/azure-sql/migration-guides/database/sql-server-to-sql-database-overview?view=azuresql
- https://learn.microsoft.com/en-us/sql/dma/dma-sku-recommend-sql-db?view=sql-server-ver16
- https://learn.microsoft.com/en-us/sql/ssma/sql-server-migration-assistant?view=sql-server-ver16
- https://learn.microsoft.com/en-us/azure-data-studio/
- https://learn.microsoft.com/en-us/azure/migrate/
- https://learn.microsoft.com/en-us/sql/dma/dma-overview?view=sql-server-ver16

CHAPTER 7
Database Design and Modeling

Introduction

In this chapter, we will cover database design, which is a key aspect in the creation, development, implementation, and upkeep of enterprise data management systems. A well-designed database is simple to manage, increases data consistency, and saves money. The primary goals of database design in DBMS are to generate logical and physical models of the proposed database system. Independent of physical factors, the logical model focuses on data requirements and data to be kept. It is unconcerned with how the data will be saved or where it will be physically stored.

Furthermore, we will delve into the aspects of data modeling which visualizes an entire information system or parts of it to show connections between data elements and structures. It aims to highlight the different types of data utilized and preserved in the system, elucidate the relationships among various data forms, and demonstrate how data can be categorized and organized, along with its formats and attributes. Data models are tailored to fit business needs. Rules and requirements are established ahead of time based on input from business stakeholders, enabling their integration into the development of a new system or refinement during iterations of an existing one.

Structure

In this chapter, we will discuss the following topics:

- Database Design Concepts
- Database Design Best Practices and Terminologies
- Data Modeling Concepts and Tools
- Methods of Data Modeling
- Benefits and Need for Data Modeling

Database Design Concepts

Database designing is the process of transforming a data model into a physical database structure that can store and manipulate data efficiently. Database design involves choosing an appropriate data model, such as relational, hierarchical, network, or object-oriented and applying various principles and techniques to optimize the performance, security, integrity, and usability of the database.

- **Data analysis:** This involves finding out what data is needed and where it comes from and gathering and arranging the data in an orderly way.
- **Entity-relationship modeling:** This involves defining the entities (or objects) and their attributes (or properties) that represent the data and the relationships (or associations) among them. An entity-relationship diagram (ERD) is a graphical tool that shows the data model visually.

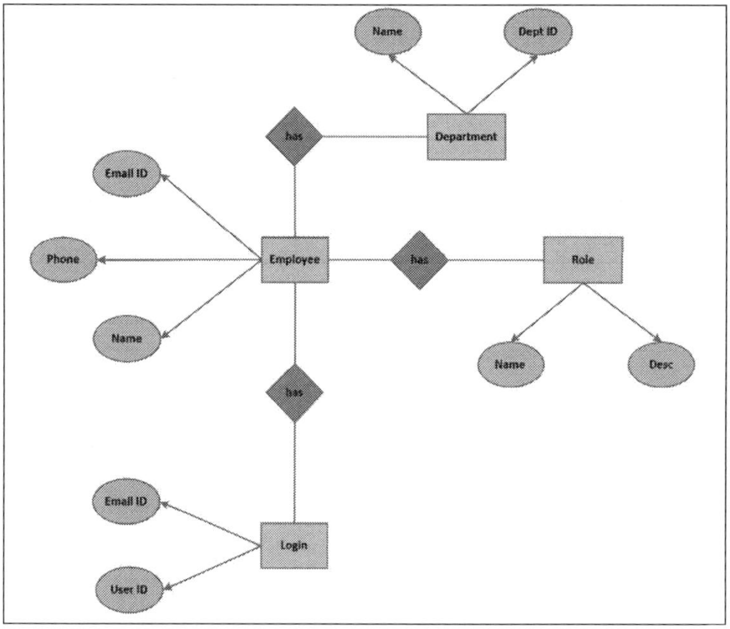

***Figure* 7.1:** *Entity Relationship Diagram*

- **Normalization:** This involves applying rules to eliminate data redundancy, inconsistency, and anomalies in the data model. Normalization results in a set of normalized relations (or tables) that have well-defined keys, attributes, and dependencies.

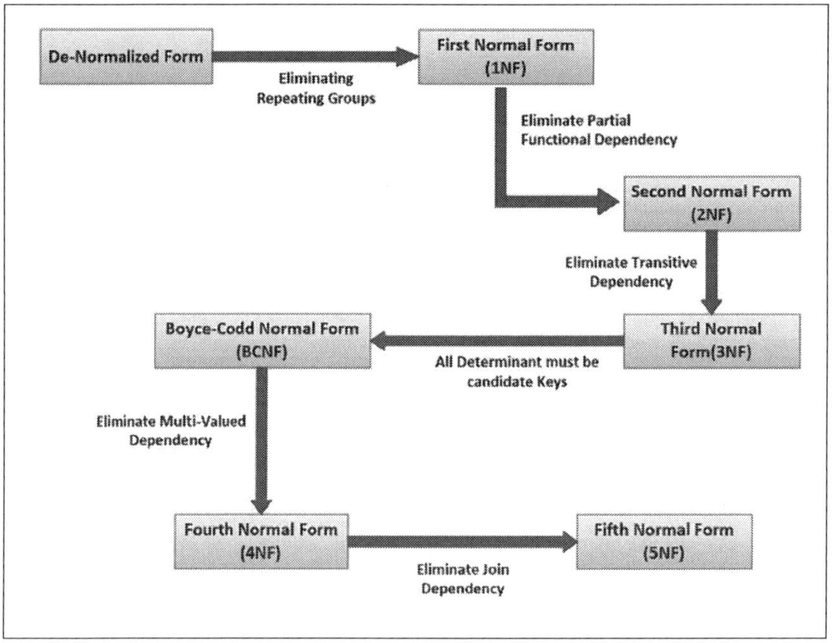

***Figure* 7.2:** *Normalization Overview*

- **First Normal Form (1NF):** In 1NF, every table column must have atomic values, which means they cannot be split into smaller values.

Let us try to understand the Normalization concepts by the following example where we have an unnormalized table that stores the data of orders placed by customers.

Order ID	Customer Name	Products Purchased
1	Ramesh	Pen, Paper, Rubber
2	Suresh	Sharpener, Scale
3	Jayesh	Notebook, Stapler
4	Paresh	Pencil, Sticky Notes

***Table* 7.1:** *Unnormalized Table*

Table 7.1 fails to meet the 1NF criteria due to the Products column having a list of products. To conform to 1NF, we must divide the products into individual rows.

Order ID	Customer Name	Product Purchased
1	Ramesh	Pen
2	Ramesh	Paper
3	Ramesh	Rubber
4	Suresh	Sharpener

5	Suresh	Scale
6	Jayesh	Notebook
7	Jayesh	Stapler
8	Paresh	Pencil
9	Paresh	Sticky Notes

***Table* 7.2:** *1NF Table*

The preceding table now contains unique values for each cell and is in 1NF.

- **Second Normal Form (2NF):** In 2NF, the primary key (the set of attributes that uniquely identifies a row) should be the only determinant for all other attributes (attributes that are not part of the primary key). For example, if a table has a primary key that consists of two attributes, both attributes should determine all other attributes, not just one.

Let's examine another example of a table which holds data regarding students and their chosen courses.

Student ID	Course ID	Course Name	Teacher Name
1	A-1	Data Engineering	Professor A
1	A-2	Data Science	Professor B
2	A-1	Data Engineering	Professor A
3	A-3	Azure Fundamentals	Professor C

***Table* 7.3:** *2NF Violation Example Table*

The table breaches 2NF since the "`Teacher Name`" field is contingent on both "`Student ID`" and "`Course ID`". For 2NF compliance, we divide the table into two distinct tables as shown in *Tables* 7.4 and 7.5:

Student ID	Student Name
1	Student-1
2	Student-2
3	Student-3

***Table* 7.4:** *2NF Example – Students Table*

Course ID	Course Name	Teacher Name
A-1	Data Engineering	Professor A
A-2	Data Science	Professor B
A-3	Azure Fundamentals	Professor C

***Table* 7.5:** *2NF Example – Courses Table*

So by splitting the tables into two, now we have the Teacher Name attribute only to being dependent on the Course ID only. We have achieved 2NF now.

- **Third Normal Form (3NF):** 3NF requires that all non-key attributes only depend on the primary key and not on other non-key attributes. This reduces data duplication and inconsistency. A common practice is to normalize a database to 3NF or higher. However, this does not mean that you should ignore higher levels of normalization, depending on the data complexity and the application needs.

Higher levels of normalization, such as Boyce-Codd Normal Form (BCNF) or Fourth Normal Form (4NF), can eliminate more redundancy and dependency in database design, resulting in better storage and enhanced data integrity. Applying normalization beyond the Third Normal Form (3NF) may be beneficial in complex data situations, where ensuring data accuracy and avoiding anomalies are essential, such as in banking systems or medical databases.

If we continue with our example in 2NF, we still don't have a relation being set between which students are enrolled on a specific course or courses. For better understanding, let's introduce a new table to make it in 3NF.

Student ID	Course ID
1	A-1
1	A-2
2	A-1
3	A-3

Table 7.6: *3NF Example Table*

- **Boyce-Codd Normal Form (BCNF):** BCNF or Boyce-Codd Normal Form is a higher level of normalization than 3NF that eliminates more redundancy and dependency in the database design. BCNF ensures that every determinant or attribute that determines another attribute is a super key or a minimal set of attributes that can uniquely identify a tuple. This means that there are no partial or transitive dependencies in the relation. A relation in BCNF has only one candidate key, which is also the primary key.

For example, consider a table that stores the names, departments, and salaries of employees. The employee's name is the primary key, but the department name also determines the salary as shown in *Table 7.7*:

Employee Name	Department	Salary
A-1	Data Engineering	1100
A-2	Data Science	1000
A-3	Data Engineering	1100

Table 7.7 (1): *BCNF Example Table - 1*

This is a transitive dependency since the salary depends on the department, which depends on the name. To convert this table to BCNF, we can split it into three tables, one for employee names and departments and one for departments and salaries.

This way, each determinant is a super key and there are no transitive dependencies. BCNF is useful for improving data consistency and avoiding updating anomalies.

Employee ID	Employee Name
1	A-1
2	A-2
3	A-3

***Table* 7.7 (2):** BCNF *Example Table* – 2

Department	Salary
Data Engineering	1100
Data Science	1000

***Table* 7.7 (3):** BCNF *Example Table* – 3

Employee ID	Department
1	Data Engineering
2	Data Science
3	Data Engineering

***Table* 7.7 (4):** BCNF *Example Table* – 4

- **Fourth Normal Form (4NF):** A relation is in 4NF if it is in BCNF and has no multi-valued dependency. A multi-valued dependency occurs when a table has two or more independent attributes that depend on the primary key. For example, if a table stores the names and hobbies of students and a student can have multiple hobbies, then there is a multi-valued dependency between the student's name and the hobby. To avoid this, we can split the table into two tables, one for student names and one for hobbies, and link them with a foreign key. This way, we can eliminate redundancy and inconsistency in the data. 4NF is useful for maintaining the atomicity of the attributes and avoiding data anomalies.
- **Fifth Normal Form (5NF):** A relation is in 5NF if it is in 4NF and does not contain any join dependency. A join dependency occurs when a table can be decomposed into two or more tables and then joined back together using the primary keys of each table, without losing any information. For example, if a table stores the names, addresses, and phone numbers of customers, and a customer can have multiple addresses and phone numbers, then there is a join dependency between the three attributes. To

avoid this, we can split the table into three tables, one for names, one for addresses, and one for phone numbers and link them with foreign keys. This way, we can eliminate redundancy and inconsistency in the data. 5NF is useful for maintaining the integrity and independence of relations and avoiding data anomalies.

- **Denormalization:** This involves introducing some controlled redundancy in the data model to improve the query performance and reduce the number of joins. Denormalization should be done carefully to avoid compromising the data integrity and consistency.

  This can be achieved by a real-time example, let's say, we have three tables and we need to find some data by joining these tables but is resulting in poor query performance. What we can do is create a new denormalized table by joining two tables and then re-write the query by joining the new table and third table.

  Denormalization can be implemented in three ways:

  1. Merge rows across various tables to eliminate the need for **`JOIN`** queries.
  2. Execute aggregate functions such as **`SUM()`**, **`COUNT()`**, or **`MAX()`**, to avoid using queries with a **`GROUP BY`** clause.
  3. Precompute resource-intensive calculations to prevent the necessity of queries containing elaborate expressions in the select-list.

- **Indexing:** This involves creating indexes on one or more columns of a table to speed up data retrieval and sorting. Indexes can be clustered or non-clustered, depending on how the data is physically stored and organized.

  SQL Server indexes are data structures that improve the performance of queries by allowing faster and more efficient access to the data in the tables. Indexes can be created on one or more columns of a table, and they store the values of those columns in sorted order, along with a pointer to the corresponding row in the table. Indexes are used to quickly locate, filter, sort, or group the data without scanning the entire table.

The following are the main types of indexes in the SQL Server:

- **Clustered Index:** A clustered index determines the physical order of the data in the table, and each table can have only one clustered index.
- **Non-clustered Index:** A non-clustered index does not affect the physical order of the data but creates a separate structure that references the data in the table. A table can have multiple non-clustered indexes, each with a different sorting order or combination of columns.
- **Columnstore Index:** Columnstore indexes are ideal for storing and querying large data warehousing fact tables. This index uses

column-oriented storage and query processing to improve query performance in your data warehouse by up to 10 times compared to traditional row-based storage. You can also improve data compression by up to 10 times compared to the uncompressed data size.

- **Columnstore:** Columnstore format organizes data into columns, with each housing value of a single attribute. Its primary advantage lies in enabling high compression ratios and lessening I/O and memory usage due to often similar column values that compress well with methods, such as dictionary and run-length encoding. Furthermore, it's designed for quick query handling in analytical tasks that involve large-scale aggregations, scans, and joins, thanks to features like vectorized processing and column elimination.
- **Rowstore:** A rowstore is data with a logical structure of a table with rows and columns and a physical structure of a row-wise data format. This format is the conventional way to store relational table data. In SQL Server, rowstore means a table where the underlying data storage format is either a heap, a clustered index, or a memory-optimized table.

○ **Clustered columnstore Index:** A table's whole data is physically stored in a clustered columnstore index.

SQL Server's deltastore feature supports hybrid storage, maintaining both row and column formats for a single table. It operates as an independent structure that preserves the changes or '*deltas*' occurring post-table conversion to a columnar format. These deltas are kept in a row-based layout and intermittently consolidated with the main column-oriented data during the tuple-mover operation. The amalgamation of these storage methods allows SQL Server to adeptly handle transactional and analytical workloads simultaneously, optimizing both performance and storage use.

○ **Nonclustered columnstore Index:** A nonclustered columnstore index and a clustered columnstore index work in a similar manner. The difference is that a nonclustered index is an additional index created on a rowstore table, while a clustered columnstore index is the main storage for the whole table.

The nonclustered index contains a copy of some or all the rows and columns in the base table. The index is defined by one or more columns of the table and has an optional condition that filters the rows.

A non-clustered columnstore index allows real-time operational analytics where the OLTP workload uses the underlying clustered index while analytics run simultaneously on the columnstore index.

Creating and maintaining indexes can improve the query performance but has some drawbacks, such as:

- Indexes consume disk space and memory resources, which can affect the storage capacity and performance of the database.
- Indexes increase the overhead of data modification operations, such as insert, update, or delete, because the indexes need to be updated as well.
- Indexes can become fragmented over time, which means that the data in the index is not stored contiguously and efficiently. This can degrade the index performance and require periodic reorganization or index rebuilding.
- The cardinality of the column is the number of distinct values in the column. Columns with high cardinality, such as unique identifiers, are good candidates for indexing because they can narrow down the search results quickly. Columns with low cardinality, such as gender or status, are not good candidates for indexing, because they can return too many rows and cause unnecessary scans of the index or the table.
- The selectivity of the column is the percentage of rows that match a given condition on the column. Columns with high selectivity, such as dates or prices, are good candidates for indexing because they can filter out most irrelevant rows. Columns with low selectivity, such as names or states, are not good candidates for indexing, because they can return too many rows and cause inefficient joins or sorts.
- The frequency and type of queries determine how often and how the data is accessed. Columns frequently used in the where, order by, or join clauses of the queries are good candidates for indexing, because they can improve the query performance and reduce the CPU and I/O costs. Columns rarely or never used in queries are not good candidates for indexing, because they can waste the index space and increase the overhead for maintaining resources.

To create an index in SQL Server, the create index statement can be used, with the following syntax:

```
create index [index_name] on [table_name] (column1, column2, ...)
```

The **index_name** is the name of the index, which should be unique and descriptive. The **table_name** is the name of the table on which the index is created. The column list specifies one or more columns of the table that are included in the index, along with an optional sort order (asc for ascending or desc for descending). By default, the index is created as a non-clustered index. To create a clustered index, the keyword clustered can be added before the column list.

To create a clustered index on the **employee_id** column of the employees table, the following statement can be used:

```
create index idx_employee_id on employees (employee_id) clustered
```

To create a non-clustered index on the **last_name** and **first_name** columns of the employees' table, the following statement can be used:

```
create index idx_name on employees (last_name, first_name)
```

To drop an index in the SQL Server, the drop index statement can be used, with the following syntax:

```
drop index idx_name on [table_name]
```

The **index_name** is the name of the index to be dropped, and the **table_name** is the name of the table on which the index is defined.

To drop the **idx_name** index from the employees table, the following statement can be used:

```
drop index idx_name on employees
```

The "**Include**" clause:

An optional component that can be appended to the create index statement in SQL Server is the include clause. This enables the inclusion of extra non-key columns at the leaf level of the index. Utilizing this clause can enhance query performance for selecting these columns by allowing the data to be obtained directly from the index, omitting the need to interact with the table. The basic structure for the include clause is as follows:

```
include (column3, column4, ...)
```

The columns listed in the include clause should not duplicate any that are already defined as key columns. Additionally, it's important to note that the include clause is exclusive to non-clustered indexes.

To illustrate, if one wishes to generate a non-clustered index for the **last_name** and **first_name** columns within the employees' table and concurrently include the email and phone columns in said index, the subsequent code will apply:

```
create index idx_employee_name on employees (last_name, first_name)
include (email, phone)
```

- **Constraints:** This involves defining rules and conditions that enforce the data validity and integrity. Constraints can be primary keys, foreign keys, unique keys, check constraints, default values, and so on.
- **Views:** This involves creating virtual tables that show a subset or a combination of data from one or more base tables. Views are used to simplify data access, provide data security, and hide the complexity of the underlying data model.
- **Stored procedures:** These are blocks of code that are stored in the database and executed automatically or on demand. Stored procedures can perform complex operations on the data, such as calculations, validations, or transformations.

- **Triggers:** SQL Server triggers can execute stored procedures or other actions when certain events occur, such as data insertion, deletion, or modification.

  SQL Server triggers are a type of stored procedures that are executed automatically in response to certain events on a table or view. For example, a trigger can be invoked when a row is inserted into a table or when a column is updated on a view.

  Triggers are useful for enforcing business rules, maintaining data integrity, auditing data changes, or performing custom actions. However, triggers can also affect the performance and scalability of the database and hence they should be used with caution and tested thoroughly.

  SQL Server supports two types of triggers: DML triggers and DDL triggers.

DML Triggers

DML triggers are triggered by data manipulation language (DML) statements, such as **`INSERT`**, **`UPDATE`**, or **`DELETE`**.

DML triggers are further classified into three subtypes: After triggers, Instead of triggers, and Nested triggers. The After triggers are executed after the triggering DML statement has been completed. The Instead of triggers are executed in place of the triggering DML statement. The Nested triggers are triggers that invoke other triggers, either directly or indirectly.

DDL Triggers

DDL triggers are triggered by data definition language (DDL) statements, such as **`CREATE`**, **`ALTER`**, or **`DROP`.** DDL triggers can be used to monitor and control the schema changes in the database. They are also used to perform additional actions, such as sending notifications, logging events, or rolling back transactions.

To create a trigger, the **`CREATE TRIGGER`** statement is used. The syntax of the statement varies depending on the type and subtype of the trigger, but it generally follows this format:

```
CREATE TRIGGER trigger_name ON {table | view} [WITH]

{FOR INSTEAD OF} {[INSERT] [,] [UPDATE] [,] [DELETE]}

AS

{sql_statements | EXTERNAL NAME}
```

The options clause can specify one or more of the following options: **`ENCRYPTION`**, **`EXECUTE AS`**, **`NOT FOR REPLICATION`**, or **`DISABLE`**. The method specifier can be used to invoke a CLR function or stored procedure as the trigger body.

To modify a trigger, the **ALTER TRIGGER** statement is used. The syntax is as follows:

```
ALTER TRIGGER trigger_name ON {Table name or view name}
[WITH <Options>] {FOR | AFTER | INSTEAD OF} {[INSERT], [UPDATE], [DE-
LETE]
AS {sql_statements}
```

To delete a trigger, the **DROP TRIGGER** statement is used. The syntax is as follows:

```
DROP TRIGGER [IF EXISTS] {trigger_name | trigger_schema.trigger_name}
[,...n]
[ON {object name ALL SERVER}]
```

To view the definition of a trigger, the **OBJECT_DEFINITION** function or the **sys.triggers** catalog view is used. To view the properties of a trigger, the **sp_helptrigger** system stored procedure or the **sys.triggers** catalog view is used.

To enable or disable a trigger, the **ENABLE TRIGGER** or **DISABLE TRIGGER** statement is used. The syntax is as follows:

```
{ENABLE | DISABLE} TRIGGER {trigger_name [,...n] | ALL}
ON {object name ALL SERVER}
```

To test a trigger, the appropriate DML or DDL statement can be executed on the table or view that the trigger is associated with. The results of the trigger execution can be verified by querying the affected table or view or by checking the output messages, error messages, or log files.

Database Design Best Practices and Terminologies

Database Design is the process of planning and creating a database. To do this well, there are some important things to consider, such as:

- Accurate and consistent data
- Reduced repetition
- Quick search using indexes
- Using the Normalization and de-normalization rules explained earlier
- Ensured security by applying different integrity rules
- Data stored in small pieces of information in the most basic format possible

The following are the best practices when it comes to designing a good database:

- Clarify the objective of your database and communicate well with the stakeholders (if any). Knowing the goal of a database will help in considering different scenarios, where the issue may occur, and how to avoid it.

- Identify all the entities that will be included in the database and how they relate to each other by using an ER diagram.
- Arrange the data into separate tables that have no or minimal repetition.
- Avoid repeating data in every table. The uniqueness of records in any relation is an important aspect of database design that helps us eliminate redundancy. Choose the key attributes to distinguish every row from columns. You can apply different key constraints to ensure the uniqueness of your table. Remember, that uniquely identifying records should use as little space as possible and should not have any `NULL` values.
- When all the tables have a clear structure and the information is arranged, use Normalization Forms to find any anomalies that might occur and redundancy that might lead to inconsistency in the database.

Key Terminologies while designing a good database:

- **Redundancy**: Redundancy means repetition of the data. There can be certain situations when we want or don't want redundancy in our database. For example: If we have a banking system application, then we may need to avoid redundancy in our database.
- **Schema**: A schema is a logical container that defines the structure and organizes the data stored in it. It has rows and columns with data types for each column.
- **Records or Tuples:** A record is a Tuple, the place where we store the data in our tables in the database.
- **Indexing**: Indexing is a technique that uses data structures to improve the efficiency of retrieving data from our database.
- **Data Integrity and Consistency:** Data integrity refers to the quality of the data stored in our database and consistency refers to the accuracy of the data stored.
- **Data Models:** Data models provide us with visual techniques to represent the data and the relationship among them. For example, model, network model, object-oriented model, hierarchical model, and so on.
- **Functional Dependency:** Functional dependency is a relationship between two attributes of the table, that is, the value of one attribute can be determined by another.
- **Transaction:** Transaction is a single logical unit of work. It indicates that some changes are being made to the database. A transaction must satisfy the ACID or BASE properties (depending on the type of database).

- **Scheduling:** Scheduling is the process that defines the order of the transactions in which they are executed by one or more users. It goes hand in hand with the functional dependency between the two objects or between two columns or the same object as well.
- **Concurrency:** Concurrency refers to allowing multiple transactions to run simultaneously without interfering with each other. This is being done to improve the overall processing time of transactions, and it is only possible when we do not have any functional dependencies and ensure there is no violation of any referential integrity constraints.

Data Modeling Concepts and Tools

The first step in designing a database is data modeling, which is the process of creating a conceptual representation of the data and its relationships. Data modeling helps to ensure the data is accurate, consistent and meets the business requirements.

Data modeling is the process of creating a conceptual representation of the data and its relationships for a specific domain or purpose. Data modeling can be divided into three levels: conceptual, logical, and physical. The conceptual level describes the main entities and their relationships in the domain, the logical level specifies the data types, constraints, and operations on the data, and the physical level defines how the data is stored and accessed in a specific system or platform.

The three levels of data modeling are explained as follows:

- **Conceptual data model**: This is the highest level of abstraction and describes the main entities and their relationships in the domain. It does not include any details about how the data is stored or implemented. The conceptual data model is usually represented by an entity-relationship diagram (ERD), which shows the entities, attributes, and relationships using graphical symbols.
- **Logical data model**: This is the next level of detail and describes the structure and constraints of the data, such as data types, primary keys, foreign keys, cardinality, and normalization. An ER Diagram further illustrates the logical data model, offering enhanced clarity and details. The logical data model does not depend on any database management system (DBMS) or technology.

  The logical data model design specifies the layout of data and how they are connected to each other. The main elements of logical design are:

  - **Data Models**: Data modeling is a graphical method used to get a general view of our database. Data models help us comprehend the needs and requirements of our database by designing our database through diagrams, for example, model, network model, relational model, and object-oriented data model.

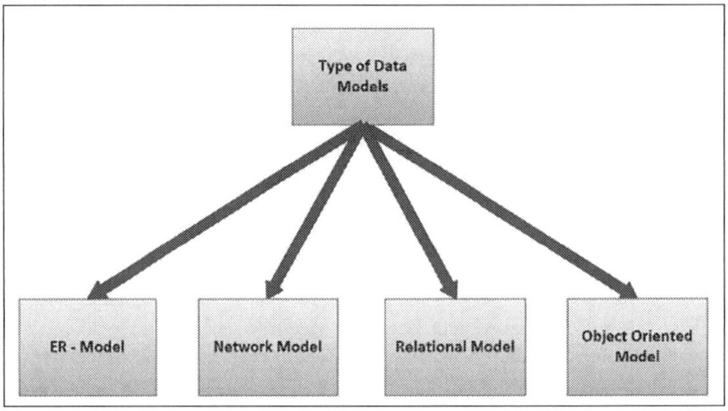

Figure 7.3: *Types of Data Models*

- **Entity**: A real-world object is called an entity, and it can have some characteristics. These characteristics are the attributes of that entity.
- **Relationships**: The way data is logically connected to each other determines the relationship of that data with other entities. In other words, the connection of one entity with another is explained here.

  Unary, binary, and ternary relationships are three types of cardinalities that describe how many instances of one entity can be associated with another entity. Cardinality is the number of possible occurrences of an entity in each relationship.

  - **A unary relationship** is a relationship between instances of the same entity. For example, a person can be married to another person, or a product can be like another product. A unary relationship is also called a recursive relationship because it involves recursion on the same entity set.
  - **A binary relationship** is a relationship between instances of two different entities. For example, a student can enroll in a course, or an employee can work for a department. A binary relationship is the most common type of relationship in data modeling.
  - **A ternary relationship** is a relationship between instances of three different entities. For example, a supplier can supply a product to a customer or a student can take an exam in a subject. A ternary relationship is more complex than a binary relationship and may require additional attributes to capture the details of the association.
- **Attributes**: Attributes are simply characteristics of a certain entity that determine how it acts. For example, an employee can have unique employee ID, name, city, passport ID, date of birth, salary, department, manager, client ID, and so on.

- **Normalization:** Normalization helps to eliminate data anomalies, such as insertion, deletion, and update anomalies, that may arise when data is duplicated or inconsistent across tables. Normalization can also improve the performance and efficiency of queries, as well as the maintainability and extensibility of the database design.

- **Physical data model:** This is the lowest level of detail and describes how the data is stored and implemented in a specific DBMS or technology. The physical data model includes table names, column names, data types, indexes, views, triggers, stored procedures, and other physical features. The physical data model is dependent on the chosen DBMS or technology and may vary depending on the performance, security, or scalability requirements.

Data modeling is an iterative and collaborative process that involves multiple stakeholders, such as business analysts, data architects, database developers, and end users. Data modeling can help to improve the quality, efficiency, and usability of the data and the database applications that use it.

Physical design is mainly concerned with executing the logical design, that is, displaying the database layout with all the columns and their data types, rows, relations, and relationships among data and explicitly specifying how relations are connected to each other.

The following are the steps taken in physical design:

1. Entities are transformed into tables or relations that have their properties (attributes).

2. Enforce integrity constraints: create foreign key, unique key, and composite key relationships among the data and apply different constraints.

3. Entity names are changed into table names; property names are changed into attribute names, and so on.

4. Apply normalization techniques based on the database design and system requirements and adapt accordingly.

5. Finalized based on the entities and attributes derived in logical design.

Methods of Data Modeling

Data modeling tools help to create and maintain these types of data models and generate scripts or code to implement them in the database. Some examples of data modeling tools for the SQL Server are:

- **SQL Server Data Tools (SSDT):** This is an integrated development environment (IDE) that allows data professionals to design, develop, test, and deploy SQL Server databases, as well as data-related projects such as Analysis Services,

Integration Services, and Reporting Services. SSDT supports both online and offline database development and provides graphical designers and editors for creating and modifying data models.

- **SQL Server Management Studio (SSMS):** This graphical tool provides a unified interface for managing and administering SQL Server instances and databases. SSMS enables users to create and edit database objects, query, and analyze data, perform backup, restore operations, and monitor, and troubleshoot database performance and health. SSMS also includes a diagramming feature that can be used to create and view simple data models based on existing tables and foreign key constraints.
- **Erwin Data Modeler:** This third-party data modeling software that supports various database platforms, including the SQL Server. Erwin Data Modeler allows users to create and manage conceptual, logical, and physical data models, as well as generate database scripts and documentation from the data models. Erwin Data Modeler also supports data governance, data quality, and data lineage features that help to ensure the accuracy and consistency of the data across the enterprise.

Benefits and Need for Data Modeling

Data modeling is the process of creating a representation of data structures and relationships in a database, using graphical or textual notation.

Data modeling can help to:

- Define the business requirements and rules for the data
- Design the logical and physical structure of the database
- Optimize the performance and scalability of the database
- Ensure the data quality and integrity of the database
- Facilitate communication and collaboration among the stakeholders of the database

Data modeling is an essential step in any data engineering project, as it can help to:

- Understand the data sources and their characteristics
- Identify the data transformations and integrations needed for the ETL process
- Design the data warehouse or data lake schema and architecture
- Implement data loading and extraction methods and tools
- Support the data analysis and reporting needs of the end users

Conclusion

In this chapter, we have learned about the database design and modeling concepts and tools available to perform effective data modeling, and how each of them impacts the design of any data engineering solution and its architecture.

We also learned about various components of a SQL Server database system and their importance and need in a database system.

The foundation of a robust database management system (DBMS) is good database design. It determines how data is governed, stored, and accessed. The system's performance and reliability depend on the quality of the database. When designing a database, you should consider data organization, standardization, performance, integrity, and more to suit your organization and your users' needs.

In the next chapter, we will be understating in detail the data security fundamentals and their importance while designing a database system and some of the key aspects of performance best practices.

Key Terms

- **Data Model:** A data model is a conceptual representation of the structure, relationships, and constraints of the data in a database system.
- **Database Designer**: The Database Designer is a visual tool that allows you to design and visualize a database to which you are connected. When designing a database, you can use Database Designer to create, edit, or delete tables, columns, keys, indexes, relationships, and constraints.
- **Deltastore**: A columnstore index can have more than one delta rowgroup. All the delta rowgroups are collectively called the deltastore.

References

- https://learn.microsoft.com/en-us/sql/ssms/visual-db-tools/design-database-diagrams-visual-database-tools?view=sql-server-ver16
- https://learn.microsoft.com/en-us/sql/relational-databases/indexes/columnstore-indexes-overview?view=sql-server-ver16

CHAPTER 8
Performance Best Practices and Data Security

Introduction

In this chapter, we will cover the performance best practices and data security related aspects of data engineering. Performance is one of the very critical aspects of database engineering as every data engineering project at every stage of the process needs a time-bound and effective solution to meet the data inputs and processing (ETL) timing requirements to be able to supply the data to underlying downstream systems for it to be used according to the end user needs which will be used for data extraction, analysis and reporting at various levels for an effective decision-making process.

Data security is another aspect where we need to have robust security mechanisms taken care of at each stage, be it data pull, transformations, data storage with proper encryption needs and security access at various reporting levels.

Structure

In this chapter, we will discuss the following topics:

- Performance Best practices
- Performance Improvement Configurations
- Query Performance Improvement Configurations
- Indexing Design
- Monitor and Tune the Performance
- Data Encryption and Security

Performance Best Practices

The performance of any RDBMS system or specifically if we talk about SQL Server is dependent on several factors, including how the instance configuration is done and how the database design and related aspects of the components of a SQL Server database are done. What are the recommended pre and post-requirements to ensure that the performance is not hampered or affected and is suitable for the majority of the workload types that suit most organizations, be it small, medium, or large based on factors, such as overall data size, daily transactional data volume, memory requirements, CPU requirements, data latency, and so on?

Some effective ways to improve the performance of relational database management systems and SQL Server are:

- Choosing the appropriate data types and avoiding unnecessary conversions or casts
- Simplifying the database schema to avoid repeated data and enhance data quality
- Creating indexes on frequently queried columns and tables to speed up data retrieval
- Updating statistics and rebuilding indexes regularly to maintain optimal query plans
- Using set-based operations more and cursors, loops, and row-by-row operations less
- Creating business logic and lowering network usage with stored procedures, views, and functions
- Tuning queries by analyzing execution plans, identifying bottlenecks, and applying optimization techniques such as joins, subqueries, filters, and hints
- Implementing caching, partitioning, and compression strategies to reduce I/O and memory usage
- Monitoring and troubleshooting performance issues using tools, such as SQL Server Profiler, Performance Monitor, Extended Events, Query Store, and Dynamic Management Views
- Configuring hardware, network, and server settings to match the workload and resource requirements of the database system
- Optimizing the query plans and avoiding expensive operations, such as table scans, nested loops, or hash joins
- Wrapping complex logic in stored procedures, views, and functions for better code reuse and maintenance
- Partitioning large tables and indexes to improve scalability and manageability

- Implementing caching and buffering strategies to reduce disk access and network latency
- Selection of row-store or column-store by understanding the table usage patterns
- Separation of log files and data files
- Creation of multiple data files, make use of file groups
- Creation of multiple tempDB data files as per the best practice suggested by Microsoft

Performance Improvement Configurations

Some configuration options at the SQL Server Database Engine level can change database engine performance. Microsoft takes care of most optimizations for Azure SQL Database; however, it's important to choose the right configuration settings to match your specific workload type and requirements.

Next, we will look closely at some of the top tips and suggestions to enhance and keep up the performance of the SQL Server Database Engine and Azure SQL Database.

Below are some of the best practices and recommended configurations for SQL Server On-Premises only

- **Disk Configurations:** Choosing the right RAID level for SQL Server is the key factor in disk configuration. RAID is an acronym for Redundant Array of Independent Disks, and it is a technology that merges multiple physical disks into a logical unit to achieve data redundancy and performance enhancement. Different RAID levels exist, such as RAID 0, RAID 1, RAID 5, RAID 6, RAID 10, and so on, each with its own pros and cons.
    - **RAID 0:** This level has no duplication and distributes data among several disks (striping). It has the highest performance but the lowest reliability, as any disk malfunction will cause data loss. Therefore, it is not advisable for SQL Server data or log files, unless a dependable backup plan is in place.
    - **RAID 1:** This level uses mirroring, which means that data is copied to two disks simultaneously. It offers good performance and high availability, as one disk can break without affecting data integrity. However, it also increases the cost of storage, as it needs twice the number of disks. RAID 1 is appropriate for SQL Server log files, as they are write-intensive and need fast recovery.
    - **RAID 5:** This level uses parity, which means that data is distributed over multiple disks and another disk is dedicated to store parity information, which can help recover data if a disk fails. It provides reasonable performance and availability, as it can survive one disk failure but also adds

some extra work for writing and reading parity. RAID 5 is appropriate for SQL Server data files, as they are more read-heavy and can handle some performance loss.

- **RAID 6:** This level is like RAID 5 but has two disks for parity instead of one. It has higher availability than RAID 5, as it can survive two disk failures but also has more overhead and lower performance. RAID 6 is appropriate for SQL Server data files that need very high availability and can accept lower performance.
- **RAID 10:** This level uses RAID 1 and RAID 0 together, so data is split across disks that are mirrored. It has the best performance and availability because it can handle more than one disk failure if they are in different pairs. But it needs the most disks and costs the most. RAID 10 is good for SQL Server data and log files that need the best performance and availability.

The choice of RAID level for SQL Server should also consider the impact of other factors, such as the size and type of disks, the I/O patterns and workload characteristics, the backup and restore strategies, and the availability and performance requirements. Additionally, some storage solutions may offer different RAID implementations or alternatives that may affect the performance and availability of SQL Server. Therefore, it is advised to test and benchmark different RAID configurations, before making a final decision.

For more disk configuration information, see this Microsoft document: https://learn.microsoft.com/en-us/previous-versions/sql/sql-server-2008-r2/ms190764(v=sql.105)?redirectedfrom=MSDN

- **Options for configuring data and log files:** This rule checks that the data and log files must be placed on separate logical drives. If both data AND log files are on the same drive, it can cause contention for that drive, resulting in poor performance. Having the files on different drives allows the I/O activity to occur simultaneously for both the data and log files.

One best practice is to use different drives for the data and logs when you make a new database. If you want to relocate files after the database is made, the database needs to be offline. Use one of these methods to move files:

- Use **`RESTORE DATABASE`** with **`WITH MOVE`** to recover the database from backup.
- Detach and then attach the database with different locations for the data and log devices.
- Run **`ALTER DATABASE`** with **`MODIFY FILE`** to change the location and then restart SQL Server.

One of the most effective ways to secure your data files and log files is to use access control lists (ACLs) to restrict who can access them. Apply the ACLs to the top-level directory where the files are stored.

View or change the default locations for database files:

1. Right-click your server in Object Explorer and select **`Properties`**.
2. Click **`Database settings`** on the left side of the **`Properties`** page.
3. See the current default paths for new data and log files under Database default locations. To change a path, type a new one in the Data or Log box or click the **`browse`** button to choose one.

- **`tempdb` settings:** How big the **`tempdb`** database is and where it is located on the disk can influence how well a system works. As an illustration, if the **`tempdb`** is too small, each time you boot up the SQL Server instance, system-processing capacity might be reallocated to enlarge the tempdb to accommodate the demands of the workload.

Here are some tips and recommended practices to improve the **`tempdb`** performance in SQL Server:

- For faster performance of data file expansion, use instant file initialization.
- Set the file size for all tempdb files to a bigger value that can handle the usual workload in your environment. This way, you can avoid frequent **`tempdb`** expansion that slows down performance. The tempdb database should be on autogrow mode to allow more disk space for unexpected situations.
- All data files within each filegroup should have the same size because SQL Server allocates space to files that have according to the available free space. Having multiple tempdb data files with equal size helps to improve parallel efficiency for operations that use **`tempdb`**.
- Choose a reasonable size for the file growth increment and make it consistent in all data files to prevent the tempdb database files from growing by too small an amount. If the file growth is too small compared to the data being written to tempdb, tempdb might need to expand often through autogrowth events. Autogrowth events hurt performance.
- **Server configuration options:** The server-level configuration settings must be handled with utmost care unless stated otherwise.
- **Max worker threads:** The number of worker threads that SQL Server can use to handle query requests are login, logout, and similar application requests.

This is a subsection termed as processor level configuration option under server configurations.

The following conditions are ensured by SQL Server, which uses the operating systems' native thread services:

- Each network that SQL Server supports has one or more threads running simultaneously

- One thread manages database checkpoints
- A group of threads serves all users

  By default, max worker threads are 0. This lets SQL Server set the number of worker threads when it starts. This is usually best for most systems. But you might get better performance by changing max worker threads to a specific value, depending on your system.

  Only experienced or certified SQL Server professionals should change this advanced option. Worker thread availability does not usually cause performance problems. It is mostly the activities that take up worker threads but don't free them, for example, long-running queries or system bottlenecks (I/O, blocking, latch waits, network waits) that cause queries to wait a long time. You should find the root cause of a performance issue before changing the max worker thread setting. We will explain how to identify the need for the change in "*Monitor and Tune the Performance*" section later in this book.

- **Memory configuration options:** The SQL Server Database Engine uses memory within a range of configuration settings, min server memory (MB) and max server memory (MB). Under normal conditions and over time, SQL Server will try to acquire memory up to the limit set by max server memory (MB).

These options have the following minimum values and preset settings:

Option(s)	Default	Min. Allowed	Recommended
min server memory (MB)	0	0	0
max server memory (MB)	2,147,483,647 megabytes (MB)	128 MB	Keep 75% of system memory free from other processes, such as other instances.

Table 8.1: *Memory Configuration Options*

SQL Server can adjust its memory needs automatically depending on the available system resources. Here are some of the suggested practices for the memory settings:

- If you set the max server memory (MB) value too high, a single SQL Server instance might use excessive memory and interfere with other OS processes and other SQL Server instances, in case multiple instances run on the same host.
- But if you set the max server memory (MB) too low, you miss a chance to improve performance and the SQL Server instance might have memory issues and performance issues.
- The SQL Server might not start if you set the max server memory (MB) to

the minimum value. If this happens, use the **-f** startup option to start the SQL Server and change the max server memory (MB) back to what it was before.

  - It's not recommended to set the max server memory (MB) and min server memory (MB) at or near the same values for SQL Server instances because it can lead to memory issues and impact performance. If they're too similar, SQL Server can struggle to manage its memory needs effectively, leading to potential errors, slow response times, or crashes. Additionally, it might hinder SQL Server's ability to adjust to varying workloads and resource requirements, resulting in poor performance or wasted resources. To avoid these problems, set the max and min server memory values with sufficient variance, allowing SQL Server to handle memory allocation dynamically. Optimal settings depend on many factors such as hardware, SQL Server version, database details, and workload, requiring tailored configurations guided by general best practices.

- **Fill factor configuration:** This is a component of the index settings. Fill factor is a feature that allows you to adjust how the index data is stored and performed. When you make or rebuild an index, the fill-factor value decides how much space on each page at the leaf level is used for data and how much is left as free space for later expansion.

  Following are the steps to follow to configure the fill factor option:

  - Open a connection to the Database Engine
  - Click **New Query** on the Standard bar
  - Copy and paste the following example into the query window and click **Execute**. It uses **sp_configure** to set the fill factor option to 100.

```
sp_configure 'show advanced options', 1;
GO
RECONFIGURE;
GO
sp_configure 'fill factor', 100;
GO
RECONFIGURE;
GO
```

- **Minimum Memory per Query Configuration:** The minimum memory per query option determines the smallest amount of memory (in kilobytes) reserved for running a query. This is also called the minimum memory grant. For example, if the minimum memory per query is set to 2,048 KB, the query is assured to get at least the same total memory. The default value is 1,024 KB. The minimum value is 512 KB, and the maximum is 2,147,483,647 KB (2 GB).

Recommendations:

- The query processor tries to balance memory use for queries. The minimum memory per query option lets you set the lowest memory each query gets. Queries often get more memory if they have big hash and sort operations. Raising the minimum memory per query value might help some smaller or medium-sized queries, but it could also make memory resources scarcer. The minimum memory per query option counts memory for sort operations too.
- Avoid setting the minimum memory per query option too high, especially on very busy systems, because the query must wait for the minimum memory it asked for or until the query wait option time runs out. If there is more memory than the minimum needed for the query, the query can use the extra memory if it helps the query.

- **max degree of parallelism setting:** The SQL Server **`MAXDOP`** option should be set according to the number of CPUs in a non-uniform memory access (NUMA) node for one or more SQL instances. This option restricts the number of processors to use for parallel plan execution and prevents queries from affecting database performance by using all available CPUs.

  NUMA node in SQL Server refers to an architecture where system memory and processors are split into nodes, with each having its own resources but able to interact via an interconnect bus. This can enhance performance for systems with many processors and memory but requires SQL Server to manage workload distribution, limit memory transfers between nodes, and allocate threads wisely for parallel queries. SQL Server automatically adjusts to the server's NUMA setup, yet certain settings like max degree of parallelism, which controls the processor count for a parallel query, need fine-tuning to ensure optimal performance. Deciding on the appropriate max degree of parallelism involves considering the NUMA node's CPU count and the number of SQL Server instances on the system to optimize resource use and minimize cross-node communication.

  Context and Best Practices:

  - The guidance presented here is appropriate for typical SQL Server workloads. There are some scenarios in which different Max Degree of Parallelism values may be appropriate.
  - If your SQL Server hosts databases for web application products, such as SAP, BizTalk, or SharePoint, consult the product documentation for guidance on MaxDOP settings. In some cases, the benefits offered by

parallelism are outweighed by the overhead, required to coordinate multiple processors.

 - Validate any changes to the MaxDOP setting in a test environment to ensure that any expected performance gains are realized before you change the setting in a production environment.

 Recommendations: For most workloads, you should set the Max Degree of Parallelism (MAXDOP) configuration option to the number of logical processors on the machine running SQL Server. In virtualized environments, ensure the MAXDOP value does not exceed the number of virtual processors allocated to the virtual machine.

- **Optimize for ad hoc workloads:** This option makes the plan cache more efficient for workloads with many one-time ad hoc batches. When this option is set to 1, the Database Engine saves a small, compiled plan stub in the plan cache when a batch is first compiled, instead of the full compiled plan. This option might help to save memory by preventing the plan cache from filling up with unused compiled plans. However, this option might make it harder to troubleshoot single-use plans.

 Suggestions: We should refrain from having many one-time plans in the plan cache.

 Following are the major reasons:

 - Query parameters with unclear data types can cause different plans. This mainly affects the length of strings and any data type with a limit, precision, or scale. For example, if a parameter **`@BookDE`** is **`nvarchar (100)`** in one call and **`nvarchar (200)`** in another call, each parameter size makes a new plan.
 - Non-parameterized queries can lead to a multitude of query plans for the same query, as they contain constant values for certain parameters that are sent to the Database Engine. These plans might vary according to the query parameters' data types and sizes.

- **Backup compression:** The backup compression default option sets whether the server instance makes compressed backups by default. When SQL Server is installed, the backup compression default option is off. By default, compression greatly raises CPU usage and the extra CPU used by the compression process might negatively affect concurrent operations. Therefore, you might want to create low-priority compressed backup where CPU usage is already high, and this can be controlled via Resource Governor.

 Recommendations:

 - You can use a different option than the server-level default when you make a single backup, set up a log shipping configuration, or create a maintenance plan.

   - Backup compression works for both disk and tape backup devices.

- **Database compatibility Level:** Database compatibility level is a useful tool to help with database modernization by allowing the SQL Server Database Engine to be upgraded while keeping the same functional state for connecting applications by preserving the same pre-upgrade database compatibility level.

  You can upgrade from an older SQL Server to SQL Server or Azure SQL Database (including Azure SQL Managed Instance) without changing your application (only database connection would be changed).

  Maintaining the previous database compatibility level is a reasonable option if the application doesn't need features that are only supported in a higher database compatibility level while upgrading to the latest SQL Server Database Engine.

  When a stored procedure/SQL Code runs, it uses the current compatibility level of the database in which it is defined. When the compatibility setting of a database is changed, all its stored procedures are automatically recompiled accordingly.

  For details on the compatibility level settings, please refer to - https://learn.microsoft.com/en-us/sql/t-sql/statements/alter-database-transact-sql-compatibility-level?view=sql-server-ver16

- **Index and Table Partitioning:** These are two methods that can enhance the efficiency of SQL Server queries by lowering the amount of data that needs to be searched, ordered, or merged. Index partitioning splits a big index into smaller groups that are kept in defined filegroups, while table partitioning does the same for a big table. This lets SQL Server use only the appropriate partitions for a specific query, and to do concurrent operations on several partitions.

  Following steps are required to implement index and table partitioning in SQL Server:

   - Create a partition function that assigns the rows of a table or index to partitions according to the values in each column. For instance, a partition function can split a sales table into monthly partitions based on the order date column.
   - Define a partition scheme that specifies which filegroup will hold each partition created by the partition function. For example, a partition scheme can assign each monthly partition of the sales table to a different filegroup.
   - Create a table or index on the partition scheme, specifying the column that the partition function uses as the partitioning column. For example, create a table or index on the sales partition scheme, using the order date column as the partitioning column.

By using index and table partitioning, SQL Server can optimize queries that filter or aggregate data based on the partitioning column, as well as queries that join tables that have the same partitioning scheme. Additionally, index and table partitioning can facilitate data management tasks, such as loading, archiving, maintaining or restoring data, by allowing operations on individual partitions rather than the whole table or index.

For more information on index and table partitioning in SQL Server, please refer to the following link: https://docs.microsoft.com/en-us/sql/relational-databases/partitions/partitioned-tables-and-indexes?view=sql-server-ver15

Query Performance Improvement Configurations

Before we dive deep into the configurations and details on how to improve the query performance in SQL Server by implementing some of the best practices and recommended configurations, let's understand how query execution happens in SQL Server.

The next sections explain how SQL Server runs queries and how it improves query performance by reusing execution plans through caching.

There are two different processing modes that the SQL Server Database Engine can use to handle Transact-SQL statements:

- **Row mode execution:**

Row mode execution is a query processing method for conventional RDBMS tables that store data in row format. When a query retrieves data from row store tables, it reads each required row along with all the columns defined in the table schema, using the execution tree operators and child operators. SQL Server then selects the columns that are needed for the result set from each read row, based on a **SELECT** statement, JOIN predicate, or filter predicate. Row mode execution works very well for OLTP scenarios but can be less effective when scanning large amounts of data, for example, in Data Warehousing scenarios.

- **Batch mode execution:**

Batch mode execution is a method of processing queries that operate on multiple rows simultaneously (hence the name batch). Each column in a batch is stored as a vector in a separate memory location, so batch mode execution relies on vectors. Batch mode execution also uses algorithms that are optimized for modern hardware that has multi-core CPUs and faster memory access.

Batch mode execution was first associated with and enhanced for the columnstore storage format. But from SQL Server 2019 (15.x) and in Azure SQL Database, batch mode execution can work without columnstore indexes.

Batch mode processing works on compressed data when possible and avoids the exchange operator that row mode execution uses. The result is better parallelism and faster performance.

When a query runs in batch mode and accesses data from columnstore indexes, the operators and their children in the execution tree read many rows together in column segments. SQL Server only reads the columns that are required for the result, as specified by a `SELECT` statement, `JOIN` predicate, or `Filter` predicate.

Batch mode execution is very efficient for Data Warehousing scenarios, where large amounts of data are read and aggregated.

Understanding Basics of Query Processing

Executing a `Transact-SQL` statement is the simplest way SQL Server runs `Transact-SQL` statements. When a statement has more than one logical operator, it evaluates NOT first, then **AND**, and then **OR**. It handles arithmetic, and bitwise, operators before logical operators.

By using parentheses to evaluate the **OR** expression earlier, you can alter the meaning of the query. Parentheses can make queries easier to read and understand and prevent errors that might occur because of operator precedence. Parentheses do not have a big impact on performance.

A simple `SELECT` statement does not tell the database server the exact steps to follow to get the data requested. The database server must examine the statement and find the best way to access the requested data. This process is called Making the `SELECT` statement more efficient. The part that does this process is the Query Optimizer. The Query Optimizer takes the query, the database schema (definitions of tables and indexes), and the database statistics as input. The Query Optimizer produces a query execution plan, sometimes called a query plan or execution plan, as output.

Optimization means picking one execution plan out of many possible alternatives. The Query Optimizer is an essential component of the Database Engine. The Query Optimizer spends some resources to analyze the query, and choose a plan; generally, this is beneficial when the Query Optimizer discovers an efficient execution plan.

The SQL Server Query Optimizer is an optimizer that uses cost as a criterion. It calculates the cost of each possible execution plan in terms of the computing resources required. The Query Optimizer must compare the possible plans and choose the one with the lowest estimated cost. Sometimes if we have a complex `SELECT` statement, then it may have thousands of possible execution plans. For these cases, the Query Optimizer doesn't evaluate all possible combinations. Instead, it uses advanced algorithms to find an execution plan that has a cost that is reasonably close to the minimum cost.

The SQL Server Query Optimizer has a dual goal: It chooses the execution plan that delivers the results with a reasonable resource cost and produces the results as fast as possible. For instance, executing a query in parallel usually consumes more resources than running it sequentially, but reduces the query time. The SQL Server Query Optimizer will opt for a parallel execution plan to output results if the server's performance isn't adversely affected.

Other statements in `Transact-SQL` such as `INSERT`, `UPDATE`, and `DELETE` follow the same basic steps as `SELECT`, `UPDATE`, and `DELETE` need to specify the rows to modify or delete. This is the same as selecting the source rows for the output of a `SELECT` statement. `UPDATE` and `INSERT` statements may have `SELECT` statements inside of the `INSERT` and `UPDATE` statements that provide data values to update or insert.

Any statements that are Data Definition Language (DDL), such as `CREATE PROCEDURE` or `ALTER TABLE`, are eventually changed into a set of relational operations on the system catalog tables and sometimes (such as `ALTER TABLE ADD COLUMN`) on the data tables.

Stored Procedure and Trigger Execution

SQL Server only retains the source code for stored procedures and triggers, not the compiled code. The first time a stored procedure or trigger runs, its source code is turned into an execution plan. The relational engine uses the same plan if the stored procedure or trigger executes again before the plan is dropped from memory. If the plan is not in memory, a new one is created. This is the same as what SQL Server does for all Transact-SQL statements. The main benefit of stored procedures and triggers in SQL Server over dynamic Transact-SQL batches is that their Transact-SQL statements never change. Therefore, the relational engine can easily find matching execution plans. Stored procedures and trigger plans are more reusable.

Stored procedures and triggers have their own execution plans that are different from the ones for the batch that calls them. This makes the execution plans of stored procedures and triggers easier to reuse.

Execution Plan Caching and Reuse

SQL Server has a memory pool that holds both data buffers and execution plans. The memory pool is divided between data buffers and execution plans dynamically, depending on the system's state. The part of the memory pool that holds execution plans is called plan cache.

Before SQL Server runs any Transact-SQL statement, the Database Engine looks in the plan cache to see if there is already an execution plan for the same Transact-SQL statement. The Transact-SQL statement is the same if it is identical to a previously run

Transact-SQL statement with a cached plan, character by character. SQL Server uses the existing plan if it finds one, avoiding the extra cost of re-compiling the Transact-SQL statement. If there is no execution plan, SQL Server makes a new execution plan for the query.

Recompilation of Execution Plans

When a database undergoes certain changes, they can affect the efficiency or validity of an execution plan, depending on the new state of the database. SQL Server identifies the changes that make an execution plan invalid and marks the plan as such. The next time a connection runs the query, a new plan must be recompiled.

Parallel Query Processing

SQL Server speeds up query execution and index operations on computers with multiple CPUs using parallel queries. This means that SQL Server can divide a query or index operation into several work units and give them to different worker threads of the operating system so that the operation can be completed quickly and more effectively.

When SQL Server optimizes a query, it evaluates the query or index operation, which could be improved by parallel execution. For these queries, SQL Server adds exchange operators to the query execution plan to prepare the query for parallel execution. An exchange operator is a part of a query execution plan that handles process management, data redistribution, and flow control. The exchange operator has Distribute Streams, Repartition Streams, and Gather Streams as subtypes of logical operators, which are shown in the Show Plan output of a parallel query's query plan.

Please refer the following link for more details: https://learn.microsoft.com/en-us/sql/relational-databases/query-processing-architecture-guide?view=sql-server-ver16

Indexing Design

Indexes improve database application performance, but they require good design. Bad or missing indexes can lead to many issues and slowdowns. In this part of the performance best practice chapter, you will see how the indexes function and gets some advice on how to create suitable indexes for your application requirements.

Let us presume we have a basic knowledge of the index types available in SQL since we covered the indexes extensively in the earlier chapters.

If you still want to read about them in more detail, please go through the following link https://learn.microsoft.com/en-us/sql/relational-databases/indexes/indexes?view=sql-server-ver16

Basic Concepts of Indexes in SQL Server

An index is a way of storing data on a disk or in memory that helps to speed up the access of rows from a table or view. A rowstore index has keys based on one or more columns in the table or view. For rowstore indexes, these keys are organized in a tree structure (B+ tree) that allows the Database Engine to find the rows or range of rows with key values quickly and efficiently.

A rowstore index maintains data in a logical arrangement akin to a table with rows and columns, and it is physically stored as either rowstore 1, which organizes the data by rows or as columnstore, which organizes the data by columns.

Choosing the best indexes for a database and its workload is a difficult balance between query speed and update cost. Disk-based rowstore indexes that are narrow or have few columns in the index key, use less disk space and maintenance overhead. Wide indexes, however, include more queries. You should test different designs to find the most efficient index. Indexes can be modified, added, or removed without changing the database schema or application design. So, feel free to try different indexes.

Role of Query Optimizer in Indexing

The query optimizer of the Database Engine usually chooses the best index for each situation. You should create different indexes for the query optimizer to pick from and trust its choice. This makes analysis faster and performance better in various scenarios. To see which indexes the query optimizer uses for a query, choose Include Actual Execution Plan on the Query menu in SQL Server Management Studio.

Using an index does not always mean good performance and good performance always means good index use. If an index always helped performance, the query optimizer would have an easy job. Also, a bad index choice can make performance worse. So, the query optimizer's goal is to use an index or some indexes, only when it improves performance and to avoid using an index when it hurts performance.

Recommended Best Practices for Index Designing

1. To begin with, comprehending the traits of the database is essential to identify the most effective indexing strategies.
    - How to manage a lot of data changes and keep high performance for an online transaction processing (OLTP) database? Memory-optimized tables and indexes can work well in this situation using a design that avoids latches.
    - Columnstore indexes are ideal for big data sets that require quick processing for a Decision Support System (DSS) or data warehousing (OLAP) database. Columnstore indexes can enhance the data warehousing

experience for users by enabling faster performance for common data warehousing queries such as filtering, aggregating, grouping, and star-join queries.

2. Learn the features of the queries that are used most often. For instance, if a common query combines two or more tables, you can figure out the best indexes to use.

3. Understand the characteristics of the columns you include in the queries. For example, a column that has an integer data type and is also not null or unique is ideal for an index. Additionally, for columns with distinct subsets of data, you can use a filtered index in SQL Server 2008 (10.0.x) and later versions.

4. Consider what index options could improve performance when the index is made or updated. For example, using the ONLINE index option would help to create a clustered index on an existing large table. The ONLINE option lets the underlying data remain accessible while the index is being built or reorganized.

5. The storage location of the index depends on its type: clustered or nonclustered. A nonclustered index can be stored in the same filegroup as its table or in a different filegroup. The choice of where to store indexes can affect how fast queries run, by affecting disk I/O performance. For example, storing a nonclustered index on a different disk than the table filegroup can make queries faster, because more disks can be used simultaneously. Also, both clustered and nonclustered indexes can use a partition scheme across multiple filegroups. When you consider partitioning, decide if the index should be aligned, that is, partitioned in the same way as the table or partitioned differently.

6. To see which indexes are missing, use DMVs like **`sys.dm_db_missing_index_details`** and **`sys.dm_db_missing_index_columns`**. Sometimes, a table may have similar indexes for the same column(s). Check the table's existing indexes before creating new ones and don't make duplicates.

7. When you create indexes, consider if the data for the index key column should be sorted in ascending or descending order. Ascending is the default and is compatible with older versions of the Database Engine. The **`CREATE INDEX`**, **`CREATE TABLE`**, and **`ALTER TABLE`** statements let you use the keywords **`ASC`** (ascending) and **`DESC`** (descending) for each column in indexes and constraints. The order of the key values in an index can help when queries that use the table have **`ORDER BY`** clauses that specify different orders for the key column or columns in that index. In these cases, the index can prevent a SORT operator in the query plan; this makes the query faster.

8. When to use non-clustered Index and when to use clustered index: singleton operations, lookups, include clause, decision about the selection of clustered

Index columns and how it affects the other non-clustered indexes, deletion of unused indexes and duplicate indexes.

Index Characteristics

When you decide that a query can benefit from an Index, you can choose the Index that suits your case most.

Index characteristics include:

- Grouped or ungrouped
- One column or more than one column Index
- Increasing or decreasing order on the columns in the index
- Whole-table or filtered for ungrouped indexes
- Column-based or row-based Indexes
- Clustered or non-clustered Index
- Hash or ungrouped for tables stored in memory

Another way to improve the performance or maintenance of the index is to set an option such as **`FILLFACTOR`** that adjusts the initial storage characteristics of the index. You can also use filegroups or partition schemes to choose the index storage location and optimize performance.

Clustered Index

Clustered Indexes sort and store the data rows in the table based on their key values. A table can contain only one clustered Index, as the data rows can be sorted in just a single way. Except in rare situations, it is generally recommended for every table to have a clustered index set on the column or columns that provide the following:

- Can be used for frequently used queries
- Ensures a strong level of originality
- The column or columns having a PRIMARY KEY constraint automatically get a unique index. This index is clustered by default, but you can choose a nonclustered index when you make the constraint.
- Suitable for queries that specify a range
- The Database Engine automatically adds a 4-byte column that is unique to the table when the clustered index does not have the UNIQUE property
- Every segment of a clustered index, identified by an **`index_id`** of 1 within sys.partitions, possesses a single row and a unique B+ tree configuration containing only the data from that specific partition. By default, a clustered index is created with a single partition. For example, if a clustered index is

divided into four partitions, it will result in four separate B+ tree structures, one for each partition.

- The query can be quicker if the columns in the **ORDER BY** or **GROUP BY** clause are indexed, because the data may be sorted already. The Database Engine might not need to sort it again.
- Columns that often change their values are not good candidates for clustered indexes, because this causes the entire row to relocate, as the Database Engine needs to maintain the physical order of the data values in the rows. This is a major issue in high-volume transaction processing systems where data updates frequently.

Nonclustered Index

A nonclustered index has index key values and row locators to show where the table data is. You can make more than one nonclustered index for a table or indexed view. Use nonclustered indexes to speed up common queries that the clustered index doesn't help with.

Like a book index, the query optimizer finds a data value by checking the nonclustered index to locate the data value in the table and then retrieves the data from there. This makes nonclustered indexes good for exact match queries because the index has entries that tell the exact position in the table of data values queries want.

- Nonclustered indexes on tables use the same B+ tree structure as clustered indexes, but they also differ from clustered indexes in some ways, as explained in the following points.
- The non-clustered keys do not sort or store the table's data rows.
- Index pages, not data pages, make up the leaf level of a non-clustered index. The key columns and included columns are stored in the index pages on the leaf level of a nonclustered index.
- A heap table has no clustered index, so the row locator is a pointer to the row that includes the file ID, page number, and row number on the page. This pointer is a Row ID (RID).
- When the table has a clustered index or the view is indexed, the row locator is the key to the clustered index for the row.
- Each partition of a nonclustered index has its own row in sys.partitions with an **index_id** greater than 1. A non-clustered index generally has one partition and can have more. A partitioned non-clustered index is characterized by a B+ tree structure that holds the index rows allocated for each specific partition.
- Databases or tables with a lot of data but few updates can benefit from using many nonclustered indexes to speed up queries. Consider creating filtered indexes for subsets of data to increase query performance, reduce

index storage costs, and reduce index maintenance costs compared with nonclustered indexes that span the whole table.

- You can use many nonclustered indexes for Decision Support System applications and databases that mostly read data. This gives the query optimizer more choices to access the data faster.
- Tables with frequent changes in Online Transaction Processing (OLTP) applications and databases should have few indexes. Also, indexes should be narrow, with few columns.
- Many indexes on a table slow down **`INSERT`**, **`UPDATE`**, **`DELETE`**, and **`MERGE`** statements because they all must be updated when the table data changes.

Indexes in database systems are not simple and require more thought and examination depending on your business/workload needs and scenario. For a more comprehensive review of the SQL Server Indexes, please see this link:

https://learn.microsoft.com/en-us/sql/relational-databases/sql-server-index-design-guide?view=sql-server-ver16

Monitor and Tune the Performance

Monitoring databases means measuring how well a server functions. Monitoring involves taking regular measurements of current performance to find problematic processes and collecting data over time to see performance trends.

Continuous assessment of database performance helps you lower response times and increase throughput, achieving optimal performance. Efficient network traffic, disk I/O, and CPU usage are crucial for peak performance. You need to evaluate the application requirements carefully, understand the logical and physical structure of the data, examine database usage, and balance tradeoffs between conflicting uses such as online transaction processing (OLTP) versus decision support.

Microsoft SQL Server and Microsoft Windows have utilities to check the database status and track performance changes. You can use different tools and methods to monitor Microsoft SQL Server.

Monitoring SQL Server lets you:

- Assess if you can enhance your performance. For instance, by tracking the response times for common queries, you can see if the query or the indexes on the tables need to be modified.
- Assess user activity. For example, by observing users who attempt to access an SQL Server instance, you can evaluate whether security is configured properly and examine applications or development systems. Another example is to observe SQL queries while they run and check whether they are formatted correctly and yield the desired outcomes.

- Resolve issues or fix errors in application components, such as stored procedures or any set of custom SQL scripts or queries that could be embedded and directly called from any application or any other scheduled or manual process.

Monitoring Performance in a Dynamic Environment

Performance varies depending on the conditions. You can observe how performance changes when there are more users, different user access and connection methods, larger database content, new client applications, more complex queries, and higher network traffic. Using tools to track performance, you can link performance changes to changing conditions and complex queries.

- You can assess the need for modifying the query or the indexes on the tables where the query runs, by measuring how long it takes for common queries to get a response.
- You can check if the Transact-SQL queries are correct and give the desired outcomes by watching them run.
- By checking the users who attempt to access an SQL Server instance, you can assess the security level and verify applications or development systems.
- Response time is how long it takes for the user to see the first row of the result set as a visual sign that a query is in progress. Throughput is how many queries the server can process in each time frame.
- When more users access a server, its resources become scarcer, which leads to longer response time and lower overall performance.

Data Encryption and Security

Encryption is the method of hiding data with a key or password. This method can make the data worthless without the matching decryption key or password. Encryption doesn't resolve access control issues but improves security by reducing data loss even if access controls are violated. For example, if the database host computer is poorly configured and a hacker gets sensitive data, that stolen data might be worthless if it's encrypted.

Encryption can help to improve security, but it's not essential for all data or connections. When you're deciding to use encryption, consider how users access data. If users access data over a public network, data encryption could help to protect security. If only secure intranet access is allowed, encryption is not necessary. Any use of encryption should also have a plan to manage passwords, keys, and certificates.

SQL Server allows encryption for connections, data, and stored procedures.

SQL Server protects data with a layered encryption and key management system. It uses certificates, asymmetric keys, and symmetric keys to encrypt each lower layer. Asymmetric keys and symmetric keys can be stored in an Extensible Key Management (EKM) module that is not part of SQL Server.

Data Encryption Concepts

- For the best performance, use symmetric keys instead of certificates or asymmetric keys to encrypt data.
- The Service Master Key is the protector of database master keys. The Windows Data Protection API (DPAPI) encrypts the Service Master Key, which the SQL Server setup creates.
- It is possible to use other encryption hierarchies with more layers.
- An extensible key management (EKM) module keeps symmetric or asymmetric keys outside the SQL Server.
- To use Transparent Data Encryption (TDE), a symmetric key called the database encryption key needs to be protected by an asymmetric key in an EKM or a certificate secured by the master database's database master key.
- The Service Master Key and the Database Master Keys for each database are all symmetric keys.

Certificates

A certificate is a digital document that confirms the relationship between a public key and the identity of its owner, who could be a person, device, or service. The owner has the corresponding private key. A certification authority (CA) is the entity that creates and signs certificates. The recipient of a certificate from a CA is the subject of that certificate.

Asymmetric Keys

An asymmetric key consists of a private key and a corresponding public key. Each key can decrypt data that the other one has encrypted. Asymmetric encryption and decryption require more resources but offer more security than symmetric encryption. An asymmetric key can encrypt a symmetric key so that it can be saved in a database.

Symmetric Keys

A symmetric key is a type of key that can encrypt and decrypt data. Encryption and decryption with a symmetric key are fast and suitable for frequent use with secret data in the database.

Transparent Data Encryption

Transparent Data Encryption (TDE) is a kind of encryption that uses a symmetric key. TDE encrypts an entire database with this symmetric key, which is known as the database encryption key. The database encryption key is protected by other keys or certificates, which are either protected by the database master key or by an asymmetric key in an EKM module.

TDE encrypts data and logs files for SQL Server, Azure SQL Database, and Azure Synapse Analytics. This encryption is called encrypting data at rest.

TDE encrypts and decrypts data and logs files on the fly. The encryption relies on a database encryption key (DEK). The key is kept in the database boot record for recovery purposes. The DEK is a symmetric key and is protected by a certificate in the server's master database or by an asymmetric key in an EKM module.

The following are some of the common features of TDE:

- TDE protects data at rest, which includes the data and log files. It helps you follow many legal, regulatory, and industry standards. This feature enables software developers to encrypt data using AES and 3DES encryption algorithms without changing existing applications.
- You cannot use TDE for system databases. It doesn't work on master, model or msdb. When a user database has TDE enabled, tempdb is encrypted automatically, but you can't encrypt it directly.
- TDE also doesn't encrypt data when it moves across communication channels.
- A database file is encrypted by the page. The pages in an encrypted database are coded before they go to disk and are decoded when they come to memory. TDE doesn't make the encrypted database bigger.
- Azure SQL Database creates the server-level certificate that is stored in the master database automatically when you use TDE. You can move a TDE-enabled database to Azure SQL Database without decrypting the database for the move operation.
- TDE ensures data files and log files are secure when they are not in use. After turning on TDE for a database that was not encrypted before, it takes a lot of time and system resources to encrypt the whole database.
- When any database on the SQL Server instance applies TDE to protect its data, the tempdb system database is also protected with encryption. This encryption might have an impact on the performance of other databases on the same SQL Server instance that are not encrypted.
- Replication doesn't encrypt the data from a database that has TDE enabled by default. You need to enable TDE separately if you want to secure the distribution and subscriber databases.

Always Encrypted Feature

Always Encrypted is a feature that safeguards data that is confidential, such as credit card numbers or national/regional identification numbers in all the PaaS databases, that is, Azure SQL Database, Azure SQL Managed Instance, and SQL Server databases. With Always Encrypted, clients can encrypt data in client applications and hide the encryption keys from the Database Engine. This separates the data owners who can view the data from the data managers who should not access on-premises database administrators, cloud database operators, or other high-privileged unauthorized users.

Thus, Always Encrypted enables customers to keep their confidential data in the Cloud with confidence and reduces the chance of data being compromised by malicious insiders.

Always Encrypted allows secure queries on encrypted data that involve equality checks.

With Always Encrypted, applications don't have to deal with encryption. A driver on the client computer that supports Always Encrypted does it by encrypting and decrypting sensitive data in the client application. The driver encrypts data in sensitive columns before sending it to the Database Engine and changes queries to keep the same meaning as the application. The driver also decrypts data in encrypted database columns in the query results.

Data Masking

Data masking, another key feature of SQL Server's data security and encryption tools, conceals sensitive information from those without permission by displaying fictitious or blurred data instead. It doesn't modify the actual database content but only changes the data presentation. Data masking is beneficial for activities like testing, developing, or analyzing, where actual data isn't necessary.

SQL Server provides two types of data masking:

- **Dynamic data masking**: This technique masks data in real-time as query results are generated, depending on the access rights of the user running the query.
- **Static data masking**: This method involves creating a duplicate version of the database containing masked data for use in non-production activities. It provides greater security compared to dynamic data masking, ensuring no risk of original data exposure.

Ledger in SQL Server

SQL Server provides a ledger feature, which is designed for auditing and ensuring the integrity of data changes. It uses cryptographic hashes to create an unchangeable record of all transactions altering data in a table, aiding in the detection and prevention of data tampering, fraud, or corruption. This feature also aligns with regulatory compliance demands for data reliability and responsibility.

Employing a hidden system table, the ledger keeps hash values, digital signatures, and timestamps for every transaction. These elements form a sequenced chain reflecting transaction order and specifics. A protected memory area called a secure enclave safeguards the signature-generating certificate against unauthorized access. The timestamp comes from a credible external time server, maintaining its accuracy.

Users can validate data accuracy and wholeness by querying the ledger table, verifying hash values, and checking signatures. The ledger is also useful for temporal analysis or detailed inquiries, enabling data state reconstruction at any moment. Furthermore, it ensures consistency across databases by matching ledger records. This ledger function enhances security for tables dealing with critical information such as fiscal transactions, health records, or legal agreements.

Encryption at Network Layer Using TLS

Encryption at the network layer is another method to keep data secure while being transmitted. SQL Server offers support for Transport Layer Security (TLS), which encrypts data packets and establishes the identity of the communicating entities. By doing so, TLS helps to prevent interception, alteration, and identity theft attacks, ensuring that only legitimate parties can access and modify the data.

SQL Server necessitates acquiring a server certificate, authenticated either by a certified authority (CA) or through self-issuance for utilizing TLS encryption. This certificate confirms the server's identity to the client and facilitates a protected link. While clients have the option to use a certificate for server authentication, this is not mandatory. SQL Server offers settings to mandate encryptions for all inbound connections or to permit a combination of both encrypted and unencrypted connections. Clients, too, can insist on encryption during the establishment of their connection with SQL Server, achievable through specific connection strings or application interfaces.

Employing TLS encryption adds an extra security dimension for SQL Server, mainly when data traverses public or insecure networks. However, the trade-off involves some overhead and potential effects on performance due to the CPU and bandwidth resources required for encryption and decryption activities. Hence, it's crucial to weigh the security requirements against performance implications for each situation and thoroughly assess the influence of TLS encryption on the system before integrating it into a live environment.

Conclusion

To summarize, SQL Server has strong data security and encryption capabilities that can safeguard important information. Encryption is an essential layer of protection, ensuring that the data stays confidential even if other security measures are breached. SQL Server provides tools to encrypt data both when it is stored and when it is transferred with features like Transparent Data Encryption (TDE) and Always Encrypted. Furthermore, the use of encryption requires a thorough key management strategy to preserve the integrity and accessibility of encrypted data.

SQL Server's encryption features are not meant to be applied uniformly but rather customized to suit the specific context of each environment. It is important to assess the type of data, the possible threats, and the legal obligations when choosing the right encryption method. By using SQL Server's encryption features efficiently, organizations can greatly improve their data security level and establish confidence with their stakeholders, knowing that their data is well-guarded against unauthorized access.

How can we present the data in a more appealing, easily accessible and readable way to influence and make the key business decisions quicker and reliable with the usage of visual representations and analysis? In the next chapter, we will cover the final and one of the most critical aspects of data engineering which is to build effective visualization and its related tools.

Key Terms

- **Encryption**: Process of transforming data into an unreadable form using a secret key, so that only authorized parties can access the original data.
- **Transparent Data Encryption (TDE):** TDE is a SQL Server feature that scrambles the database files, both data and log files. TDE guards the data at rest, so if the database files or backups are taken, then they need the encryption key to be read.
- **Index:** It is a database object that enables faster data retrieval from a table or view. An index creates an entry for each value or combination of values in the indexed columns and provides a pointer to the location of the corresponding rows in the table or view. Indexes can improve the performance of queries that use the indexed columns in the `WHERE` clause, `JOIN` condition, or `ORDER BY` clause.
- **Certificates:** A certificate is a digital signature that connects the value of a public key to the identity of the owner of the related private key, whether it is a person, device, or service.

References

- https://learn.microsoft.com/en-us/sql/relational-databases/performance/performance-center-for-sql-server-database-engine-and-azure-sql-database?view=sql-server-ver16
- https://learn.microsoft.com/en-us/sql/relational-databases/performance/monitor-and-tune-for-performance?view=sql-server-ver16
- https://docs.microsoft.com/en-us/sql/relational-databases/partitions/partitioned-tables-and-indexes?view=sql-server-ver15
- https://learn.microsoft.com/en-us/sql/relational-databases/indexes/indexes?view=sql-server-ver16
- https://learn.microsoft.com/en-us/sql/relational-databases/sql-server-index-design-guide?view=sql-server-ver16
- https://learn.microsoft.com/en-us/sql/relational-databases/query-processing-architecture-guide?view=sql-server-ver16
- https://learn.microsoft.com/en-us/sql/relational-databases/security/sql-server-security-best-practices?view=sql-server-ver16
- https://learn.microsoft.com/en-us/azure/azure-sql/database/security-best-practice?view=azuresql

Chapter 9
Data Visualization and Application in Real World

Introduction

In this chapter, we will cover the concepts of data visualization and its application in real-world scenarios. Data visualization assists data professionals in telling a story using data. Here is a comprehensive guide on data visualization. The depiction of information and data using charts, graphs, maps, and other visual tools is known as data visualization. These visualizations let data professionals quickly identify patterns, trends, and outliers in a data set. Data visualization also makes data accessible to specific target audiences who lack technical skills. The goal of data visualization is to aid in informed decision-making and bring color to an otherwise dull database.

Data visualization also helps in providing a broader and quicker perspective that data can be interpreted more effectively and easily.

The interpretation can be depicted in multiple ways based on the audience and the purpose of the report. One report can be built to suit the needs of any target audience, be it a developer or a software engineer, a team manager, or a C-suite executive.

Structure

In this chapter, we will discuss the following topics:

- Data Visualization Needs and Concepts
- Principles of Data Visualization
- Benefits of Data Visualization
- Data Visualization Tools
- SSRS vs Power BI Desktop and Power BI App

- Publishing Reports on Cloud
- Scheduling Data Refresh and Security as Per Roles

Data Visualization Needs and Concepts

Data visualization is the practice of converting data into visual or interactive formats that can convey information, patterns, trends, and connections more clearly than numbers or text alone. Data visualization can assist users in examining, investigating, and comprehending large and complex datasets, as well as sharing their results and suggestions with others.

Below are some of the aspects of data visualization

- Choosing the right type of chart or graph for the data and the message. For example, line charts are good for showing changes over time, while pie charts are good for showing the proportions of a whole.
- Using color, shape, size, and other visual cues to enhance the meaning and clarity of the data. For example, using contrasting colors to highlight differences or outliers, or using consistent colors to group related data.
- Balancing simplicity and complexity to avoid cluttering or oversimplifying the data. For example, removing unnecessary elements or details that distract from the main point, or adding annotations or labels to explain the data.
- Designing for the audience and the purpose of the data visualization. For example, using appropriate language and terminology, providing context and background information, and choosing a suitable format and style.
- The capability to tell a story using visual elements or themes that convey more depth than mere words alone.

Data visualization is a potent and flexible technique that can help data professionals convey their findings, convince their audience, and examine their data in a deeper and more informative way.

Data visualization can be used for different purposes, such as:

- **Exploratory analysis:** Data visualization helps data professionals explore the data and discover patterns, trends, anomalies, and relationships that might otherwise be hidden or overlooked. Exploratory data visualization can also help generate hypotheses and questions for further investigation.
- **Explanatory analysis:** Data visualization helps data professionals explain their findings and conclusions to others, using visual elements to highlight the main points, support the arguments, and provide evidence. Explanatory data visualization can also help convey the implications and recommendations based on the data analysis.

- **Interactive analysis:** Data visualization helps data professionals create interactive and dynamic visualizations that allow the users to manipulate the data, filter the information, zoom in and out, and drill down to the details. Interactive data visualization can also help engage the users and invite them to explore the data on their own.

To create effective data visualizations, data professionals need to understand the basic concepts and principles of data visualization, such as:

- **Data types and variables:** Data types are the categories of data that can be measured or observed, such as numerical, categorical, ordinal, or temporal. Variables are the specific instances of data types that represent a characteristic or attribute of the data, such as age, gender, revenue, or date. Different data types and variables require different types of visualizations and scales.
- **Visual encoding and channels:** Visual encoding is the process of mapping the data values to visual attributes, such as position, size, shape, color, or texture. Visual channels are the specific ways of using visual attributes to represent the data, such as bars, lines, points, areas, or maps. Different visual channels have different strengths and weaknesses in conveying the data and facilitating the perception and cognition of the users.
- **Design and aesthetics:** Design and aesthetics are the aspects of data visualization that relate to the appearance, style, and layout of the visual elements, such as fonts, colors, backgrounds, legends, titles, annotations, or interactions. Design and aesthetics can influence the readability, clarity, and appeal of the data visualization, as well as the emotions, attitudes, and preferences of the users.
- **Audience and context:** Audience and context are the factors that determine the purpose, scope, and format of the data visualization, such as the type of data, the message, the goal, the medium, the environment, or the expectations of the users. Audience and context can affect the choices and decisions of data professionals in selecting, transforming, encoding, designing, and presenting the data visualization.

Principles of Data Visualization

By following some basic principles, you can turn raw data into clear, useful visuals that show insights and attract viewers.

These principles are essential for good data visualization and help establish a clear understanding of the data insights being portrayed.

Improved Understanding and Clarity Towards Data

The principle of simplification and clarity stresses the need to make complex data into clear, easy-to-understand visualizations. It requires eliminating extra details, making visual elements simpler, and showing data directly to ensure viewers can easily and quickly understand the main message without confusion.

Visual Encoding and Perception

Visual encoding and perception are the aspects of data visualization that relate to the representation, interpretation, and cognition of visual information, such as shapes, sizes, colors, positions, or movements. Visual encoding and perception can influence the effectiveness, accuracy, and efficiency of the data visualization, as well as the attention, memory, and reasoning of the users.

The principle of visual encoding and perception stresses the need to use appropriate visual variables, such as length, area, angle, hue, saturation, or texture, to encode different types of data, such as nominal, ordinal, interval, or ratio. It also requires considering the perceptual properties, such as contrast, salience, grouping or ordering of the visual variables to ensure viewers can easily and correctly perceive the patterns and relationships in the data.

Choosing the right visual encodings is essential for data visualization. It highlights the need to fit data types with proper visual representations. Whether using bars for categories or lines for time series, using the appropriate visual elements ensures the message is clear and understandable.

Sometimes your data might be very effectively cleaned and processed but if the right representational visual is not chosen that can tie back to the story we are trying to convey or the message we are trying to pass to the end user, then no matter how effective your data and your knowledge of techniques were the visualization will not end up passing the message.

As data becomes more important for decisions and communication, we expect data visualization to keep changing and innovating.

Data Accuracy and Consistency

Data visualization projects rely on consistency and accuracy as basic principles. By being consistent in design elements, such as color choices and labels, viewers can understand the data in a coherent manner. At the same time, accuracy in data display, including honest scales and exact labels, establishes credibility with the audience, strengthening the dependability of the visualization.

Interaction and Exploration

Interaction and exploration are the aspects of data visualization that relate to the manipulation, navigation, and discovery of visual information, such as zooming, panning, filtering, selecting, or highlighting. Interaction and exploration can influence the functionality, flexibility, and interactivity of the data visualization, as well as the engagement, curiosity, and user satisfaction.

The principle of interaction and exploration stresses the need to provide useful and intuitive features, such as tooltips, legends, menus, buttons, or sliders, to enable users to interact with the data visualization and explore different aspects, dimensions, or perspectives of the data. It also requires considering the user needs, tasks, and feedback to ensure the interaction and exploration are meaningful, relevant, and responsive.

Different Types of Data Visualization

Visuals are the graphical elements that display the data in a data visualization, such as charts, graphs, maps, diagrams, or tables. Visuals can vary in their complexity, structure, format, and style, depending on the type, amount, and quality of the data, as well as the purpose, audience, and message of the data visualization.

The principle of types of visuals emphasizes the importance of choosing the appropriate and effective visuals that match the data and the story, as well as the design principles of clarity, consistency, and aesthetics.

- **Bar chart**: A chart that uses horizontal or vertical bars to compare the values of different categories or groups of data.

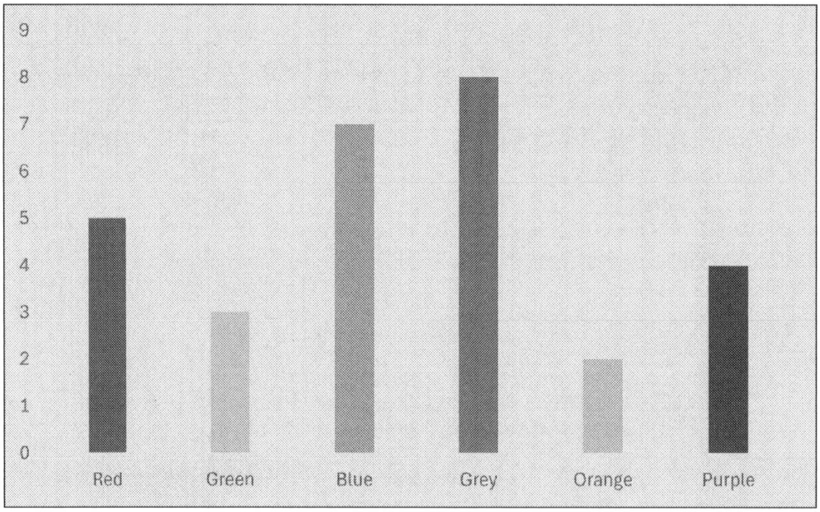

Figure 9.1: *Bar Chart*

- **Line chart:** A chart that uses lines to show the change or trend of one or more variables over time or across a continuous scale.

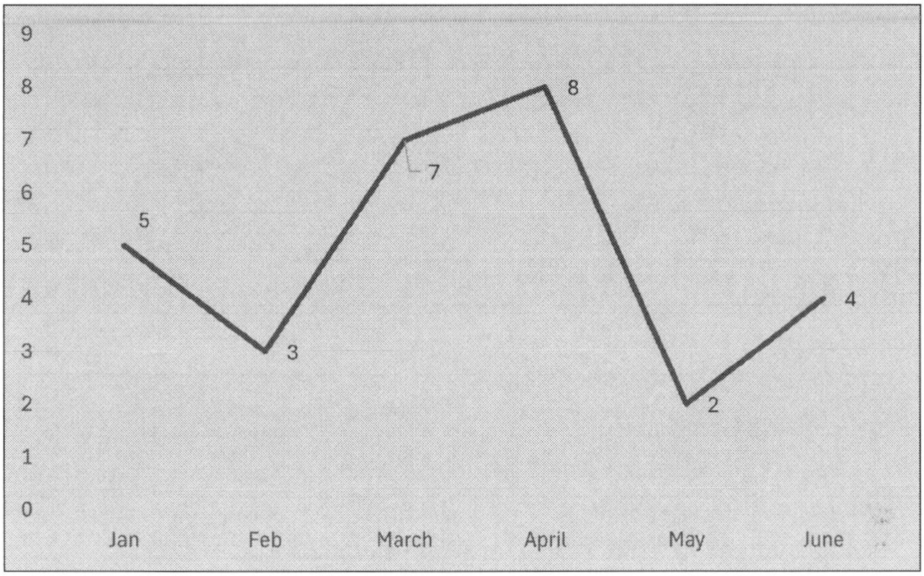

Figure 9.2: *Line Chart*

- **Pie chart:** A circular chart that uses segments or slices to show the proportion or percentage of each category or group of data in relation to the whole.

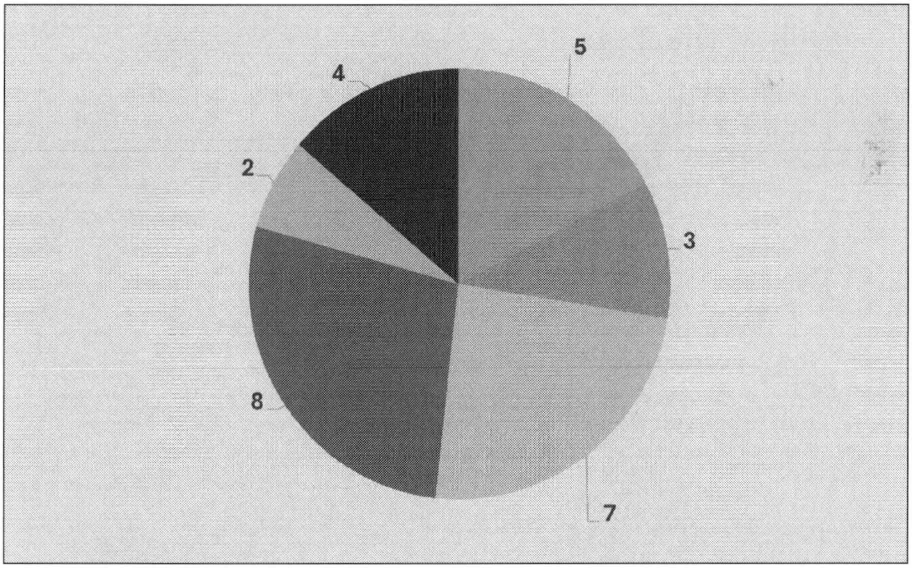

Figure 9.3: *Pie Chart*

- **Scatter plot:** A chart that uses dots or points to show the relationship or correlation between two numeric variables on a horizontal and vertical axis.

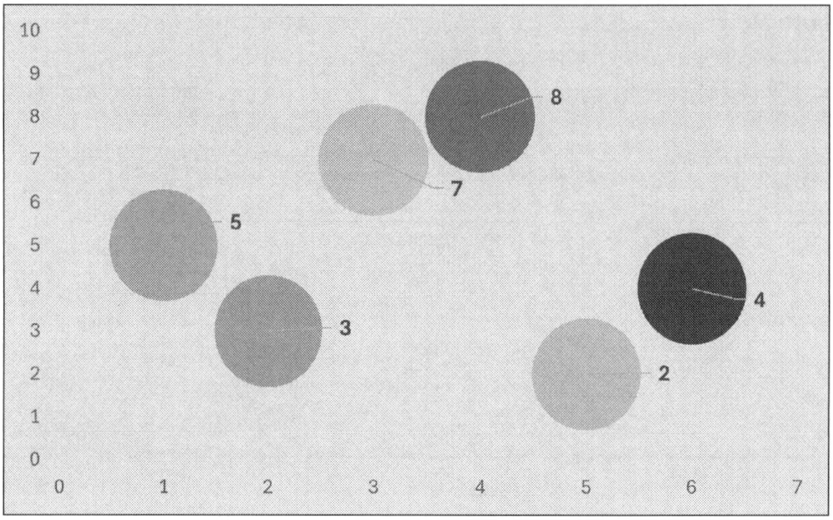

Figure 9.4: *Scatter Plot Chart*

- **Histogram:** A chart that uses bars to show the frequency or distribution of a single numeric variable over a range of intervals or bins.

The horizontal axis of a histogram chart represents the values or categories of the variable, and the vertical axis represents the frequency or count of each value or category.

A histogram chart visualizes the shape, spread, center, and outliers of a data set, as well as compares different data sets or groups.

A histogram chart also shows the density or probability of the variable by using relative frequencies or proportions instead of counts on the vertical axis.

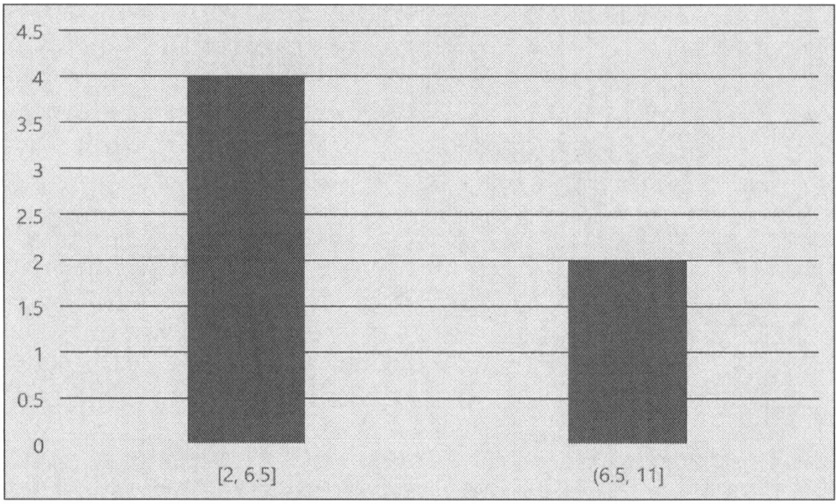

Figure 9.5: *Histogram Chart*

- **Sankey chart:** A Sankey chart is a flow diagram that shows the flow of energy, material, or information from one source to another. The width of the branches or links in the diagram is proportional to the amount of flow or quantity involved. Sankey charts are often used to visualize complex systems, such as energy production and consumption, supply chains, or web traffic.

In the following example shown in *Figure* 9.6, we showcase the co-relation between the countries dealing in a specific segment of market. For example, here we can see that all countries deal in all the markets shown.

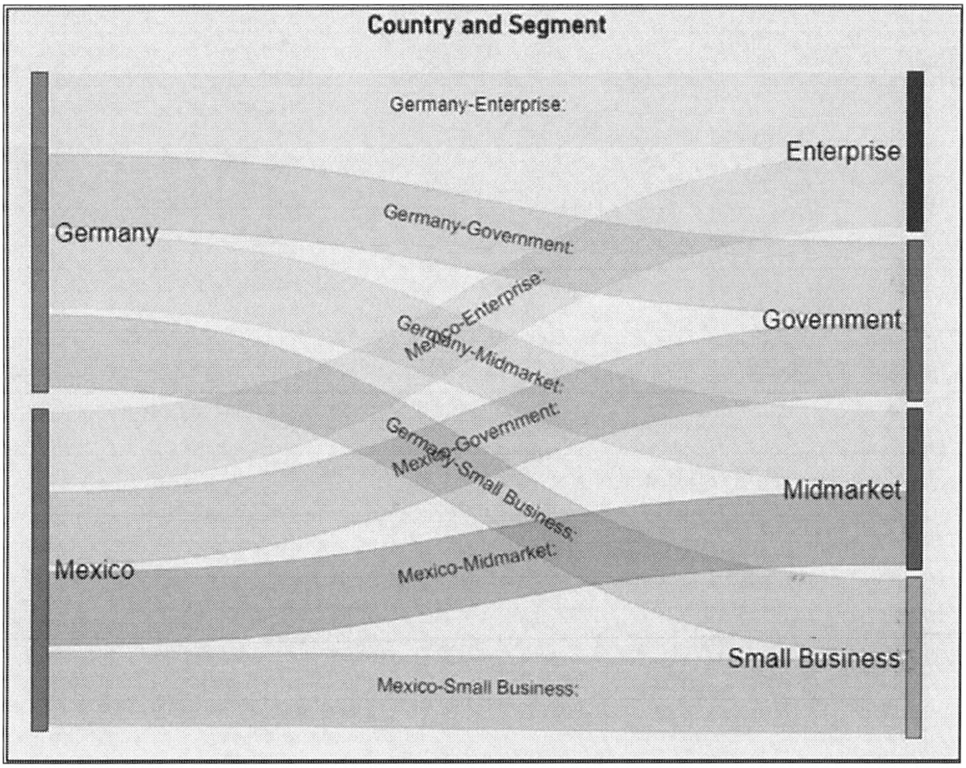

***Figure* 9.6**: *Sankey Chart*

- **Table:** A visual representation of data that uses rows and columns to organize and display values, labels, or categories.

This is the simplest of the visuals and is most used as well, for all the above types of charts shown, the end users will still be interested in seeing what's behind to be able to drill down to the details to analyze the patterns and outcomes further for taking right decisions and root level.

There are two types of table visuals: Regular Table and Matrix Table.

A regular table visual is a simple table visual that shows data in rows and columns. Each row is an item or a record, and each column is a field or an attribute. A regular table can have measures and dimensions but no hierarchies or aggregations. You can sort, filter, and slice the data but not drill down. A regular table is good for showing the data without summary or grouping. For example, you can show profits and discount bands for each country. *Figure* 9.7 is a regular table visual.

Country	Sum of Profit	Discount Band
Canada	1,020,566.79	Low
Mexico	713,359.05	Medium
France	566,200.03	Low
Mexico	474,067.32	Low
United States of America	333,781.15	Low
Germany	331,521.28	Medium
France	326,196.73	Medium
Canada	309,644.29	Medium
United States of America	276,406.49	Medium
Germany	177,833.38	Low
Total	**4,529,576.50**	

Figure 9.7: *Regular Table Visual*

A Matrix table is a table visual that shows data in a grid with rows, columns, and values. A matrix table can have more than one level for both rows and columns and shows totals for each group. You can also change the color or size of the values in a matrix table based on rules. A matrix table is good for showing complex and multidimensional data in a small and tidy manner. For example, you can use a matrix table to show how different products sold in different regions and time periods. *Figure* 9.8 is an example of a matrix table visual.

Country	Low	Medium	Total
⊟ **Mexico**	**474,067.32**	**504,754.56**	**978,821.88**
VTT	308,113.24	80,376.77	**388,490.01**
Paseo	9,495.84	343,880.74	**353,376.58**
Amarilla	141,740.00	36,998.20	**178,738.20**
Velo	14,718.24	43,498.85	**58,217.09**
⊟ **Canada**	**770,617.52**	**203,903.56**	**974,521.08**
Paseo	346,260.32	36,638.40	**382,898.72**
VTT	165,269.25	106,815.94	**272,085.19**
Amarilla	219,432.00	40,020.00	**259,452.00**
Velo	39,655.95	20,429.22	**60,085.17**
⊞ **France**	**372,879.40**	**165,438.93**	**538,318.33**
⊞ **United States of America**	**188,311.11**	**283,113.24**	**471,424.35**
⊞ **Germany**	**77,302.06**	**313,980.58**	**391,282.64**
Total	**1,883,177.41**	**1,471,190.87**	**3,354,368.28**

Figure 9.8: *Matrix Table Visual*

There are a few more very effective visuals that can be used widely like stacked column charts, clustered bar charts, donut charts, tree maps and many more. We will understand the usage and details of the same while discussing the features of Power BI in the later sections of this chapter.

Benefits of Data Visualization

There are numerous benefits of data visualization using various types of charts, graphs, and even other forms of displaying the data taking inputs from various non-visual data formats, for example, flat files, data stored in the form of tables in databases, structured or unstructured raw data, and so on.

Some of the key benefits are listed as follows:

- **Simplification of Complex and Unmanaged Data:** Data visualization converts big and complex datasets into visual forms, making them simpler to comprehend and analyze. By showing data visually, it becomes more manageable and user-friendly for decision-makers.
- **Displaying Data Patterns and Trends:** Visual formats like graphs, charts, and others help to see patterns, correlations, and trends that may not be easy to spot in plain numbers. Finding these patterns quickly can lead to better decisions and save resources.
- **Supports Decision Making:** Data visualization shows important insights that help make decisions quickly and efficiently. Businesses can assess performance, competition, customer behavior, and market trends, allowing informed strategic choices.
- **Improves Memory and Engagement:** Visual data is more attractive and memorable than plain data. Well-designed visualizations tell compelling stories about the data, making them great tools for presentations, reports, and stakeholder communication.
- **Makes Data More Accessible:** Visual representations make data easier to understand for a broader audience. Whether it's executives, analysts, or non-technical stakeholders, anyone can comprehend the information better through visualizations.
- **Allows Real-Time Monitoring:** Visual dashboards enable real-time monitoring of important metrics, allowing timely responses to changing conditions.
- **Detects Areas for Improvement:** Visualizations highlight areas that require attention or improvement. Whether it's finding bottlenecks in a process or detecting anomalies visual data guides corrective actions.
- **Supports Predictive Analysis:** Visualizing historical data helps find trends and patterns that can inform predictive models. It helps in forecasting future outcomes.
- **Improves Storytelling Experience and Methodology:** Well-crafted visualizations improve storytelling. They convey complex narratives briefly, making data-driven stories more persuasive.

- **Improves Productivity by quick Interpretation:** When data is presented visually, it reduces the time spent deciphering complex reports. Teams can focus on analyzing insights rather than struggling with raw data.
- **Risk Management ability:** Visualizations provide a clearer picture of risks, allowing organizations to manage them proactively. Whether it's financial risk, operational risk, or compliance issues, visual data aids risk assessment.

Figures 9.7 and 9.8 in the previous section of the same chapter show two examples of data visualization tools that can create different types of charts, tables, and dashboards. *Figure* 9.7 shows a regular table visual that displays data in rows and columns, while *Figure* 9.8 shows a matrix table visual that displays data in a grid with hierarchical rows and columns. Both visuals can be useful for showing numerical values, but they have different advantages and disadvantages depending on the data and the user's needs.

Data Visualization Tools

Data visualization tools are software applications that can help you create, customize, and present graphical representations of your data. Data visualization tools can help you explore your data, discover patterns and trends, communicate your findings, and support decision-making. Data visualization tools can range from simple spreadsheet programs like Excel or Google Sheets to specialized tools like Tableau, Power BI, or Qlik Sense, to coding-based tools like Jupyter, R Markdown, or D3.js.

A good way to start combining data visualization tools with data engineering tools is to pick tools that work well together or that have APIs, connectors, or plugins to link them easily. For example, if you use a cloud-based data warehouse, such as Snowflake or Big Query for your data engineering, then use a data visualization tool to connect to these platforms, such as Tableau, Power BI, or Looker. Or, if you use a data engineering tool that supports SQL, such as Apache Spark or PostgreSQL, then use a data visualization tool that can access data directly from SQL.

The choice of a data visualization tool depends on several factors to be considered, which are as follows:

- **The nature and scale of your data:** You may require a different tool for data that is structured or unstructured, for datasets that are small or large, or for data that is static or streaming.
- **Your visualization's purpose and kind:** You may require a different tool depending on whether you want to explore or explain your data, describe or forecast outcomes, or create different kinds of plots, diagrams, maps, or dashboards.
- **The degree of personalization and engagement:** You may require a different tool for basic or intricate visuals, fixed or changing visuals, or interactive or non-interactive visuals.

- **The user-friendliness and learning process:** You may require a different tool based on your technical abilities, experience with the tool, or access to documentation and support.
- **The price and accessibility:** You may have to choose a different tool based on how much you can spend, what kind of license you have, or how easy it is to obtain the tool.

There is no single best data visualization tool for every situation. You can use different tools for different tasks or combine multiple tools to achieve your goals. What is important is to choose a tool that suits your data, audience, and objective. To help you with this, we will review some of the most popular and widely used data visualization tools in the following sections. We will compare their features, advantages, and disadvantages, and provide some examples of how they can be used. We will also discuss how to combine data visualization tools with data engineering tools to create a complete data pipeline.

The following section will cover how Microsoft's BI suite has covered the visualization aspects of data engineering from on-premises tools like SSRS (SQL Server Reporting Services) to Power BI Applications.

SSRS vs. Power BI Desktop and Power BI App

To combine data visualization tools and data engineering tools to work together and share your findings with your team or organization to benefit from the shared knowledge and feedback of your data community, you can use the collaboration and sharing features of your data visualization tool or use other tools that can help with communication and documentation.

For example, if you use Tableau or Power BI for data visualization, you can use their online or server versions to publish, share, and comment on your visuals. Or, if you use Jupyter or R Markdown for data visualization, you can use tools like GitHub or Google Collab to store, version, and work together on your notebooks.

You can ensure reliability and scalability by monitoring and optimizing the performance of your data pipelines and visualization. This can be done by using the monitoring and logging features of your data engineering and data visualization tools, or by using external tools that can track and alert on metrics such as data quality, latency, errors, usage, and costs.

In this section, we will cover the two major Microsoft reporting tools, such as SSRS and Power BI.

SQL Server Reporting Service (SSRS)

SSRS is a data visualization tool that is part of the Microsoft SQL Server suite. With SSRS, you can create, manage, and deliver different kinds of reports using data from various sources, such as relational databases, multidimensional databases, or web services. SSRS can work with report formats such as paginated reports, mobile reports, or interactive reports. You can also design your own report templates and layouts with the Report Designer or the Report Builder tools.

With SSRS, you can upload your reports to a web portal called the Report Server, where you can arrange, secure, and distribute them to your audience. You can also set up the report delivery, create subscriptions, or export the reports to other formats, such as PDF, Excel, or Word. SSRS also offers a REST API that allows you to access and manipulate the reports and the Report Server programmatically.

SSRS has the advantage of being compatible with other Microsoft products, such as Power BI, SharePoint, or Visual Studio. You can create and share dashboards that contain SSRS reports with Power BI or display and manage the reports with SharePoint. You can also develop and distribute SSRS projects with Visual Studio or use the SQL Server Data Tools (SSDT) extension to work with SSRS in a comfortable setting.

Downloading and Installing SSRS

An earlier version of SSRS used to come as a part of Microsoft's business intelligence development studio (BIDS) which later got upgraded to SQL Server Data Tools (SSDT) and now we have the extensions coming as a part of the Visual Studio 2022 as the latest version.

SQL Server Data Tools (SSDT) is a Microsoft Visual Studio tool that builds business intelligence solutions. SSDT has the Report Designer, where you can work with Reporting Services paginated report elements, such as report definitions, shared data sources and shared datasets.

Once you have the Visual Studio 2022 installed on your machine you can then download the SSRS extensions from the marketplace at the following link: *https://marketplace.visualstudio.com/items?itemName=ProBITools.MicrosoftReportProjectsforVisualStudio2022*

Basic Report Creation and Deployment in SSRS

There are various tools to make and publish reports, such as Report Designer in Visual Studio, Report Builder, or Power BI Report Server.

To make a report, you need a data source that connects to your database and a dataset that specifies the query and fields for your report.

You can use the Report Wizard to make a data source and a dataset automatically or make them yourself using the Data Sources and Datasets windows in Visual Studio.

When you have a data source and a dataset, you can add a report item to your project, such as a table, matrix, chart, map, or gauge. You can drag and drop fields from your dataset to the report item and change its look and layout using the Properties window and the Toolbox.

You can also add other things to your report, such as a title, header, footer, logo, or parameter. You can use expressions to set dynamic values or calculations for your reporting needs.

Let's explore a step-by-step process, starting from the creation of an SSRS project, transitioning to the design phase, and concluding with the deployment of the SSRS report onto the Reporting Server, ensuring accessibility for end users.

Step 1: Create a SSRS project from Visual Studio.

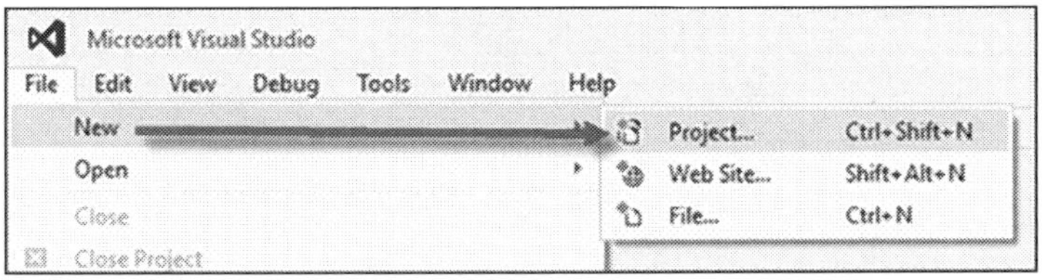

Figure 9.9: *Create new SSRS project from Visual Studio*

Step 2: Select the Appropriate project type from the options provided under SSRS section.

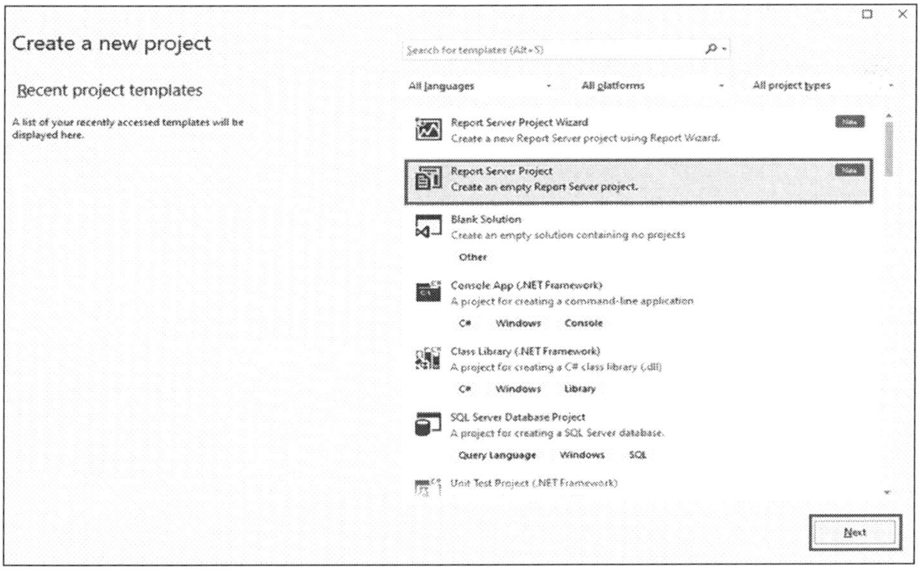

Figure 9.10: *Select Report Server Project (Reporting Services)*

Step 3: Create a new report by selecting the "`Add Report`" Option which is the "`.rdl`" file under the reports section and get a report designer view with design and preview tabs on the top and a report data section on the left-hand side.

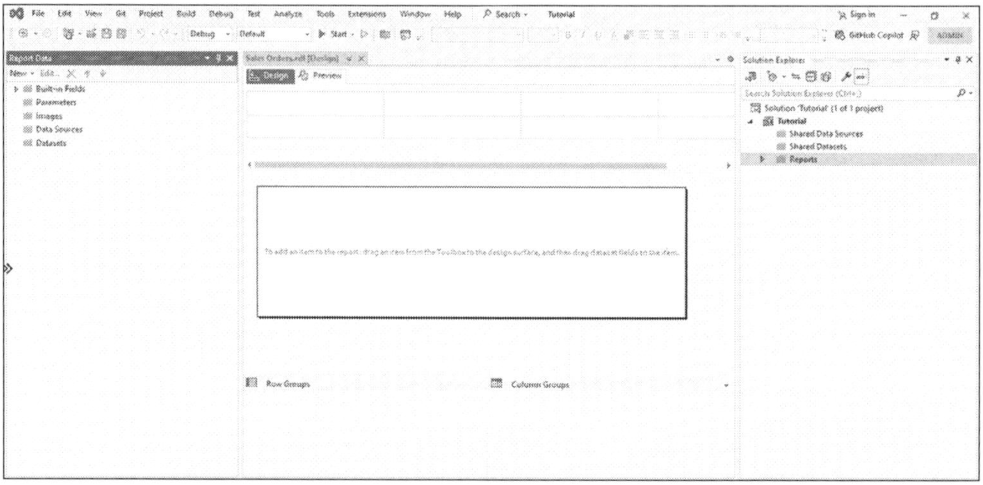

***Figure 9.11:** Add New ".rdl" Report*

- **Step 4:** Define a data source which is our input data to be shown in the report.
  - We can have multiple data sources which is used for a single report.
  - Then add data sets to the report which is either a set of tables, views or custom queries that can act as an individual dataset.

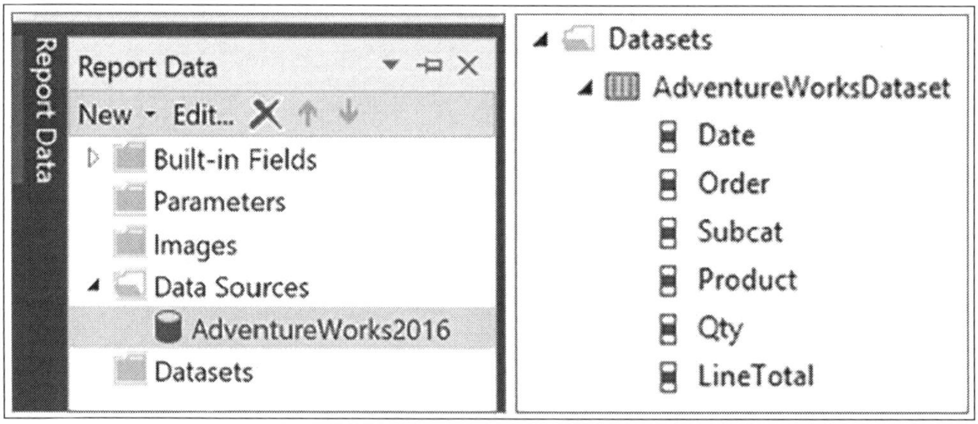

***Figure 9.12:** Data Source and Datasets in a SSRS Report*

- **Step 5:** Once the preceding steps are done, design the first report by adding the required visuals to the report which can be a table, graph, line chart, and so on.

  Some of the common design options include:

  - Formatting the table by adding borders, formatting the text or headers by making them bold, Italic, or adding color to text or the complete text box.
  - Adding totals based on rows or columns to the tables.
  - Adding Custom Images, such as a logo or some other background images as watermark, and so on.

  Once done, we can preview the report to verify if it's according to our expectations and business requirements.

- **Step 6:** Once finished with the report building, we are now ready to publish this report to the report server to be able to share this with the end users.
  - First, let's ensure we have provided the correct Target Server details before publishing.
    - If we are publishing to a local server then we should use: *https://localhost/reportserver/*
    - If we are publishing the report on the report server then we should use: *http://<targetservername>/reportserver/*
  - We need to publish this report from the SSDT \Visual Studio by selecting the deploy option.

If you want to migrate your SSRS reports to Power BI, then first migrate the SSRS database to the Power BI report server database and then we need to change the database configuration to point to the Power BI report server.

For details on this, please refer to https://learn.microsoft.com/en-us/power-bi/report-server/migrate-report-server

Power BI

Power BI is a cloud-based service that allows you to explore and display data with various features. You can link to different data sources, such as SQL Server, Excel, or web services, and make interactive reports and dashboards with the data. You can also save the data in the Cloud as Power BI datasets that refresh automatically or whenever you want.

One way to have your SSRS reports on Power BI is to use the Power BI Report Server, which is a special type of SSRS that can host both Power BI reports and regular SSRS reports. You can also use the Power BI Report Builder, which is a tool that helps you create and publish paginated reports to the Power BI service. Paginated reports are like SSRS reports, yet they differ in format and present certain constraints when compared with SSRS reports. For example, paginated reports can only use Power BI datasets for data and do not support sub-reports, drill-throughs, or custom code.

Power BI enables you to take advantage of the cloud benefits, such as scalability, accessibility, and security, by hosting your reports on the Cloud. You can also integrate your reports with other applications, such as SharePoint Online, Microsoft Teams, or custom websites, using the Power BI embedding feature. Additionally, you can view and interact with your reports on your phone or tablet using the Power BI mobile app. Power BI also offers a REST API that lets you access and manage your reports and datasets with code.

Downloading and Installing PowerBI

You can download and install the latest version of the different flavors of power BI reporting tool from Microsoft's official download center site: https://powerbi.microsoft.com/en-us/downloads/

There are three major types of power BI setup that you can download and install based on your requirements and business needs which are as follows:

1. **Microsoft Power BI Desktop:** The Power BI Desktop lets you see your data in different ways with a flexible canvas, modern visualizations, and simple report creation.

   Download link: https://aka.ms/pbidesktopstore

2. **On-premises reporting with Power BI Report Server:** Share and publish Power BI reports that are interactive—and paginated reports that are conventional—inside the security limits of your organization's firewall.

   Download link: https://go.microsoft.com/fwlink/?LinkId=2235079&clcid=0x409

3. **Microsoft Power BI Report Builder:** Make paginated reports that look the same on paper or digital formats, with a trusted experience used by thousands of report creators.

   Download link: https://go.microsoft.com/fwlink/?LinkId=2086513&clcid=0x409

The best part is that you can install both Power BI Desktop and Power BI Desktop for Power BI Report Server, on the same computer simultaneously.

To ensure that you are using the latest version of Power BI Desktop for the Power BI Report Server, the best thing is to launch it from the web portal of your report server.

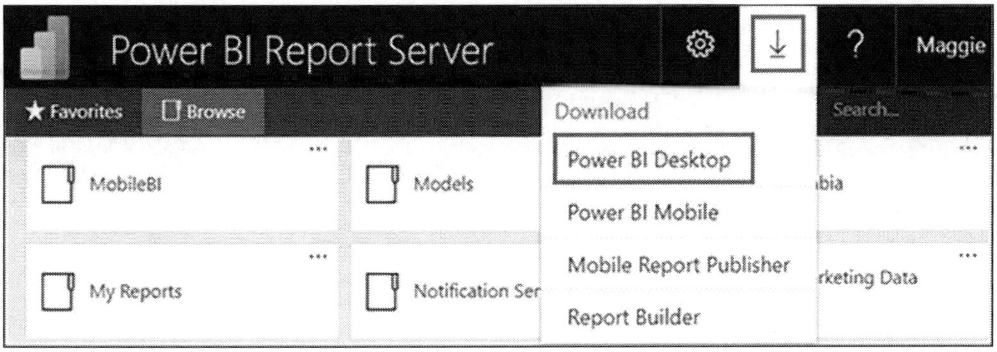

Figure 9.13: *Downloading the latest Power BI Version from Report Server*

Once you are done with the download and installation of the latest version of your choice of the Power BI software, start building some of the coolest and most impactful reports and dashboards for our businesses to ensure the data that we have got into our warehouses after following all the necessary steps of data engineering is now available to end users in a more easily readable, accessible, and visually appealing way to cater to the decision-making process for business enhancement and a better user experience.

Basic Report Creation and Deployment in Power BI

In this section, we will see how to make a simple report with Power BI Desktop and upload it on the Power BI cloud service. A report is a set of visualizations that show data from one or more datasets in a consistent and understandable way. A report can have multiple pages, each with its own design and style. You can also add filters, slicers, and other interactive features to your report to improve the user experience and allow data analysis.

A report requires a dataset that has the data you want to show. You can either bring in the data from different sources into Power BI Desktop or use an existing dataset on the Power BI cloud service or another online place. For this example, we will use a sample dataset that Power BI Desktop provides, called Retail Analysis Sample. This dataset has sales data for a made-up retail company.

To create a report using this dataset, follow these steps:

1. **Step 1:** Launch Power BI Desktop and select Get Data in the Home tab. A dialog box will show up with different data sources that you can pick from.

   Figure 9.14 shows different ways to choose data for your first Power BI report. You can import from an Excel file, a CSV or a TXT file. You can also select from SQL Server, which is a prominent source on the main screen or from many other databases.

In our case study, we can use sample data that comes with the downloaded version. It will appear on your right-hand side under the data section when you click this option.

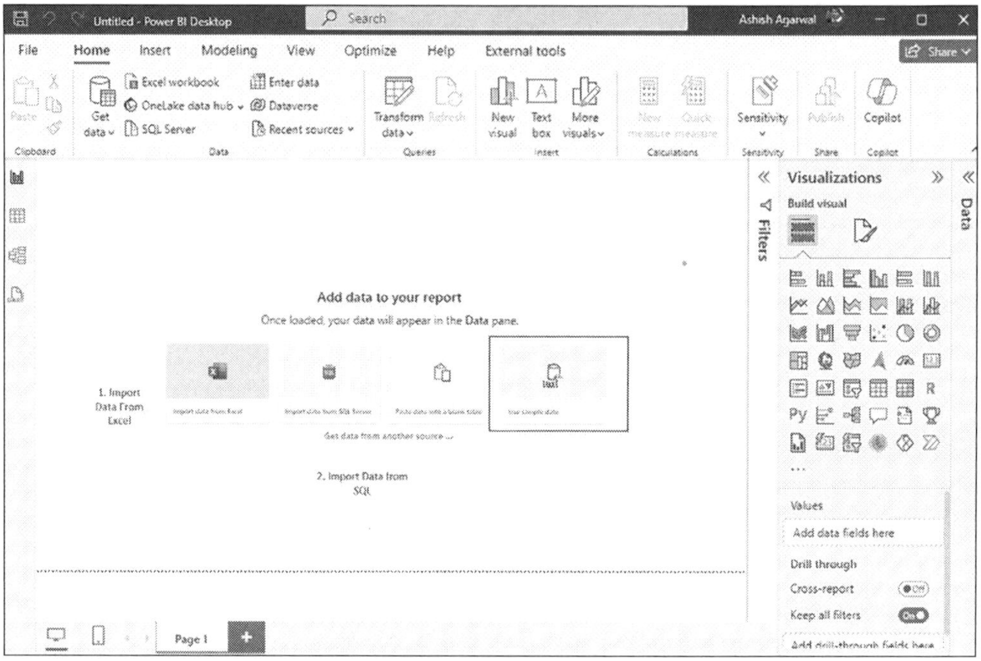

Figure 9.14: *Get Data from Various Sources for a Power BI Report*

2. **Step 2:** As discussed earlier, let's start with the sample data as our source to start building our first Power BI Report, choose "**`Use sample data`**" and then click on "**`Load sample data`**" as shown in *Figure* 9.15.

   This action will load the sample "*financial*" data to work and develop reports. It will have some sample facts and dimensions data which will be available for either direct load or transformation like data type changes for columns or creating additional calculated columns, and so on.

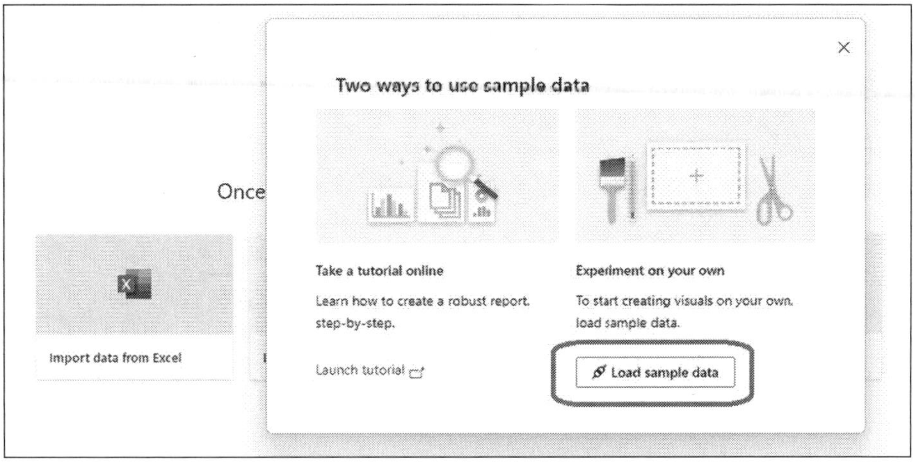

Figure 9.15: *Load Sample Data for a Power BI Report*

The data will be available for us to use under the data tab as a single table for now which you can enhance by adding more tables if needed from various others or same sources as well.

Now, we will have three major sections to be used:

- **Data:** This will contain the tables or datasets imported or directly queried based on the mode selected for us to build reports.
- **Visualizations:** This tab contains options for us to select from a variety of visualizations to build our reports. The most used ones are filter visuals, Stacked Column charts, Pie charts, Bar charts, Heat Maps, and so on which we have already covered in earlier sections.
- **Filters:** This section is used to apply filters on our data based on certain business rules or requirements.

  There are three types of filters that can be used in a Power BI report or dashboard:

  - **Visual Level Filter** works only on a specific visual in a report.
  - **Page Level Filter** works across all filters on a specific page in a report only.
  - **All Page Level Filter** works across all pages in a report including all visuals on each page. This can be used in "`Sync`" mode where if we change a filter on any page, then it will be automatically applied on all pages.

3. **Step 3:** To create a visualization, let's say, a stacked column chart, drag and drop fields from the **`Fields`** pane to the **`Report`** canvas or the **`Visualizations`** pane.

For example, drag and drop the "**`Sales`**" and "**`Profit`**" fields to the Y-axis of the Report canvas and "**`Country`**" field to the X-axis of the visual properties. A column chart will be created showing the total units sold and total profit by country.

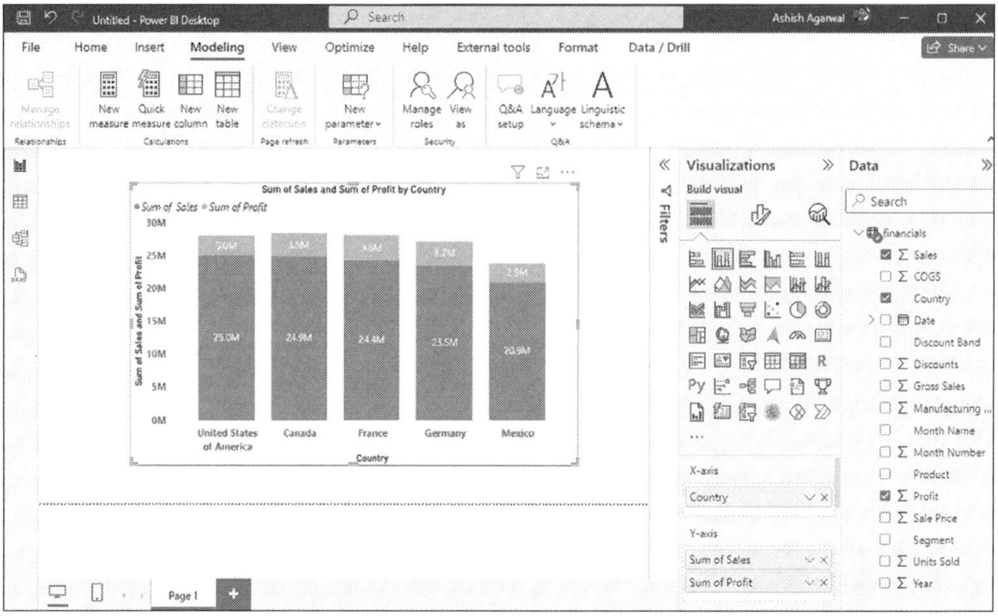

***Figure 9.16**: Stacked Column Chart Visual in Power BI with Sales and Profit Data*

With this, your report is now ready and can be used as it is or enhanced by using some of the wide range of options/features available to us to make a world-class report.

Following is the list of features:

- Power BI enables us to easily transform the type of visualization by selecting the visual and then clicking on the icons in the Visualizations pane. For instance, click on the Line chart icon to convert the column chart to a line chart.
- You can also add more fields to the visualization to add more details or dimensions to your visualization, for example, if you want to showcase a number of units sold as well then drag and drop the "`Units Sold`" metric and you will see another stack with a new color being added. You can change the color of new metric or even existing metrics from the formatting section under the visualizations head.
- You can also customize the appearance of the visualization by using the options in the Format tab in the Visualizations pane. For example, you can modify the title, colors, labels, axes, and other features of the chart.
- You can create a new page for the report by clicking on the **+** icon at the bottom of the screen as shown in the preceding *Figure* 9.16; to change the name of the page, double-click on the default name and type a new one.
- You can create more visualizations for the report by following the same steps as earlier. You can also move visualizations from one page to another by copying

and pasting them or using the toolbar buttons in the Home tab to organize, line up, group, or sort the visualizations.

Once the report is built and the customizations done, you need to save the file in a safe location.

To save the file, Click File and Save to save the report. Choose a name and a location for the "`.pbix`" file. You can open it again in Power BI Desktop.

This file can be shared with other people on your team by attaching it to an email, sharing via OneDrive, or even over an FTP. If the other user has access to the source data, then he or she can also view the report or modify it, but the modifications might not reflect on your side unless it is done on a OneDrive shared location.

Creation of the Report Using Copilot Feature in Power BI

Power BI has recently introduced the copilot feature that leverages natural language queries to construct reports. This innovative tool uses AI to grasp your data and fabricate visualizations that are both relevant and insightful in response to your questions. It is accessible through the "**`Ask a question`**" button found in the Home tab of the ribbon, or by pressing "**`Ctrl+Q`**".

For optimal use of the copilot feature, ensure you have a structured data model present in Power BI Desktop. Once prepared, input your question into the query box and the copilot aims to deliver the most accurate answer using your data. The feature also supports filters, aggregations, calculations, and comparisons within questions, provided they align with your data model capabilities. For instance, queries such as:

- What's the total sales figure for a specific region?
- How does profit margin change across different product categories?
- What's the average order size per customer segment?
- Which products rank highest and lowest in customer satisfaction scores?

The copilot will present the optimal visualization for your query, which can be a chart, table, map, or card. To switch the type of visualization, you can click on the icons in the Visualization pane or utilize the "**`Change visualization`**" button on the toolbar. Additionally, the visualization's characteristics like title, color scheme, labels, axis details, and filters can be altered using the Format pane.

To expand your report with more inquiries, select the "**`Add tile`**" option in the toolbar or use the shortcut "**`Ctrl+N`**". It will generate a fresh tile on your report canvas for posting new questions. Tiles can also be repositioned or resized within your report by dragging and dropping to suit your preferred layout.

When your report meets your standards, it can be saved in the **`.pbix`** format and shared as previously outlined. Furthermore, publishing it to the Power BI service unlocks additional functionalities, including dashboards, apps, workspaces, and Q&A. To publish, hit the "**`Publish`**" button in the Home tab of the ribbon, log in to your Power BI account, opt for an appropriate workspace destination for your report, and hold to complete the upload process. Afterwards, you can access your report online, sharing it via a link or embedding code.

Publishing Reports on Cloud

Providing availability of the reports and dashboards to the end users in the best possible and easily accessible way is to put the visualizations in your applications so that you can offer data-based insights to your users or stakeholders. You can do this by using the embedding functions of your data visualization tool or by using a custom web framework that can show the visualizations.

For instance, if you use Dash or Streamlit as your data visualization tool, you can make interactive web applications that display the visualizations and then launch them using a web server or a cloud service. Or, if you use Plotly or Bokeh as your data visualization tool, you can create HTML files that have the visualizations and then insert them in your applications using iframe tags.

Publishing a Power BI Report to the Cloud

In an ideal organizational setup, it is expected that the reports are centrally managed and published once developed so that anyone who wants to see the report or use it to make any decisions or for some analysis perspective can be able to do so seamlessly without needing to worry about the data source, access to source data, raw files, business logic or rules application, and so on.

Once the report is built by considering all the above factors and providing access to the business users, they can easily access these reports from the Power BI Cloud service.

To publish the report on the Power BI cloud service, follow these steps:

1. Before you publish your report, you will be asked to save it on your device if you have not done so already. Pick a name and location for your report file and click **`Save`**.
2. In the **`Home`** tab, select **`Publish`**. A dialog box will prompt you to sign in. If you already have a Power BI account, type your email ID and select **`Sign in`**. If you need a Power BI account, you can sign up for free by selecting **`Start Free`**.
3. Once you sign in, a dialog box will appear that asks you to choose where you want to save your report. You can pick a workspace that you already have or

make a new one. A workspace is where you store your reports, dashboards, and datasets in the Power BI cloud service. Click on **Select** to finish your selection.

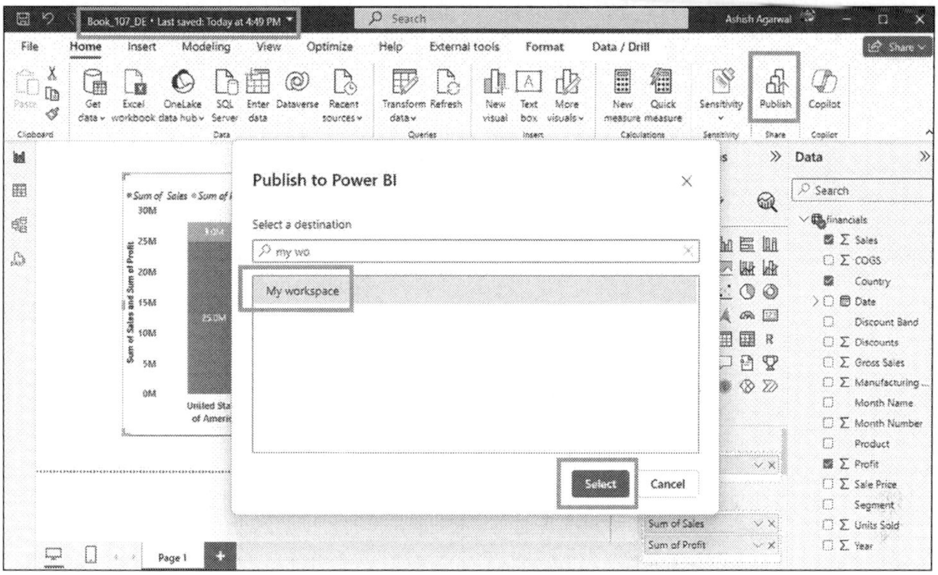

Figure 9.17: *Publishing a Power BI Report to Server*

4. Select the destination to publish the report to the chosen workspace. You will get a message that tells you that the report and the dataset are being transferred to the Power BI service. After the process is completed, you will see a link to view the report online.

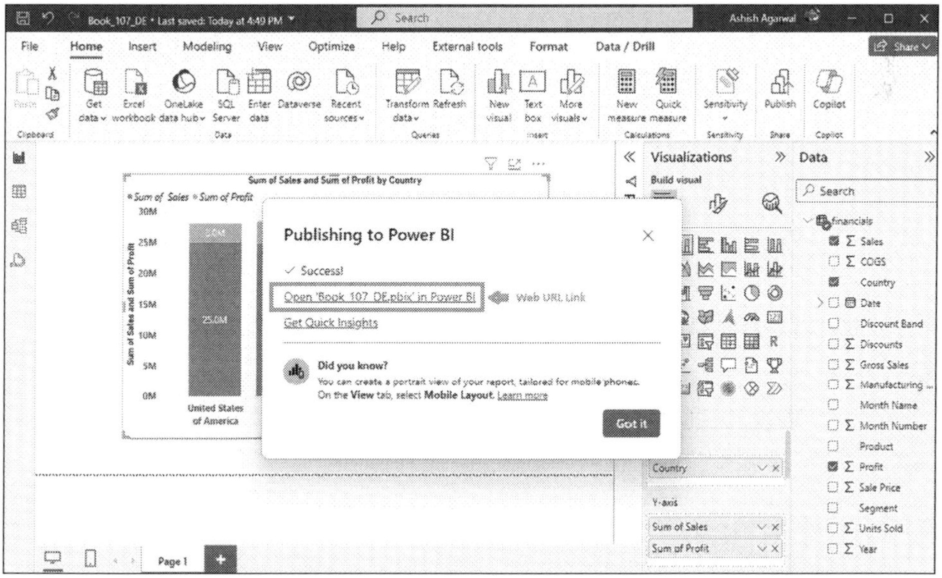

Figure 9.18: *Power BI Report Publish Confirmation with Web Link*

5. To access and control your published report, visit the Power BI cloud service website at https://app.powerbi.com and log in with your account. You will find your workspace and the report you uploaded in the left navigation pane. You can select the report to view it in the browser or right-click on it to explore more options, such as editing, sharing, or deleting the report.

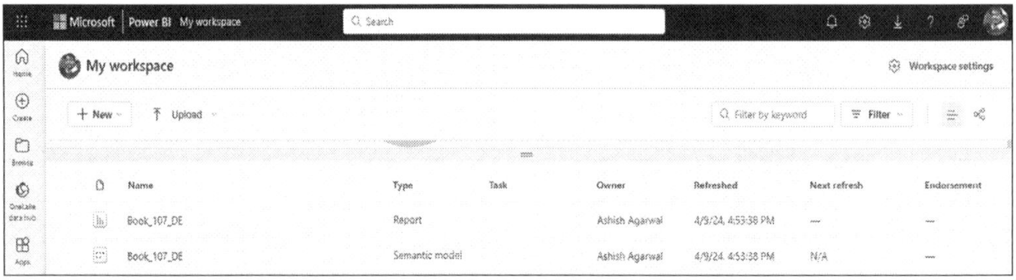

Figure 9.19: *Viewing Published Report on Power BI App Workspace*

Here you see a second file with the same name has been published with the type as "`Semantic model`". Let's understand what a semantic model is and its importance.

Power BI Semantic Model

A semantic model is a method of arranging and displaying data in a way that makes sense to users and allows them to explore and examine it easily. A semantic model establishes the connections, levels, computations, and metrics that are important for a specific business area or situation. A semantic model also ensures a uniform view of data across different reports and dashboards.

You have two options to create a semantic model in Power BI: Power BI Desktop or Power BI Dataflows. With Power BI Desktop, you can access various data sources, shape, and cleanse the data and design a data model with tables, columns, relationships, and measures. You can also use Data Analysis Expressions (DAX) to perform complex calculations and logic in your model. With Power BI Dataflows, you can create and manage data entities in the Cloud and use them as data sources for your Power BI reports and dashboards.

When you publish a report from Power BI Desktop to the Power BI service, you also publish the underlying semantic model. This means other users can access and explore the same data and calculations you have defined in your report, without having to recreate them. You can also use the Power BI service to edit or enhance your semantic model, such as adding new measures, changing data types, or modifying relationships. Additionally, you can use the Power BI service to create datasets from your semantic model and share them with other users or apps. Datasets are reusable data collections that can be used as the basis for multiple reports and dashboards.

A semantic model in Power BI can support both import and DirectQuery modes. Import mode means data is imported into Power BI and stored in a compressed and optimized format. DirectQuery mode means data remains in the original source and Power BI queries it on demand. You can also use a hybrid mode called *Composite Models*, which allows you to combine data from both import and DirectQuery sources in the same semantic model.

Power BI semantic models enable you to create powerful and interactive reports and dashboards that leverage the full potential of your data. By using a semantic model, you can ensure that your data is consistent, accurate, and easy to understand for your users. You can also benefit from the performance and scalability of Power BI, which can handle large and complex data models efficiently.

Power BI Dashboards

A dashboard is a page that shows key data and insights from reports. You can customize a dashboard by adding visualizations, images, text, or web content from your existing reports or Quick Insights. You can also change how your dashboard looks and works and see your dashboards on the Power BI service homepage or mobile app. You can also share or embed your dashboards.

Here are the steps to make a dashboard from the report that you have published:

1. To view the report in the Power BI service, choose the visualization you'd like to pin to the dashboard. You'll see a pin icon emerge on the top right corner of the visualization.
2. Click on the pin icon and select an existing dashboard or make a new one. You can also give the tile a title and a subtitle.
3. Do this for each visualization that you want to put on the dashboard. You can pin visualizations from different reports to the same dashboard.
4. To see your dashboard, go to the left navigation pane and select **`Dashboards`**. You will see a list of your dashboards and you can click on the one you made.
5. To change your dashboard, hover over the dashboard name and click on the ellipsis (...) icon. You will see options such as **`Rename`**, **`Share`**, **`Delete`**, etc. You can also click on the **`Edit`** mode button on the top right corner of the dashboard to adjust the layout, size, and position of the tiles. You can also add new tiles by clicking on the Add tile button and choosing the content you want to show.

Scheduling Data Refresh and Security as per Roles

One of the most critical aspects of keeping data visualization tools and data engineering tools in sync is to ensure the data refreshes are automated so that the visualizations always show the most recent and correct data. This can be achieved by setting data pipelines to run periodically or activating them based on events or changes in the data sources. For instance, if you use Apache Airflow or Prefect as your data engineering tool, you can build workflows that perform data transformations and load data into your data warehouse or database and then initiate data refreshes in your data visualization tool, such as Tableau or Power BI, using their own APIs or webhooks.

Scheduling and Refreshing a Power BI Report

The last and most important part of any data engineering final output is to make sure that the data and reporting requirements of the business users and various other stakeholders are met in a timely manner with the latest updated data with all the embedded business logic at a fixed interval or duration (be it daily, weekly any custom frequency).

To achieve this, we need to schedule the refresh of data for our Power BI reports from the Power BI app.

This is how you can set up a Power BI report to refresh automatically:

1. On the **`Home`** page of Power BI, go to **`My Workspace`** and pick the report that you want to keep updated.
2. Click on the "**`Semantic Model`**" settings icon in the top-right corner of the report. This will take you to the Dataset settings page where you can view data source details and credentials for your report.
3. Under **`Data source credentials`**, check that your credentials are valid and current. If not, click on **`Edit`** credentials and enter the necessary information.
4. Under **`Scheduled refresh`**, switch on the Keep your data up to date toggle. This will allow you to set frequency and time zone for your refreshes.
5. Select whether you want to refresh your data daily or weekly and choose the days and times that work for you. You can also set an email notification option to get alerts when the refresh fails or completes successfully.
6. Click on **`Apply`** to save your settings.

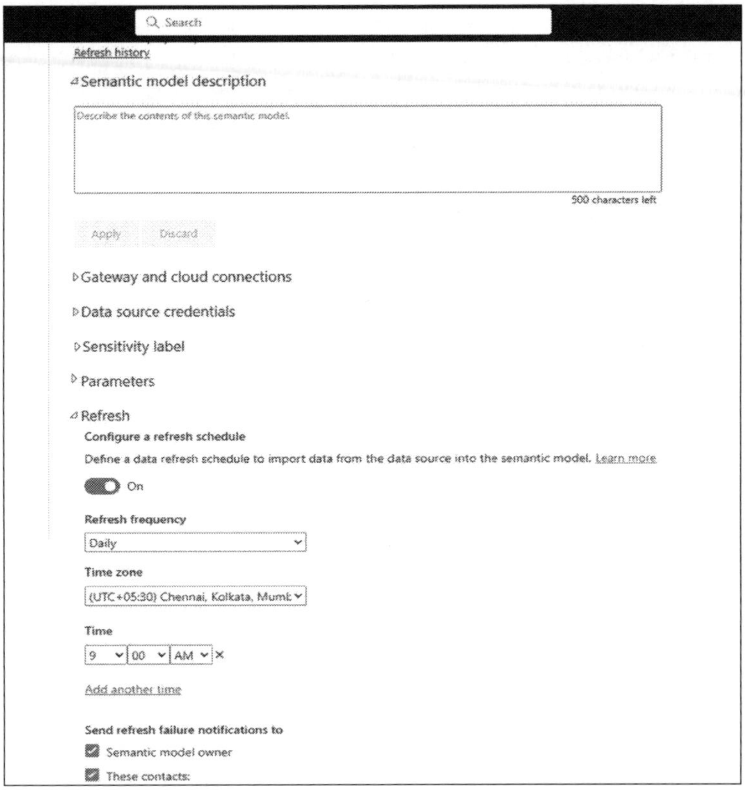

Figure 9.20: *Scheduling a Power BI Report Refresh*

Depending on your Power BI license type, you have different limits for how often and how long you can refresh data.

See this link for more details: https://docs.microsoft.com/en-us/power-bi/admin/service-premium-incremental-refresh#refresh-limits

Conclusion

In this chapter, we have learned that data visualization, especially when used in real-time, is a game-changer across industries. It enhances understanding, drives efficiency, and enables proactive decision-making. Whether you are a data analyst, scientist, or business professional, mastering this skill opens doors to impactful insights and informed decision-making.

We also learned in detail about various aspects of data visualization and understood the most widely used visuals and their respective usage along with the effective tools which can help build industry's best dashboards and reports.

With this chapter, we conclude the various aspects of data engineering right from the stage of analysis on the raw source side till the final goal of presenting the data in the most impactful form to support the business needs going through all the interim stages of source data analysis, ETL, creating an automated process to cater for the daily data needs and most importantly how the process varies from on-premises to Cloud (Azure) and respective tools usage.

In the next and final chapter of this book, we will cover how we can leverage what we have learnt from this book to ace some of the most effective data engineering and fundamental certifications and how one can prepare for the certification with the right approach and mindset.

Key Terms

- **SSRS:** SQL Server Reporting Service is a reporting tool that comes as a part of Microsoft's business intelligence suite and is widely used for reporting across various businesses.
- **Power BI:** It is a cloud-based business intelligence service that enables users to create, share, and consume interactive dashboards and reports. Power BI can be accessed through a web browser, a desktop application, or a mobile app.
- **Publishing:** It is the process of uploading and sharing the reports online using a cloud service, such as Power BI service or Azure SQL Reporting Services. Publishing to the Cloud can enable users to access the reports from anywhere and on any device, as well as collaborate and interact with the data in real-time.
- **Scheduling:** It is the process of setting up and managing the frequency and time of data refreshes for reports. Scheduling can help ensure that the reports always display the latest and most accurate information from the data sources.

References

- https://learn.microsoft.com/en-us/sql/reporting-services/create-deploy-and-manage-mobile-and-paginated-reports?view=sql-server-ver16
- https://learn.microsoft.com/en-us/power-bi/create-reports/
- https://learn.microsoft.com/en-us/power-bi/visuals/power-bi-visualization-types-for-reports-and-q-and-a
- https://learn.microsoft.com/en-us/power-bi/consumer/end-user-paginated-report
- https://learn.microsoft.com/en-us/power-bi/consumer/end-user-dashboards
- https://learn.microsoft.com/en-us/power-bi/report-server/migrate-report-server
- https://learn.microsoft.com/en-us/power-bi/create-reports/desktop-excel-stunning-report

Chapter 10
Data Engineering Certification Guide

Introduction

In this chapter, we will cover data engineering certifications and how one can approach acquiring certifications as a part of personal skill checks and enhancements or to fulfil organizational mandates for a specific role.

Certifications are very crucial aspects for any data engineer to ensure that they have an overall understanding of the subject as often, we don't get a chance to work on all the technological aspects of data engineering as part of our daily roles and responsibilities and hence certifications help us to keep updated with the latest technologies and advancements.

One of the most popular cloud platforms for data engineering is Microsoft Azure, which offers a range of services and tools for building, managing, and analysing data pipelines.

To demonstrate their skills and knowledge, Azure data engineers can pursue various certifications from Microsoft. These certifications validate the ability to work with various Azure data technologies and design optimal data solutions on Azure.

Structure

In this chapter, we will discuss the following topics:

- Certifications: Overview and Journey
- The Most Influential Certifications
- Choosing the Right Certification for Your Career Aspirations
- Applying for a Certification Exam

Certifications: Overview and Journey

Certifications are a way of validating your skills and knowledge in a specific domain or technology. They can help you stand out from the crowd of candidates as the certifications demonstrate your commitment, expertise, and ability to handle real-world challenges. They boost your career prospects, as they open up new opportunities, increase your salary, and enhance your professional credibility.

Certifications are not only beneficial for individuals but also for organizations. Employers can use certifications as a criterion for hiring, promoting, and retaining data engineers, as they can ensure that their teams have the necessary skills and qualifications to deliver high-quality solutions. Certifications also help organizations align with industry standards, best practices, and emerging trends, as they can keep their data engineers updated and relevant in the fast-changing data landscape.

Figure 10.1 shows how one can effectively plan a journey toward acquiring an Azure data engineer certificate if he/she is aspiring to become a certified Azure data engineer.

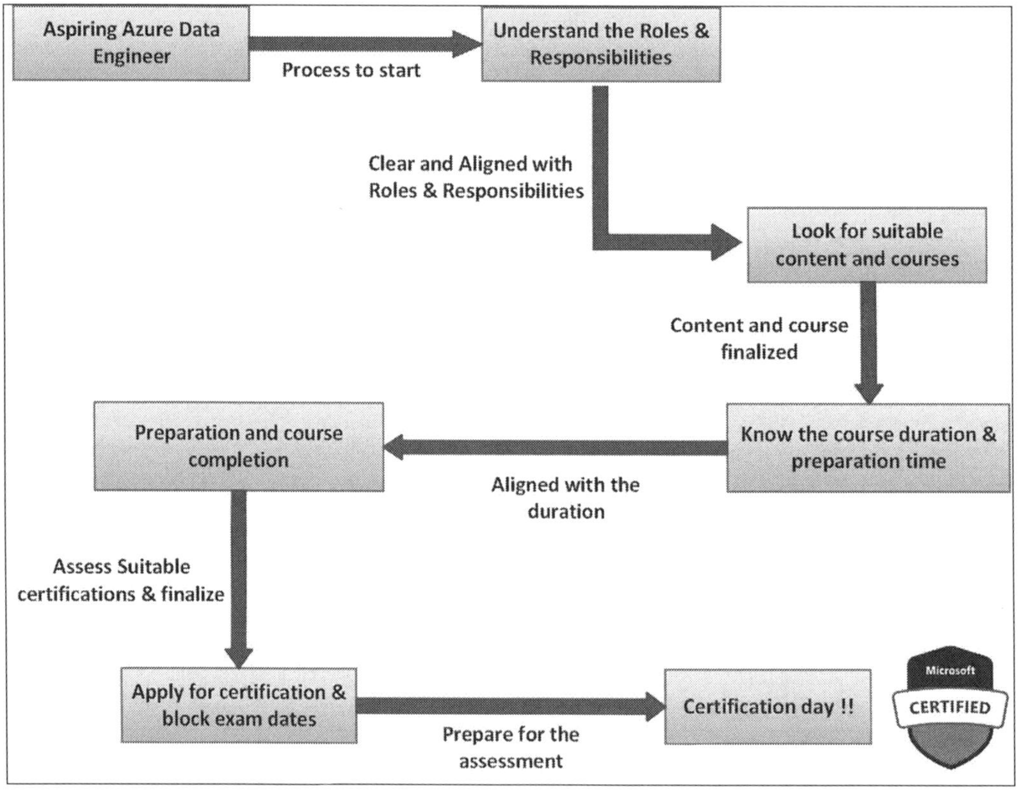

Figure 10.1: *Azure Certification Journey*

The Most Influential Certifications

Although there are a lot of certifications available from Azure for data personnel, we have a few specific ones that fit in most of the organizations' must have or required list while looking for the right candidate for a data engineer role.

In this section, we will cover some of those certification details.

There are two main Azure data engineering certifications:

- The Azure Data Fundamentals certification and
- The Azure Data Engineer Associate certification.

These certifications vary in terms of difficulty, requirements, and goals. In this section, we will describe the content and scope of each certification, how to get ready for them and what advantages they can offer for your career. We will also evaluate them and assist you in selecting the appropriate certification for your career ambitions.

The Azure Data Fundamentals Certification (AZ-900) is an optional but helpful step before the Azure Data Engineer Associate Certification and it is good for those who have little experience with Azure or data engineering. It teaches the basic concepts and principles of data engineering, such as basic data concepts, relational and non-relational data, data processing, and data analytics. The exam has 40-60 multiple-choice questions and lasts 60 minutes.

The Azure Data Engineer Associate Certification is a great choice for those who want to show their proficiency in designing and implementing data solutions on

Azure. However, there is a new certification that has taken the place of the DP-200 and DP-201 exams: The Data Engineering on Microsoft Azure (DP-203) Certification. This certification is for data engineers who use Azure Synapse Analytics, Azure Data Lake Storage, Azure Databricks, and Azure Stream Analytics to deliver complete data solutions.

The DP-203 exam includes the same topics as the DP-200 and DP-201 exams, but it also adds new content on Azure Synapse Analytics, Azure Databricks, and Azure Stream Analytics. The exam has 40-60 multiple-choice questions and takes 210 minutes. You need to pay 165 USD for the exam.

If you have already passed the DP-200 or DP-201 exam before June 30, 2021, you can switch to the DP-203 certification by taking a shorter transition exam (DP-203T00) that focuses on the new content.

Choosing the best certification for your career goals depends on your current skills and objectives. If you are new to data engineering or Azure, you may want to begin with the Azure Data Fundamentals Certification to learn the basics. If you are a skilled data engineer who wants to verify your skills on Azure, you may want to take the DP-203 exam directly or switch from the DP-200 or DP-201 exam. Either way, getting certified in data engineering on Azure can improve your confidence, credibility, and career opportunities.

If you want to show your skills in artificial intelligence and machine learning with Azure services, you can consider the Azure AI Fundamentals Certification (AI-900) and the Azure Data Scientist Associate Certification (DP-100). These certifications teach you how to use Azure to create, train, and deploy AI solutions, such as natural language processing, computer vision, speech recognition, and conversational agents.

The Azure AI Fundamentals Certification introduces the basic ideas and principles of artificial intelligence, such as machine learning, computer vision, natural language processing, speech recognition, and conversational AI. It also shows how to use Azure services and tools to apply these AI solutions. The exam consists of 40-60 multiple-choice questions and lasts 60 minutes.

The Azure Data Scientist Associate Certification is a more advanced and specific certification that focuses on using Azure Machine Learning to create and implement machine learning solutions. It covers topics such as data exploration and preparation, model training and evaluation, model deployment and consumption, and model monitoring and optimization. The exam consists of 40-60 multiple-choice questions and takes 180 minutes.

Choosing The Right Certification for Your Career Aspirations

There is no one-size-fits-all certification for your career ambitions. It depends on what skills you already have and what you want to achieve.

If you are a beginner in artificial intelligence or Azure, you may want to begin with the Azure AI Fundamentals Certification to learn the basics.

If you are a proficient data scientist who wants to validate your skills on Azure, you may try the Azure Data Scientist Exam.

Opting for DP-203 is advisable if you're specifically targeting a career trajectory in Data engineering and seeking to advance your current and future positions. It encompasses key segments of Azure data engineering and incorporates extra skills and tools within its program.

Either way, getting certified in any aspect of data, be it artificial intelligence, data science, or data engineering on Azure, can boost your confidence, credibility, and career prospects.

Additionally, choosing the best Azure data certification requires you to think about your existing skills, career aspirations, and the learning opportunities you have. Here are some tips to help you decide wisely:

- Evaluate your current abilities and knowledge of Azure data services and technologies. You can use the Microsoft Learn website to find free online courses and learning paths that cover the subjects and skills needed for each certification.

- Determine your career objectives and interests in the data field. Do you want to specialize in data analysis, data engineering, or data science? Do you want to work with specific tools or scenarios, such as Power BI, Azure Synapse Analytics, or Azure Databricks? Do you want to prove your expertise in a certain domain, such as finance, healthcare, or manufacturing?
- Compare the different certifications and see which one matches your goals and interests. You can use the Microsoft Certifications website to find the details and requirements of each certification, such as the intended audience, the exam topics, the suggested skills and experience, and the exam format and fees.
- Select the certification that meets your needs and preferences. You can also think about taking more than one certification if you want to expand your skill set and increase your employability. For example, you can combine DP-203 with DP-900 (Microsoft Azure Data Fundamentals) or DP-100 (Designing and Implementing a Data Science Solution on Azure) to show your competence in both data engineering and data science on Azure.

Applying for a Certification Exam

Once you are done with the preparation of the desired certification and feel ready to appear for the examination, you can follow the below-mentioned steps and do the following:

1. Go to the Microsoft Learn website and choose the certification you want to pursue.

   Here is the link for the Azure Data Fundamentals Certification Page - https://learn.microsoft.com/en-us/credentials/certifications/azure-data-fundamentals/?practice-assessment-type=certification
2. Read the exam details, objectives, and skills covered.
3. Book your exam online through Pearson VUE or find a test centre near you.

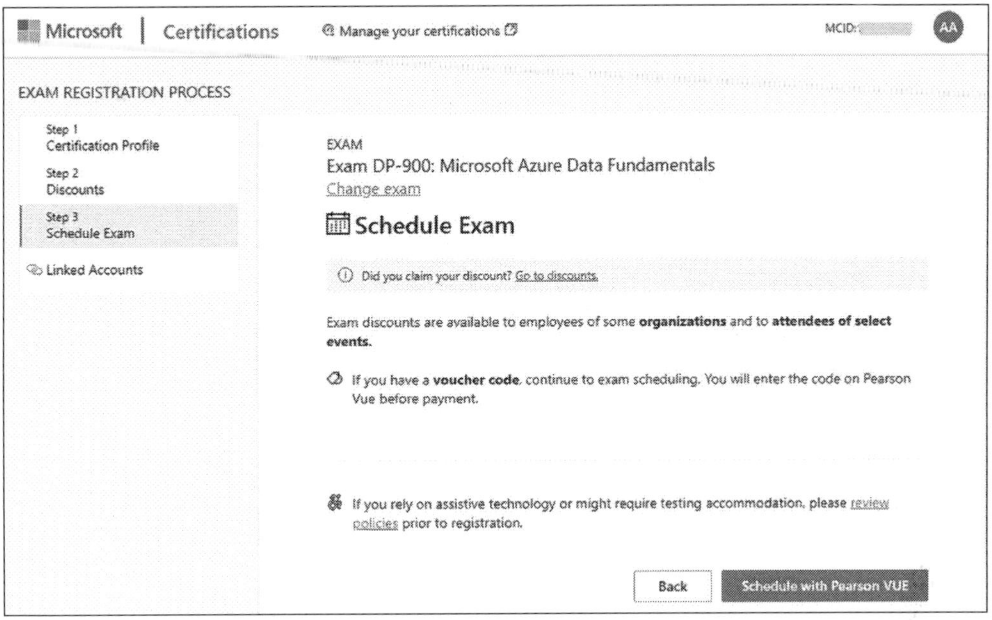

***Figure 10.2**: Azure Certification Exam Appointment*

4. Get ready for the exam by completing online courses, practice tests, and labs on Microsoft Learn or other platforms.
5. Take the exam and see your results right away. If you pass, you will get your certification within 48 hours.
6. Enjoy your accomplishment and display your digital badge with your network.

Conclusion

In this chapter, we have learned how to prepare for various Azure certifications related to data and AI in this chapter. We hope that this guide has helped you to understand the requirements, benefits, and resources for each certification. Now you can proudly showcase your digital badge and share your achievement with your network.

This chapter has introduced the different Azure certifications that are available for data engineering, data science, and artificial intelligence roles. You have also discovered the exam formats, objectives, and preparation tips for each certification.

In this chapter, we have examined the various Azure certifications that are suitable for data and AI practitioners. You have learned how to prepare for your exams, what they will cover, and where to find the best resources for each certification.

This marks the end of the book and I hope you all have enjoyed it, and it has improved your knowledge about the different facets of data engineering and related tools on Azure.

I wish you all the best for your certification exams and your career growth.

Once you have successfully completed your respective certification exams, you will also get a digital badge that you can use to show your skills and expertise. Don't forget to share your badge with your network and tell everyone about your achievement.

All the Best and Thanks!

Key Terms

- **DP-100**: This is a certification exam that validates the skills and knowledge of data scientists who use Azure Machine Learning to design and implement machine learning solutions. The exam covers topics such as data preparation, model training, model deployment, model monitoring, and responsible AI.
- **DP-203**: This is a certification exam that validates the skills and knowledge of data engineers who use Azure Data Services to design and implement data solutions. The exam covers topics such as data storage, data processing, data security, data optimization, and data monitoring.
- **Pearson Vue**: It is a company that provides computerized assessment services for professional and academic certifications. Pearson Vue is Microsoft's official partner for the delivery of Azure certification exams, such as DP-100 and DP-203. Candidates can take these exams online or at a Pearson Vue-approved test centre. To register for an exam, candidates must create a Pearson Vue account and choose a date, time, and method of delivery of the exam. Pearson Vue also offers exam preparation resources, such as tutorials, test guides, and practice assessments.

References

- https://learn.microsoft.com/en-us/credentials/certifications/azure-data-fundamentals/?practice-assessment-type=certification
- https://learn.microsoft.com/en-us/credentials/certifications/resources/study-guides/dp-203

Index

A

B

C

D

T

Made in United States
Orlando, FL
04 November 2026

90200515R00138